URBAN
HORROR

SINOTHEORY
A series edited by Carlos Rojas
and Eileen Cheng-yin Chow

HOR

Duke University Press   Durham and London   2020

URBAN
ROR

**Neoliberal Post-Socialism
and the Limits of Visibility**

Erin Y. Huang

© 2020 Duke University Press
All rights reserved
Designed by Courtney Leigh Baker
Typeset in Minion Pro by Westchester Publishing Services

Library of Congress Cataloging-in-Publication Data Names:
Huang, Erin Y. (Erin Yu-Tien), [date] author.

Title: Urban horror : neoliberal post-socialism and the limits of visibility / Erin Y. Huang.
Description: Durham : Duke University Press, 2020. | Series: Sinotheory | Extensive and substantial revision of author's thesis (doctoral)—University of California, Irvine, 2012, titled Capital's abjects : Chinese cinemas, urban horror, and the limits of visibility. | Includes bibliographical references and index.
Identifiers: LCCN 2019024134 (print) | LCCN 2019024135 (ebook)
ISBN 9781478006794 (hardcover)
ISBN 9781478008095 (paperback)
ISBN 9781478009108 (ebook)
Subjects: LCSH: Motion pictures—China—History and criticism. | Motion pictures—Political aspects—China. | Motion pictures—Social aspects—China. | Cities and towns in motion pictures.
Classification: LCC PN1993.5.C4 H824 2020 (print) | LCC PN1993.5.C4 (ebook) | DDC 791.430951—dc23
LC record available at https://lccn.loc.gov/2019024134
LC ebook record available at https://lccn.loc.gov/2019024135

Cover art: Lee Ka-sing, *Hong Kong, Someday in 1997*. Gelatin silver print. Courtesy of the artist.

Duke University Press gratefully acknowledges the University Committee on Research in the Humanities and Social Sciences at Princeton University, which provided funds toward the publication of this book.

For Pao-Cheng, Shu-Ling, and Erica Huang

Contents

Acknowledgments

This book grew from a deeply personal desire to understand and describe the spatial and temporal experience growing up in the aftermath of the Cold War in Kaohsiung, a port city and an export-processing zone surrounded by industrial factories that export goods and energy but leave behind toxic pollutions in the island nation of Taiwan. In fierce competition with other Chinese port cities and industrial zones that rapidly expanded after China entered the era of economic reform in the 1980s, Kaohsiung appears in my memory as a crowded urban space that defies the existing definitions of a political or mercantile city. Having neither historical monuments to mark the city's past political and economic significance, nor a flashy financial district to flaunt its newness as a major transportation center located between Southeast and East Asia, the urbanscape of Kaohsiung consists of the infrastructure of global movement, where endless streams of megasize container ships and trucks load and unload. Although the Taiwanese export-processing zone gradually lost its global competitiveness to the special economic zones in China and other developing countries in Southeast Asia, the space that shaped my life remains mysterious and leaves behind unanswered questions: What are the geopolitical forces that created the export-processing zone? Is space also a technology of governmentality that can be engineered and reproduced? What are the contemporary systems of power that continue to create transnational land and oceanic urbanization with not yet legible human and environmental consequences? Looking at the toxic and hazy skyline of Kaohsiung—a space whose name is unfamiliar to many people but that plays a role in the global logistic routes of supply and demand—these questions haunt me.

Yet what concerns me is not the individual case of Kaohsiung but the proliferation of spaces like Kaohsiung—a model of neoliberal experimentation with the production of space that reduces space to reproducible protocols and procedures. The zones are disposable and can always be replicated elsewhere, in a land or country that offers more competitive resources. The spatial technologies behind the practice of zoning can be further developed, providing not only a tool of economic expansionism but also the means to exert political and military control. Kaohsiung highlights the tip of an iceberg in the advancement of the technologies of space in the aftermath of the Cold War. It is a unique vantage point to see the urban transformations taking place in China, Hong Kong, and Taiwan in what I theorize in this book as the neoliberal post-socialist era. Among the Sinophone regions that I examine, two are islands located between Southeast and East Asia. The frequent references to Southeast Asia in this book are meant to pose questions about regional boundaries and explore newly emergent connections that are created under the deterritorialized imaginary of infinite economic expansion. Rather than focusing on the representations of select cities, I am drawn to the theorization of space as a reproducible sociopolitical mechanism of power that creates new types of spaces—special economic zones, special administrative regions, and science and industrial parks—that occupy central roles in Asia's post–Cold War urban transformation.

The years I spent on researching, thinking, and writing led me to the questions above. The process of writing resembles an archaeological excavation, where I peel away layers to collect the traces of thoughts that appeared in different forms and are in search of a language of articulation. There are innumerable people I need to thank in this process, for selflessly teaching me how to think, for reading numerous versions of chapters and drafts, for believing in me and my ideas when things get messy, for long conversations that open my mind, and for simply being who they are. I thank Ackbar Abbas, who has a mysterious way of reading my mind and untangling my thoughts. His love for experimenting with theory taught me the infinite possibilities of reading. I thank Hu Ying and Jennifer Terry, who taught me the foundations of feminist thinking and the importance of feminist doing. Their influence on my work cannot be described in words, and their generosity will always be passed on to my colleagues and students. I want to give special thanks to Jonathan M. Hall for inspiring my passion for film and media theory and for always pushing me to think beyond my limits.

This book underwent radical transformation in the intellectual environment of Princeton University. I am privileged to work alongside Steven

Chung and Franz Prichard. The almost daily conversations we had led to the creation of Asia Theory Visuality, an interdisciplinary platform where we dream of conducting all kinds of intellectual experiments that range from conferences and workshops to media projects and installations. Their friendship and companionship sustained me through the ambitious and challenging process of writing this book. My colleagues at Princeton gave unrelenting support to all my intellectual ventures. I thank Martin Kern, Anna Shields, Thomas Hare, Willard Peterson, Sheldon Garon, Thomas Conlan, Paize Keulemans, Federico Marcon, Amy Borovoy, Janet Chen, Atsuko Ueda, He Bian, Ksenia Chizhova, Brian Steininger, Xin Wen, Jing Wang, April Alliston, Leonard Barkan, Wendy Laura Belcher, David Bellos, Sandra Bermann, Marina Brownlee, Benjamin Conisbee Baer, Susana Draper, Karen Emmerich, Daniel Heller-Roazen, Lital Levy, Alexander Nehamas, Eileen Reeves, Anne Anlin Cheng, Zahid R. Chaudhary, Kinohi Nishikawa, Devin Fore, and Katherine Hill Reischl. I want to thank Kat especially, for initiating conversations about comparative studies of socialisms and post-socialisms. Our discussions resulted in the PIIRS-funded international conference "The Geopolitical Aesthetics of Post-Socialisms: China, Russia, and Beyond" in 2017. In addition to an intellectually stimulating environment, Princeton University generously supported a semester of leave to complete the writing of this book and awarded me the Professor Uwe E. Reinhardt and Julis-Rabinowitz Family University Preceptorship in Multidisciplinary Studies.

Whenever people ask what gives me joy in what I do, my answer has always been the opportunity to meet and grow with the most amazing people and the most brilliant minds. My writing is inseparable from the drinks and meals, laughter and tears, and the thought-provoking chats that I shared with these people: Arnika Fuhrmann, Yomi Braester, Shu-mei Shih, Carlos Rojas, Jerome Silbergeld, Peter Brooks, Xudong Zhang, Rebecca Karl, Thomas Looser, Akira Lippit, Margaret Hillenbrand, Tomiko Yoda, Alexander Zhaltan, Feng-Mei Heberer, Zhang Zhen, Lily Chumley, Michelle Cho, Kim Icreverzi, Jason McGrath, Weihong Bao, Victor Fan, Guo-Juin Hong, Jenny Chio, Luke Robinson, Calvin Hui, Pooja Rangan, Ma Ran, Jean Tsui, Corey Byrnes, Ari Larissa Heinrich, Thomas Lamarre, Yuriko Furuhata, Marc Steinberg, Joshua Neves, Wang Ban, Yiman Wang, Poshek Fu, Diane Lewis, Paul Roquet, Christine Marran, Thy Phu, Ju-Hui Judy Han, Christopher Tong, Nick Admussen, Moonim Baek, Winnie Yee, We Jung Yi, Phillip Kaffen, Olga Fedorenko, Megan Steffen, Laurence Coderre, Yun-Jong Lee, Yuka Kano, Seo Young Park, Hyun Seon Park, Chungmoo Choi, Kyung

Hyun Kim, Bert Scruggs, Eyal Amiran, Rei Terada, Jane Newman, Tiffany Tsai, Ying Qian, Li Jie, Jill Jarvis, Catherine Reilly, Qinyuan Lei, Anindita Banerjee, Heather Inwood, Guangchen Chen, Shaoling Ma, Weijie Song, Angelina Lucento, Jennifer Dorothy Lee, Ying-Fen Huang, Hwa-Jen Tsai, Sheldon Lu, Astrid Møller-Olsen, Michael Schoenhals, Jie Lu, Frederike Schneider-Vielsäcker, Loïc Aloisio, Pamela Hunt, Christina Chuang, and graduate students at Princeton who never cease to inspire me, Chan Yong Bu, Junnan Heather Chen, and Darja Filippova. Special thanks go to the filmmaker Cong Feng, who generously shared his films with me. I also wish to thank Victoria Hsieh, who did amazing work untangling my thoughts and sentences in the early stage of preparing the book manuscript. I still remember the day she sat and listened to the concept of urban horror when we were both in graduate school. The experience of writing this book is a token of our friendship.

Without the enthusiasm and unrelenting support from the people at Duke University Press, this book would not have been possible. I thank Ken Wissoker, who understood the core of this project within minutes of our conversation and gave me unlimited freedom to write. I am grateful for Carlos Rojas and Eileen Chow for generously including the book in the Sinotheory series. With utmost sincerity, I thank the book's two anonymous readers. It was an amazing experience to read and think about their eloquently composed comments that made me realize how far many ideas could actually go. Their vision for the book and their excitement for the direction it takes are the best encouragement I have ever received. At the Press, I thank Joshua Tranen, Susan Albury, and the entire team for taking great care with this project.

At last, I wish to express my infinite gratitude to my family for always giving me strength at unexpected turns of life. It was their unconditional love and kindness that made me realize the depth of humanity. They are the reason for what I do.

An earlier version of chapter 2 was published in *positions: asia critique* 27, no. 2 (2019): 333–60. An earlier and shorter version of chapter 3 was published in *Journal of Chinese Cinemas* 13, no. 1 (2019): 42–60.

Introduction. Urban Horror

Speculative Futures of Chinese Cinemas

On October 1, 2014, the National Day of the People's Republic of China, a celebration takes place in the city of Hong Kong, a former British colony now ruled as a special administrative region under China's policy of "one country, two systems." As fireworks illuminate Hong Kong's skyline, the scene on the ground reveals an entirely different landscape. The streets are filled with people and engulfed in a chemical cloud. The police are shooting tear gas at the crowd to disperse the nonviolent and unarmed demonstrators demanding democracy in what will later be called the Umbrella Movement. Against the darkness of the sky, the fireworks' brilliant colors shine above the protest zones that have been transformed into urban battlegrounds. Shots are fired and canisters of tear gas fly across crowded protest sites, where irritant chemicals touch and penetrate the demonstrators' bodies. In the opening scene of Chan Tze-woon's *Yellowing* (*Luanshi beiwang*, 2016)—a documentary that archives the Hong Kong filmmaker's intimate observations of the protesters and their lived experiences in the Occupy movement—the camera captures the chaotic scene as it gazes at Hong Kong's iconic skyscrapers lit up with celebratory slogans in red (see figure I.1). "Prosperous nation; flourishing families [*Guorong jiasheng*]," the

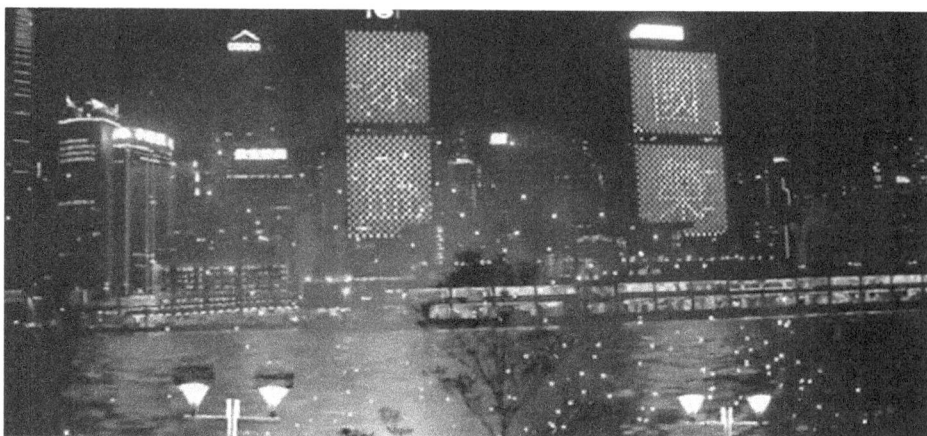

FIGURE I.1. The camera in *Yellowing* (2016) captures the chaotic scene of the Umbrella Movement as it gazes at Hong Kong's iconic skyscrapers lit up with celebratory slogans in red.

slogan says. Yet it is unclear who the families are and what defines wealth and prosperity. Accentuated as part of the ordinary landscape of post-handover Hong Kong, the image complicates the meaning of "one country, two systems," in which the imaginary coexistence of socialism and capitalism rehearses a futurity that I theorize as neoliberal post-socialism, referring to a deterritorialized form of market post-socialism and a new global system without a (proper) name that is actively reshaping the lived conditions of the present. The combination of neoliberalism and post-socialism puts the conventional definitions of these terms into question and probes the socialist origin of neoliberalism, suggesting a globally expanding market economy without laissez-faire that depends on state intervention, wherein the definition of the state and its relationship with the market undergoes radical transformations.

The Chinese state's suppression of a protest movement demanding political sovereignty and freedom in Hong Kong—a space of neoliberal post-socialist experimentation—illustrates that freedom under "one country, two systems" is a flexible façade, its meaning subject to infinite manipulation and redefinition. The gap between the freedom of free trade and the freedom to perform political sovereignty only highlights the centralized flexibility of neoliberal post-socialist state power rather than its diminishment. Putting the spatial and temporal assumptions of Chinese post-socialism into question, the script in red captured in *Yellowing* that is written into Hong Kong's urban landscape suggests a new direction of critical inquiry—specifically, a form of post-socialism in a formerly nonsocialist region of Asia that demands new understandings of what the *post-* in post-socialism means and how its versatility is deployed to dissolve and articulate new borders in the aftermath of the Cold War.

In *Yellowing*'s opening scenes, the camera wavers between the spectacles above and below, until they are merged in the same frame, contiguous and indistinguishable. The cuts and movements of the camera suggest the desire to evoke the invisible interrelations in an intensifying ecology of violence that lies beyond the literal representation of clashing police and protesters in a political and economic zone of exception. The force of the images is further conveyed through the film's soundtrack, where the sounds of exploding tear gas canisters and fireworks are mixed with the cry of the crowd, transforming distant images of the protest into an intimate sensory experience. As if tracing the imperceptible connections between two urban landscapes and their incomprehensible juxtaposition, the camera is guided and motivated by an invisible force, a public sentiment that this book investigates: the *urban horror* that springs up when the excesses of contemporary violence embedded in the neoliberal production of space overwhelm the existing frames of cognition. The visible becomes illegible and is deployed in the film to highlight the gap between conflicting realities that are associated with Hong Kong—one as the territory of China, and the other one as a sovereign land. The revolution takes place not only on the street but also in a film produced after the assembly of protesting bodies in the Umbrella Movement came to an end. Rather than a memorial of the demonstration, *Yellowing*'s treatment of footage taken during the protest is an experiment with the future of the image. The urban protest has ceased. Yet the potentiality of the image in an image-saturated world has not been fully explored. Drawing attention to urban horror allows for a discussion of the speculative forces of cinema from the 1990s to the present. *Urban horror* is the term I use to denote an emergent horizon of affects, indicating a communicative network of emotions where cumulative intensities of feelings that are searching for new forms of expression travel and disseminate through mediated informational and sensory channels. Looking at cinema from this period urges us to reimagine resistance *after* the presumed end of revolutionary times, in the aftermath of the end of revolutionary Chinese socialism and the catastrophic Tiananmen Square protest of 1989.

Urban Horror: Toward a Theory of Marxist Phenomenology

Distinct from the legible forms of Euro-American gothic literature and the Hollywood-centric horror genre that already propose a provocative history of monstrous bodies and their relations to the violence of capitalism (e.g., Dr. Frankenstein's monster, Dracula, the phantom of the opera, etc.), urban horror continues this line of inquiry but shifts focus to the post–Cold War, contemporary Sinophone world, including China, Hong Kong, and Taiwan. Here the continuities and discontinuities of socialist, post-socialist, capitalist, and neoliberal economic histories pose new questions about the relationship between aesthetics (i.e., the forms of cultural ambivalence and resistance) and politics (i.e., the geopolitical and economic system shaping global orders). This relationship is particularly relevant for the time period under discussion, in which the era of neoliberal post-socialist economic transformation corresponds to the era of hypermediality, referring to the transformations in the meaning of the image and its relation to the concept of reality, when the production of the image no longer depends on an externally existing reality and now exists in the realm of digital technologies and computer algorithms.[1] In this book about the aesthetics of cinema—with discussions of texts that were produced when the concept of the image and its power to shape reality underwent fundamental changes during the media revolution after the Cold War—the motivating question concerns how the cinematic aesthetics of urban horror play a role in dramatizing, influencing, and shaping future urban revolutions that may or may not ever be actualized.

Horror—a socially produced affect that responds to contemporaneous forms of violence and that is basically antirepresentational but requires a form of representation—has produced a new species of monstrous bodies in the Euro-American tradition since the Industrial Revolution. Proposing a Marxist sociology of the modern monster, Franco Moretti links the emergence of capitalism and nineteenth-century monsters: "The fear of bourgeois civilization is summed up in two names: Frankenstein and Dracula." Interpreting both as "totalizing" monsters that are distinct from earlier bodies of monstrosity, Moretti reads Dr. Frankenstein's monster as "a pregnant metaphor of the process of capitalist production, which forms by deforming, civilizes by barbarizing, enriches by impoverishing—a two-sized process in which each affirmation entails a negation." Whereas Frankenstein's monster resembles the conditions of the proletariat, denied a name and individuality, Dracula represents the antirepresentational Capital itself, alluding to an incorporeal vampiric body of accumulation that "impelled towards a continuous growth, an unlimited expansion of his domain."[2] Jack Halberstam further suggests a Foucauldian approach to historically shifting concepts of monstrosity when he traces a new genealogy of horror in a combined study of nineteenth-century gothic literature and twentieth-century horror films. Calling for an investigation of specific racialized and sexualized bodies and the social affects they mediate, Halberstam's analysis of gothic horror, which begins with Mary Shelley's *Frankenstein* and ends with Dr. Hannibal Lecter in *The Silence of the Lambs* (1991), illustrates that monstrosity is a historically contingent concept shaped by the technologies of representation.[3] Yet, as this genealogy of gothic horror that extends from literature to contemporary Euro-American film culture suggests, the notion of totalizing monsters whose bodies provide an identifiable form of representation amid contemporaneous, antirepresentational systems of violence has witnessed a change in recent decades. The bodies of monstrosity continue to exist but are regenrefied through waves of commodified nostalgia in the form of remakes and sequels. The bodies of hybrid humans-machines as well as vampires and zombies still serve as cultural metaphors for anxieties over capitalist accumulation, technological advancement, and the alienation of human labor. However, the emergence of cultural texts without an identifiable agent of horror, where monstrous bodies are replaced by nature, an invisible virus, or another unspecified calamity, suggests a diffusion of body-centered horror and an increasingly noticeable gap between currently existing cultural forms of representation and the excesses of contemporary systems of violence that await naming. The study of neoliberal, post-socialist urban horror takes up this gap and theorizes the historical conditions leading up to the diffusion of horror.

Before introducing the geopolitical and economic transformations of neoliberal post-socialism and the new aesthetic forms of urban horror, the term *horror* requires more careful theorization. The brief history of Euro-American gothic horror presented above complicates the meaning of *horror*, especially when the term is conflated with the study of horror as a genre. The word refers to a commodity of attraction where monstrosity is exhibited as a spectacle, producing sensationalized social affects that allow spectators to enjoy the feelings of thrill and fear that are sold as horror; it also suggests an elusive sensory communicative channel, where the excessiveness and incomprehensibility of the global systems that shape the conditions of everyday life emerge as sights and sounds that overwhelm the senses and the capacity to think. Rather than pursuing a horror genre study where the focus is often on categorizing a collection of cultural texts and figures using a legible convention—generally already defined in the aesthetic and economic traditions of Euro-American productions of body-centered horror—my interest lies in the second definition, which opens up horror as a historical mode of perception arising when the perceived external reality exceeds one's internal frame of comprehension.

To further elaborate on this definition of horror as a constantly morphing assemblage of social forces that conjure different bodies, spaces, temporalities, images, and sounds—rather than a scripted and commodified feeling that is presumed to be uniform throughout history and across languages and cultures—we can examine the history of horror in Chinese cinema. Introduced as part of urban spectacle and consumer culture in Republican Shanghai, Ma-Xu Weibang's *Song at Midnight* (*Yeban gesheng*, 1937) is recognized as the first Chinese horror film. It is modeled after Rupert Julian's Hollywood film *The Phantom of the Opera* (1925), which in turn is based on French writer Gaston Leroux's serialized novel depicting a ghost-like, disfigured man who haunts the Paris Opera House. Ma-Xu obsessed over makeup artistry, and the film's success in introducing a sensationalized grotesque body was further amplified by the technology of sound. Due to sound media's dissemination of the film's theme songs, the phantom's presence did not depend on the theatrical release of the film but could be found in any space in the urban fabric connected by sound technology. As Zhang Zhen argues, *Song at Midnight* introduced an acoustic horror to Chinese cinema, where the technologies of sound combined with the visual techniques of making monsters on screen, leading to the film's unrivaled popularity.[4] However, like the careers of many other Shanghai filmmakers of the Republican era, Ma-Xu's work was interrupted by the Chinese Civil War (1945–49) fought between the Chinese Communist Party and the Guomindang Party following the end of World War II.

The account of the horror genre's origin in China reveals, first, the displacement of a Shanghai filmmaker to Hong Kong in the postwar era, where Ma-Xu continued to make sequels to *Song at Midnight*, and, second, the obscured history of "Chinese horror" as an artistic experimentation with a Western form and a part of a globally circulating cosmopolitan urban culture that was produced in a semicolonial Chinese port city. As one of the first treaty ports opened to free trade with the West after the First Opium War in 1842, Shanghai was ruled under semicolonialism, the city divided into concessions that were ceded to foreign control. Produced under the condition of semicolonialism, the horror that was born in the city does not speak to the realities of colonialism but rather presents itself as a cinematic and technological attraction. Flaunting itself as an artistic achievement that longs for the film spectators' acknowledgment, the monster in *Song at Midnight* does not hide behind the camera but longs to be seen. To further enhance the pleasures of the Chinese phantom as a cinematic spectacle, the phantom is given the benevolent identity of a leftist revolutionary who fought against feudal landlords. Calling the Chinese phantom Song Danping a "benevolent monster," Yomi Braester further notes the creation of this Chinese monster as part of a "theatrical phantasmagoria."[5] Changing the urban setting of *The Phantom of the Opera* to an unspecified scenic countryside in *Song at Midnight*, the Chinese adaptation stays away from the space of semicolonialism, so the phantom's disfigured and scarred face can be loved as a humanized spectacle in a cinematic excursion to the countryside.

In a milieu filled with the desire to become modern—to be contemporaneous with the cultural and artistic metropolitan West without confronting the colonial West—*Song at Midnight*'s obsession with new cinematic aesthetics and technologies associated with cosmopolitan horror is representative of the political unconscious that motivated the production of Shanghai modernisms.[6] Instead of presenting a Shanghai urbanscape that was fissured and controlled by competing Western colonial powers, *Song at Midnight* is arguably celebrating the Chinese reinvention of commodified Euro-American horror. The sensationalized horror that the film associates with the phantom's disfigured body remains a part of Shanghai's New Sensationalism, which flourished before the beginning of the Second Sino-Japanese War in 1937. A critical rereading of Chinese horror's origin story reveals that the body-centered horror genre is a globally circulating commodity and an aesthetics of cultural translation. The camera's love of the phantom's face, seen in prolonged close-ups and multiperspective angle shots, evokes the fascination and allure with cosmopolitan urban culture rather than the communicative channel of emergent feelings that respond to the contemporaneous forms of systematized violence. The horror associated with *Song at Midnight* refers to a commodified thrill and not the sentiment that arises in the face of an unnamable crisis. Therefore, distinguishing horror as a commodified genre and a sensory communicative channel poses new questions about the history of horror in modern China, especially while considering the socialist era and the socialist realist cinema that indirectly banned the production of horror genre films. This distinction also opens up a new breadth of texts across multiple genres that probe the meaning of horror as the gap of cognition produced under the intensive conditions of capitalist, socialist, and neoliberal post-socialist economic developments.

According to Rei Terada's historicization of feelings in theory, drawing from the writings of Jean-Jacques Rousseau, Gilles Deleuze, and others, emotions arise from the gap between one's perceived interiority and the realities that are associated with the external world. For this reason, emotions always already exceed the limit of one's imagined subjecthood. And the emergence of emotions depends on a phenomenological process in which human feelings (i.e., the biological, the interior, the subjective, etc.) are the result of sociopolitical processes.[7] Terada's analysis sheds new light on the common narrative that emotions are an expression of an ingrained and universal human nature, leading to new questions about the normative definition of horror as the expression (i.e., externalization) of an internally existing and innate subjective feeling. For this reason, this book theorizes horror as the torsion between socially constructed interiors and exteriors and moves away from the expressive hypothesis of emotion. As illustrated in *Yellowing*'s evocation of contemporary Hong Kong as sights and sounds that are visible but incomprehensible—where a perceived externality exceeds the audience's previously existing frame of interior cognition—the question that emerges is the role of visual media in creating public sensory channels that are actively producing feelings of not knowing how to feel and disseminating sentiments and affects that are in search of reactions to a newly discovered present. Accentuating the gap between vision and cognition, contemporary urban horror is consciously produced and sustained. The emergence of horror means the paralysis of the former order of the world and its system of signification, revealing them as the structures that condition our knowledge of the world and potentially igniting what Jacques Rancière calls a revolution of the sensible world.[8]

From the comparative analysis of Euro-American and Chinese horror genres, it becomes clear that horror as a commodity genre and horror as a sociopolitical sentiment of potential dissent are distinct. Whereas the former has generated distinguished studies, thinking about the latter kind of horror requires a new genealogy of the history of feelings in political theory. The affective excess that the camera in *Yellowing* evokes highlights the social function of horror as a communicative channel of public sentiment that was already present in nineteenth-century Marxist urban theory based on industrializing European cities. The sentiments and affects that were disseminated in the critique of capitalism have a specific urban setting that probes the relationship between capitalism and the systematized production of space. To further theorize the circulation of contemporary urban horror, an early Marxist text that describes the emergence of factory towns helps shed light on, first, the phenomenological method of observing the impact of the industrialization of space, and second, the birth of an industrial horror that belongs to the modern era. Derived from Friedrich Engels's early writing, in a text that I read as a Marxist phenomenological treatise on an English factory town, horror performs the role of describing the sentiment that arises when human subjects are seen as no longer commensurable with the abstracting industrial landscape. In classical Marxian theory, questions about the modern city never have the same scope as they do in Engels's early work.[9] In *The Condition of the Working Class in England*, Engels records his experience working at his father's cotton mill in the factory town of Manchester from 1842 to 1844. In chapters that detail the urban sensoria he experienced as a young adult—from the sights and smells of workers' dwelling spaces and their deteriorating bodies, to the emergence of new slums amid the infrastructural network of industrial railways and bridges—the visible sight of Manchester paradoxically became incomprehensible. He writes, "Everything which here arouses horror and indignation is of recent origin, belongs to the *industrial epoch*."[10] "Horror," in this case, is not used to preach moralism and resentment, an approach that can obscure and paralyze the potential for radical critique. Rather, Engels's statement draws a distinction between the perceived reactive sensations and the true causes of the problem that remain in the dark. A set of implied questions emerges regarding the horror and indignation that are tied to the industrial epoch—an industrial horror. Already suggesting a Marxian structure of feeling, the affects that pervade Engels's urban treatise refer not to inherent humanist expressions but to emotive categories that are created in the abstracting system of capitalist industrial modernity. The horror is socially produced and refers to a set of social relations that materialized in a quintessentially capitalist affect that ramifies through homogenizing processes of global urbanization. The work that horror performs here is the opening of a phenomenological channel of perception that introduces the body as a perceptive surface where the external conditions of capitalist abstraction are producing a new kind of human sensation, appearing whenever a gap is opened between one's imagined interior reality and the perceived external world. Once the gap closes, horror disappears, or becomes the conventional, scripted horror that no longer unsettles the perception of reality.

The Condition of the Working Class in England represents an early Marxist critique of the capitalist production of space that also probes the potentialities of an industrial horror in rehearsing and inciting future revolutions. The text is a performative theorization of not only a capitalist affect but also the emergence of Marxist phenomenology, a method of inquiry that un-ravels the human sensorium as the torsion of interiorities and exteriorities, wherein lies the desires, anxieties, ambivalences, and potential strategies of resistance toward an invisible totality called Capital. The emphasis on capital-ism alone was further complicated, considering the histories of socialisms that competed with the capitalist mode of production that climaxed dur-ing the twentieth century. To trace the genealogy of Marxist phenomenol-ogy against the backdrop of intensifying urbanization of the last century, the writings of the urban theorist Henri Lefebvre and the phenomenolo-gist Maurice Merleau-Ponty bring into view a set of historical mediations and debates on the body as a surface of perception and a site of individual consciousness when the boundary between capitalism and socialism that produces military-industrial urbanization began to blur.

The question of individuality and individual consciousness in the Marx-ist imaginary of collective action and revolution represents a particular strand of Marxist intellectual history, present in the work of Marx, Engels, Rosa Luxemburg, Georg Lukács, and Antonio Gramsci.[11] The theoretical inquiry into the place for subjects and subjecthood in Marxist thought be-came the foundation for existential Marxism in postwar European soci-ety. Represented by the works of Jean-Paul Sartre and Merleau-Ponty, their contribution (especially the latter's) to Marxist theory remains an ongoing theoretical debate. Sartre's visit to China in 1955, for example, opens up a new intellectual horizon for thinking about Sino-French Marxist human-ism during the Cold War as an important component of the global 1960s.[12] Compared to Sartre, whose name is often associated with Marxist thinkers of the same generation, the ambiguity of Merleau-Ponty's Marxist writings and his early death contributed to the underexploration of his existential Marxism.[13] In addition to Merleau-Ponty's multiple books on the subject of Marxism in response to Lukács, G. W. F. Hegel, and the young Marx, *Phenomenology of Perception, Humanism and Terror*, and the later *Adven-tures of the Dialectic* represent an extensive body of work that wrestles with the relationship between phenomenological inquiry and Marxist historical materialism. For example, in "Marxism and Philosophy," Merleau-Ponty explains the linkage between Marxism and phenomenology: "If it is nei-ther a 'social nature' given outside ourselves, nor the 'World Spirit,' nor the movement appropriate to ideas, nor collective consciousness, *then what is, for Marx, the vehicle of history and the motivating force of the dialectic?* It is man involved in a certain way of appropriating nature in which the mode of his relationship with others takes shape; it is concrete human intersubjectivity, the successive and simultaneous community of existences in the process of self-realization in a type of ownership which they both submit to and transform, each created by and creating the other."[14] For Merleau-Ponty, the phenomenological method does not attribute human experience to reactive responses toward external stimuli, nor does it attribute human experience to consciousness that springs from an internal essence. Rather, it is a critical inquiry that theorizes the body-subject in motion and that looks at how concepts of the world are formed through mobile perspectives and intersubjectivity. Through continuously forming relations that blur the boundaries of the body-world-beyond, the phenomenological theory of the body is already a theory of perception, as Merleau-Ponty suggests in *The Phenomenology of Perception*.[15] Opening up the field of perception as the site of an infinitely expandable torsion of the exterior and interior worlds, phenomenology suggests an open-endedness and temporality to social relations that are also at the core of Marx's theory of Capital, in which Marx theorizes Capital not as a thing but as a "social relation of production."[16] A person, a thing, or a machine becomes a part of Capital only when it is entered into a social relation of production. Marxism and phenomenology's shared emphasis on intersubjectivity and social relation as infinitely expandable processes binds them together and opens up room for potential collaboration.

In the writings of Lefebvre, exemplified by *The Production of Space* (*La production de l'espace*) that critiques the competitive Cold War urban industrial development in both capitalist and socialist blocs, Marxist phenomenology can be further explored with Lefebvre's elusive theorization of "lived experience" and "lived space" as strategies of resistance. Emphasizing that "space" is not a thing but a cumulative process of rendering space reproducible, Lefebvre's Marxist urban theory moves through different spatial categories, beginning with absolute space, transitioning to abstract space and contradictory space, and ending with differential space as the site of consciousness and the locus of the performative production of differences.[17] In addition to writing against the systematized abstraction of space, *The Production of Space* is also a theory that speculates the place and role of the body in producing the space of resistance. Specifically, the meaning of the book's title is twofold: one refers to the production of "space" by rendering space into a thing-like object and repeatable procedures, and another refers to the production of the space of resistance. Appearing throughout the text, the body figures centrally as another type of space. For example, Lefebvre asks:

Can the body, with its capacity for action, and its various energies, be said to create space? Assuredly, but not in the sense that occupation might be said to "manufacture" spatiality; rather, there is an immediate relationship between the body and its space, between the body's deployment in space and its occupation of space. Before *producing* itself by drawing nourishment from that realm, and before *reproducing* itself by generating other bodies, each living body *is* space and *has* its space: it produces itself in space and it also produces that space. This is a truly remarkable relationship: the body with the energies at its disposal, the living body, creates or produces its own space; conversely, the laws of space, which is to say the laws of discrimination in space, also govern the living body and the deployment of its energies.[18]

Using a set of vocabulary that evokes the "living" body—rhythms, gestures, beyond "subject" and "object"—Lefebvre treats the body as an "enigma" that has the capacity to "produce differences 'unconsciously' out of repetitions." The capitalist production of objectified space is countered with body-centered spatial practices that can arguably take any form, as they emerge out of contingency. Lefebvre's Marxist phenomenological theorization of the body stops here, reaching a limit and leaving the "differential body" to the imagination. What the "body" means is never clarified in Lefebvre's prolific writings. Not referring to the biological body, it becomes instead an elusive synonym for a set of spatial and temporal practices that produce what Lefebvre describes as "energies," "laws of space," "occupation," and "spatiality."[19] The temporal dimension of the differential body is central to his theorization of resistance, for it implies repetition, dispersal, and dissemination—in other words, an unspecified network of communication that extends from the body to the ultimate transformation and disruption of the urban fabric, leading to the discussion of the dissemination of contemporary urban horror and cinema's role in helping to produce a *different* space.

In texts that were written in response to the global urban uprisings of 1968 with a vantage point of continental Europe, Lefebvre's elusive descriptions of the "differential body" and "differential space" that are envisioned as embodied actions and performativity of resistance against both capitalism and socialism pose old and new questions to the neoliberal post-socialist system that arose in the aftermath of the Cold War. Highlighting the indistinguishability of capitalist and socialist production of space, Lefebvre's Marxist phenomenology is already mapping the emergence of a mutative system—without a (proper) name—that thrives on the combined structure of capitalism and socialism. To elaborate on the contemporary conditions producing the "urban" in urban horror, the next section focuses on the emergence of Chinese neoliberal post-socialism, a contemporary system beyond capitalism and socialism that resides in the imaginaries of the post-.

Neoliberal Post-Socialism: A Globalizing System without a (Proper) Name

The juxtaposition of fireworks and police tear-gassing captured in *Yellowing* in a space like Hong Kong—a historical zone of exception that evolved from a colonial port city ceded to England in the nineteenth century to the PRC's special administrative region after 1997—raises questions about the deployment of horror as a public sentiment of dissent in a documentary produced in the aftermath of the Umbrella Movement and about the evocation of a new system of political and economic extraction whose name is not yet determinable. The sights and sounds of urban horror the film disseminates are produced and mediated by a unique urbanscape that is constructed by spatial technologies that already exceed Engels's description of a nineteenth-century factory town. Increasingly integrated in the archipelagoes of South China's expanding special economic zones that are creating an underexplored history of global post-socialism, Hong Kong is a case that illustrates the post-socialist spatial technology of creating and managing proliferating zones of exception in and outside of post-socialist China for the purpose of political integration and financial profitability. I will leave the detailed study of post-socialism in Hong Kong to chapter 4. The evocation of the urban that now mediates the production of affect in the media of resistance requires a more detailed introduction, beginning with a fundamental rethinking of what Chinese post-socialism means, the kinds of deterritorializing histories it engenders, and the work that post- as a sliding signifier performs. It is one task to meticulously compile a post-socialist urban history that includes architectural designs, engineering blueprints, finance reports, and environmental evaluations for the numerous megaports, bridges, expressways, dams, canals, railways, and energy plants. It is another to theorize the "production of space" under the condition of Sinocentric neoliberal post-socialism, whose complexity I present below.[20]

From the collapse of the Soviet Empire to the fall of the Berlin Wall, the past few decades have witnessed a surge of narratives recounting and imagining the end of socialism and the beginning of the neoliberal post-socialist era. However, as post- becomes a common trope used to describe the geopolitical and economic relations between the capitalist and socialist blocs after the Cold War, the imagined spatiality of post-*socialism*—especially the issue of whether it is a phenomenon happening only within formerly socialist countries—highlights an area of opacity that the emphasis on neoliberal post-socialism addresses. As the dissolution of socialist state powers swept across Eastern Europe and China, creating a diverse variety of post-socialist pathways after 1989, what is commonly perceived as the end of the Cold War was in reality the beginning of a new historical moment that we can characterize as the era of neoliberal post-socialism.[21] Distinct from the post-socialism that refers to the historical transformation of the juridical, economic, and political structures of formerly socialist states and societies, neoliberal post-socialism refers to the ongoing formation and rearticulation of the geopolitical relations between formerly socialist and nonsocialist countries in the era of the post-. Considering their intensifying economic, political, and cultural interdependence, where post-socialism begins and where it ends becomes conceptually blurred. Yet the idea of a world that has moved past Cold War divisions seeps into the political unconscious of the global post-socialist world and motivates new financial, infrastructural, technological, and transnational neocolonial projects. A new logic of the post- is at work, and calls for an excavation of the post-—a site where the anticipation of the post- generates lived global histories that expand like a rhizome with incommensurable differences—that each chapter of this book presents. The attention to lateral and comparative histories of post-socialism—with special attention to the formation of post-socialist relations between the PRC and the rest of the world—is the underlying theme that motivates this study.

To analyze the new logic of the post-, one needs to consider its proliferation in the post–Cold War era. As post-socialism became ubiquitous in describing the end of socialism during the early 1990s, the idea of post-capitalism—an information-based knowledge society that ended capitalism as the developed First World knew it—was also being introduced.[22] The coexistence of these notions emphasizes how the iterations of post–Cold War geopolitical relations are in search of a new name and a new spatial-temporal metaphor. The crisis of socialism also reflects the crisis of capitalism, highlighting a bigger issue that remains elusive and opaque. Rather than making a case for the end of either socialism or capitalism, neoliberal post-socialism considers their interrelation and reads the proliferation of the post- as the symptom of a new economic rationality: the logic of the post-X.

Although the post- is commonly associated with a mode of anticipation that evokes a different future path, the temporal logic embedded in the rhetoric of post-socialism is paradoxically hyphenated and reverts back to socialism. The anticipation is built upon a mode of regression, where the future is conceptualized through indeterminable relations with a former system that is neither alive nor dead. Rather than describing a new era to come, the post- conjoins a suspended future with a reimagined past. The result is a new mode of temporality characterized by infinite deferment and a prolonged anticipation of a future that may never come. The global post-socialist condition can thus be characterized as a perpetually extended *present* that renders the traditional categories of past, present, and future obsolete (see chapter 3).[23] Therefore, I use the post- not to describe the era following the end of the Cold War but to ask how the post- is put to work as a temporalized and spatialized imaginary in the production of post-socialism as a global reality. The new global condition that characterizes the present is not so much the end of socialisms as the emergence of a post-X logic, where the allusive power of the post- and the conjoining effect of the hyphen contribute to an extended and intensified present, leaving in question the place of the past, the role of the future, and the power of the post- that subjects both to infinite redefinitions.

The post- as an active cultural field that is continuously remade to rehearse the desires and anxieties of an era can be glimpsed from the term's intellectual history in English-language scholarship. In the year of the Tiananmen Square massacre of 1989, Arif Dirlik described post-socialism in a hopeful light, calling it "a radical vision of the future" that "offers the possibility in the midst of a crisis in socialism of rethinking socialism in a new, more creative ways."[24] Still envisioning a distinction between post-socialism and capitalism in a text written in the 2000s, Xudong Zhang describes the post- in post-socialism as a potential space of resistance against global capitalism: "Like the prefix *post-* in *post-colonialism*, the *post-* in *post-socialism* indicates a new socioeconomic and cultural-political subjectivity which prefigures the new but is embedded in an order of things that does not readily recognize the ideological claim, political legitimacy, and cultural validity of capitalist globalization for the totality of human history and its future horizon."[25] Yet in his study of emergent post-socialist cultural forms of the 1990s and 2000s and their relationship with market forces, Jason McGrath defines post-socialism as global capitalism: "I argue that not only have the forces of marketization resulted in a new cultural logic in China, but this development is part of a global condition of post-socialist modernity and must be understood in the context of the history of the global capitalist system, which not only transforms China but also is thereby transformed."[26] Rather than a stable and consistent concept, the meaning of the post- evolved from a utopianized beginning of a new era to the synonym of global capitalism, revealing the function of the post- as a sliding signifier that mediates the relationship between China's past and future, while both are subject to infinite reconstructions. Absent from these definitions is the consideration of post-socialism(s) that can no longer be contained in the territorial borders of formerly socialist countries, as a globally imagined post- shifts the course of history and spatial expansion after the Cold War.

Temporal anticipation defines the global condition of post-socialism, referring not only to the disintegration of an organized alternative to capitalism but also to an emergent post-socialist economic rationality, where the post- becomes an essential instrument for maximizing and managing a conceptual space of flexible ambiguity that aids the creation of transterritorial, neoliberal technologies of economic extraction and political integration. Instead of periodizing a bygone era that is no longer relevant in the temporal logic of global capitalism—with the assumption that post-socialism is an interchangeable synonym for global capitalism—I examine post-socialism as a present global condition affecting the entire world, with an emphasis on Chinese post-socialism as a mutative and transregional imaginary creating concrete post-socialist histories in the PRC and the Sinophone world beyond.[27] I choose the phrase *Chinese post-socialism* rather than "PRC post-socialism" to invoke the flexibility and ambiguity that are associated with the former in the creation of transregional economic integration. The post- refers to an empty signifier where tangible historical meanings and consequences are created, as the prefix is claimed and reclaimed in different geopolitical and national contexts. Evoking a future that is framed as the aftermath to an obfuscated past, the structure of the post-X—with the emphasis on the post- and a system that conjoins—captures the underlying operational techniques in the mutative system of neoliberal post-socialism, where the contingent iterations of neoliberalism depend on the condition of global post-socialism.

The term *neoliberal post-socialism* arises out of the desire to theorize an impasse in the study of the contemporary Sinophone world after China implemented economic reform policies in 1978. The crisis manifests most visibly in the static language available to describe the decades of economic and political expansions and integrations that have taken place across and beyond the Sinophone world. From socialism with Chinese characteristics to market socialism, late socialism, and post-socialism, to capitalism, late capitalism, state capitalism, and neoliberalism, the proliferation of terms and conceptual frameworks used to identify China's state-managed and globally expansionist economic development suggests a new global phenomenon that struggles to find a language of articulation.[28]

Decades have passed since China entered the era of economic reform. The events that followed signaled for many the beginning of a new era when the globalization of capitalism was conflated with the promise of individual freedom and democracy.[29] However, amid the familiar narrative describing China's liberation from a Cold War totalitarian socialist regime, the Tiananmen Square massacre of 1989 broadcast to the world that the post- in Chinese post-socialism has distinct meanings in the economic and political realms. The "freedom" associated with the "free" market economy is only a flexible façade, subject to infinite redefinition. The utopic and ambiguous myth of a democracy expanding through market forces rebounded, leaving behind shock and disappointment but also the searing inscriptions of a new post-socialist economic rationality that now creates its own kind of mutative state apparatus. Under neoliberal post-socialism, the state can no longer be understood as the centralized locus of political and economic sovereignty but has instead become what Michel Foucault describes as the *mobile effect* of multiple governmentalities that produce and organize the condition for freedom.[30] The new state in the post-socialist world is therefore best characterized by its mutative contingency rather than by a traditional decision-making center.

The question raised by acts of state violence in post-socialist times—the Tiananmen massacre, the civil unrest in Xinjiang, the Umbrella Movement in Hong Kong, the political suppression of Tibet and Taiwan, and many more that remain unnamed—is captured in the intensification of transnational Sinocentric economic integration, financial speculation, and trans-Asian infrastructural urbanization—in other words, the contradiction between economic freedom and the political undoing of freedom. Here transnational Sinocentric economic integration is used to describe Chinese post-socialism as a deterritorializing machine of desires that produces speculative fantasies of limitless and borderless economic accumulation and growth, with the PRC as the nexus of these desires. Some observers attribute contemporary state violence to the Cold War narrative of socialist totalitarianism, while others dismiss the escalating regional tension as due to China's domestic and international problems. But neither claim provides the tools to theorize an emerging system that challenges the conventional origin story that capitalism, including its advanced form of neoliberalism, emanates from the West and expands worldwide. In Foucault's theorization of neoliberalism in postwar Germany, France, and the United States, he distinguishes between liberalism and neoliberalism. The difference resides not in the state's adoption of new market-oriented policies but in a fundamental redefinition of the state itself: instead of an autonomous governing entity, the state has become the mobile effects of a new order of economic rationality.[31] Contradicting the common belief that neoliberalism is the withering away of the state through practices that maximize deregulation and nonintervention (the classic ingredients of laissez-faire economics), the neoliberal world that Foucault describes has a market economy without laissez-faire and depends on state intervention. Fundamentally, the relationship between the market and the state shifted in the neoliberal era, and the state can no longer be understood as an autonomous source of power. Foucault writes, "Government must accompany the market economy from start to finish. The market economy does not take something away from government. Rather, it indicates, it constitutes the general index in which one must place the rule for defining all governmental action. *One must govern for the market, rather than because of the market.*"[32] The overlapping intensification of state violence, surveillance, and state-managed neoliberalism in the Sinocentric post-socialist world suggests a different origin story. Yet it remains unclear what has emerged. How do we comprehend a "neoliberalism with Chinese characteristics" that exposes the assumptions of a Eurocentric capitalist and neoliberal developmentalist model? How do we decipher the intricate mechanisms and lived experiences of a Sinocentric "Chinese neoliberalism" with full acknowledgment of the flexibility and ambiguity of these terms?[33]

A new type of neoliberal state has arisen in the People's Republic of China—a regime alternately called authoritarian socialist, post-socialist, and post-capitalist—that operates according to the logic of the post-X. The shifting terms and conceptual frameworks capture the limits of the language available to describe neoliberalism, especially its relationship to an Asia that has historically been relegated to passively receiving capitalist imperialism—a history that has led Western philosophy to speculate about how the "lack" of an indigenous capitalism in Asian countries subjected these countries to the violence of imperialism. Naming this tendency the "white mythologies" of Western philosophy, Shih Shu-mei highlights the way China is discussed in Hegel, Marx, and Max Weber. These eminent figures provide interconnected theories on the lack of the concept of freedom, the depth of interiority, and the desire to conquer nature in Chinese society, all of them contributing to the notion of incommensurability between China and global capitalism.[34] Chinese historians' critiques of global capitalism during the socialist era further encouraged the idea that capitalism was a totalizing system that existed elsewhere and then entered an insulated China. Such claims are echoed in the common narrative that defines post-socialism as the final triumph of global capitalism, wherein the capitalist economic system—and more recently the neoliberal economic system—entered socialist China while transforming everything within. But this view obscures the fact that socialism and capitalism share a developmentalist logic that provides the basis for a new economic rationality in the era of the post-.

When confronted with the expansion of Chinese state power that governs *for* the market with Chinese characteristics, the crisis induced by the global condition of post-socialism shifts from the expansion of neoliberalism, assumed to be a known global phenomenon that replaces capitalism, to a problem that is perceivable only in an unnamable economic rationality and that exists in fragile connection to what was known as socialism, capitalism, and neoliberalism. In the era of economic reform, "socialism with Chinese characteristics," describing either an Asianized Chinese socialism or a late developmental stage of socialism (mirroring late capitalism), indicates the radical transformation of the state and its sociopolitical functions. The common rhetoric used to describe China's state capitalism, authoritarian capitalism, or state neoliberalism indicates not adequate frameworks or proper names but a shadow archive of conceptual proximities that capture the difficulty of remapping an emergent power structure after the collapse of existing geopolitical imaginaries in the post–Cold War world.

From state-led economic reform policies and the strategic deployment of economic and political zones of exception (e.g., special economic zones and special administrative regions) to the recent Belt and Road Initiative (*yidai yilu*) that aims to create an integrated infrastructural network connecting China to Western and Eastern Europe, the Middle East, and Central, South, and Southeast Asia, the prominent role of the Chinese state in what has been theorized as a rapidly neoliberalizing global economy has become a hypervisible blind spot.[35] In David Harvey's *A Brief History of Neoliberalism*, where China is portrayed as a key player in the global economy since the 1970s, neoliberalism in China is given special treatment in the description "neoliberalism 'with Chinese characteristics.'"[36] Unable to decipher China's state-managed neoliberalism, Harvey's term can be read as a rupture in neoliberalism's apparent origin in capitalism, since China's case clearly presents a different origin story rooted in state socialism. "Chinese characteristics" also offers more questions than answers. Namely, what does it mean to suggest that there is an "exception" to the economic model that explains the global expansion of neoliberalism? Does "neoliberalism with

Chinese characteristics" propose a specific "China model" that is replicable in other parts of the world?[37] Neither a representative history of neoliberalism nor the only text that deals with the nuanced relationship between Asia and neoliberalism, Harvey's approach to Chinese post-socialism is reminiscent of the historical tension between Asia and capitalism in theoretical discourses that continues to the present day. Narratives on the origins of capitalism tend to view it as a Eurocentric economic system that manifests in the combined forms of European colonialism and imperialism, leading to post-colonial critiques of centers and peripheries as well as the temporal grid of advancement and backwardness.[38] The assumption that a totalizing system is moving across different countries, languages, and cultures predominates and has intensified in recent years, especially in the discourse of economic development used to describe the post-socialist world, where capitalism is perceived as expanding beyond its geopolitical borders and opening up formerly closed territories.

The genealogy of the crisis in language elucidates a new global impasse: the logic of the post-X, where the post- is affixed to existing namable systems not for the purpose of clarifying a future path or relationship with the past but to create a perpetual present that allows for maximum economic and political impunity. The problem of the present moment is not how to choose the perfect or politically correct word but the fact that no proper name can be selected for the new economic rationality that shapes a predatory global system. Due to the flexibility and ambiguity of the post-, a new neoliberal post-socialist system that strategically assigns vulnerability and profits from the management of precarity has come into being.[39] The post- is strategically deployed, managed, and instrumentalized to allow for complicit participation among both formerly socialist and nonsocialist countries in the development of new state and extrastate technologies of governmentality. The logic of the post-X—a temporal iteration of a teleological future that hinges on a strategically obfuscated relationship with an infinitely reimagined past—is at the core of a new global imaginary that depends on post-socialism as a global condition with concrete histories that await genealogical excavation.

The *Urban* in the Horror

The opacity of the post-X—an intensifying focus on the current practices of expansion and extraction that fade away the past and eradicate the future—provides the condition for a new Sinocentric expansionism that has been transforming the physical landscape of China and its neighboring regions. With the aim of creating better connectivity and extending its military presence, China has been aggressively developing new spatial technologies on air, land, and maritime waters to connect old and new economic trade routes and initiate new pathways for military logistics. Expressways and train tracks cut across remote mountains and deserts, connecting Chinese cities to Central Asia and Europe. In addition, satellite megaports extend China's logistics routes to the maritime waters of South and Southeast Asian countries, while oil and gas pipelines grow between Central Asia and China. These techniques of infrastructural and urban expansionism raise new questions about how we understand post-socialist urbanization—as not only a domestic Chinese occurrence but also an expanding global phenomenon.[40]

Under the guise of a flexible post-, new technologies of spatial management proliferate, including the practice of zoning, infrastructural diplomacy, the expansion of the urban fabric, land speculation, and dispossession.[41] These technologies create new kinds of displacement that are both physical and psychical. The evocation of urban horror in the Hong Kong–produced film *Yellowing* proposes a new record of urban affect that demands a parallel examination of the spatial transformations that are produced under the neoliberal post-socialist condition, and cinema as a mediator and disseminator of emergent feelings that are produced in specific social settings. Before the question of cinematic mediation is addressed, the *urban* in the horror requires clarification.

Although Sinocentric urban development has homogeneity as its goal, it is never a homogeneous process. As new spaces are produced and rendered reproducible, new psychical structures and networks of communication emerge. Post-socialism means different opportunities—and the loss of opportunities—for various countries and groups of communities, creating dissimilar urban realities that confront distinctly gendered, ethnicized, and classed subjects. The moment has arrived to question the claim of authority given only to the *visible* evidence of urbanization that is already conditioned by a specific regime of visibility, where human subjects and other ecological actors are stripped away and rendered as blurred, omitted, and blotted blind spots by post-socialist economic rationality. The issue here is less a question of competing discourses of urban history and more the lack of critical analytical tools for remapping how the violence of space (as evolving technologies and procedures for managing and abstracting space) operates differently across the neoliberal post-socialist world.

The study of urban horror is not meant to designate the history of specific Chinese cities for two main reasons. The first concerns how space is approached in Marxist thought. Whereas Marx and Engels are invested in the space of production—the factory city, the production line, and the space and time of labor—Lefebvre extends these Marxian inquiries and draws attention to space as not merely a physical or architectural site but a process of rendering space reproducible through abstraction, homogenization, and repetition. As he points out, space is a live and mutative process of rendering rather than a stationary and unchanging object. Writing *The Production of Space* during the Cold War, Lefebvre explains the rationale for his treatise on the violence of objectification that intensifies under capitalism: "Perhaps it would make sense to decide without further ado to seek inspiration in Marx's *Capital*—not in the sense of sifting it for quotations nor in the sense of subjecting it to the 'ultimate exegesis,' but in the sense of following *Capital's* plan in dealing with space." In a speculative mode, Lefebvre's *Production of Space* and numerous books on the urban revolution do not apply Marxist thought to postwar European society, but rather take Marx and Engels's initial inquiries as methodological leads in order to confront the new technologies of space that are produced in the advanced stages of capitalism, socialism, and neoliberalism. Writing about the urban as a problematic in both capitalist and socialist systems, Lefebvre raises crucial questions about the production of space that move beyond ideologically constructed dichotomies. For example, he asks, "Has state socialism produced a space of its own?"[42] Concluding that it has not, he observes the similitude between the capitalist and the socialist production of space, paving the way for a future Marxist urban theory where we encounter Chinese post-socialism—a socialist regime that is strategically adopting and reinventing neoliberal economic techniques to manage its participation in the world market. In addition to indicating a possible socialist origin to neoliberalism, the post-X logic that characterizes the global condition of post-socialism has become the general means through which new technologies of space are deployed.

The second reason for not conceptualizing the book as an introduction to major urban transformations in specific Chinese cities is due to the elusiveness of the city as an analytical category. In the context of transnational post-socialist urbanization, where new procedures of producing, reproducing, abandoning, and marginalizing space have created numerous types of spaces (e.g., special economic zones, special administrative regions, science and industrial parks, and factory cities), the city as a historical category for analyzing urbanization provides only a limited vantage point. Rather than focusing on Beijing, Hong Kong, and Taipei as the quintessential Chinese cities, the chapters unravel the violent process of *producing* these post-X spaces through the repeated subjections to techniques of dispossession, political integration, and zoning. Cities like Hong Kong and Shenzhen, for example, have become code names for spatial software to be copied and deployed elsewhere in the global proliferation of replicated space. Urban horror addresses not the specific history of each city's evolution but the new technologies of producing space that each city helps make visible. The problems they highlight are not unique but belong to a globalizing epidemic. As these spatial techniques are revised and redeployed, dispossession and inequality are programmed into the way space is reproduced, transmitting and mutating the origins of the problem. The *urban* in urban horror therefore is not used to indicate specific city-based studies but is meant to open up the city as a process that invokes a particular treatment of space to render it reproducible according to the logic of neoliberal economic expansionism and Sinocentric post-socialism.

The emergence of Engels's industrial horror corresponds to the global proliferation of factory towns that created a new spatial technology of economic extraction and industrial colonialism. Therefore the question that contemporary urban horror poses is the emergence and evolution of new methods of producing and managing space—embedded in socialist and post-socialist factory spaces (chapter 1), apartments and urban dwelling spaces as the mechanisms of maintaining gender hierarchy (chapter 2), the compression of space and the production of an intensive present (chapter 3), zoning and the creation of economic and political zones of exception (chapter 4), and the management of precaritized bodies (chapter 5). Responding and reacting to the invisible techniques and protocols of rendering space reproducible, new aesthetic forms emerge as they provoke, convey, and rehearse the elusive sentiment of horror that belongs to the neoliberal post-socialist epoch.

The goal of the book is thus not to take horror that is loosely defined as physical fright or fear as the framework of reading contemporary Chinese cinemas, but rather to collect a wide spectrum of sentiments and feelings circulating in the sensory network of cinema and ask: What does horror mean in the neoliberal post-socialist world? What are the images, people, temporalities, and spaces that are associated with the affect of horror? What are the aesthetic forms that now accommodate the excesses of systematized violence that redraw the boundary between the visible and the invisible, and the perceptible and imperceptible worlds? Shifting the focus from body-centered horror that was produced in industrializing Euro-American societies to the diffusion of horror in contemporary Chinese cinemas, the emergence of urban horror on one hand suggests the changing scale of a global system that is no longer containable in perceivable bodies of monstrosity, and on the other hand stresses the importance of theorizing *relationalities*, where the body is a nodal point in the social network of relations that extend to the urban fabric and the manufactured environment beyond.

Speculating the Futures of Film: The Forces of Resistance in the Era of Hypermediality

To close this introduction, I return to Chan Tze-woon's *Yellowing* on Hong Kong's Umbrella Movement, a recent film that I choose to open the discussion of contemporary urban horror that explores the forces of resistance in the era of neoliberal post-socialism. In the book's collection of films from China, Hong Kong, and Taiwan—including popular post-socialist nostalgia films, feminist blockbusters, experimental documentaries, commercial horror-comedies, art house films, and more—the mixing of genres is not meant to erase individual generic traditions and filmmaking practices but to suggest a way of capturing the circulation and accumulation of urban horror and the futurity of resistance that seep into different generic forms. The Umbrella Movement represents a visible point in recent history when embodied actions were taken against an accumulating history of making Hong Kong a space of exception. However, the images of ordinary citizens taking action against the unknown and the richness of other political performativities of protests that are surging and circulating in Chinese cinemas suggest the presence of an invisible archive of public sentiments, arising as the present becomes increasingly incomprehensible.

Across different genres, the rehearsal of urban horror implies the anticipation of a different futurity that is captured in *Yellowing*'s documentary form, for instance. Composed of a series of video diaries where the same cast speaks to the camera and regularly records their thoughts and feelings during the protest, the dominant sentiment that motivates their performance is to leave records for the future—suggested by the film's Chinese title, *Luanshi beiwang* (Memorandums of troubled times)—as a reminder for themselves, for Hong Kong, and for the future world from where the revolution will be continued. Ending the film with a monologue from the aftermath of the Occupy movement, the filmmaker talks through a series of images: a shot of the wind blowing on the curtains in his studio in the present, excerpts of the protesting footage, the tents that occupied the streets, the protesters who slept on the pavements, hands held tightly together to form a human shield, and more. Has the protest changed anything? The images are the only things left, as Chan says with a melancholic tone. Yet cutting to an interview with a young adult protester, who is asked to imagine whether he will be the same person in twenty years, the film ends with his reply: "If I were different, hit me hard and wake me up. Your film will be important evidence, to show me who I had been twenty years ago." The statement is simple and common, conveying a documentary mode that treats the image as a retainer of the past. Yet the real question raised by the film that is made to visualize resistance lies in the nuanced change in the meaning of the image and image-making in the contemporary world. For the filmmaker and the filmed subjects in *Yellowing*, the Umbrella Movement refers not to the urban revolution that is contained in seventy-nine days of footage, but to a deterritorialized event that sets off a sensory revolution made up of infinite series of future virtual encounters that are mediated by the images they made. The film initiates communicational channels that expand through circulation, creating unpredictable results that are beyond the temporality and space of filmmaking. As the subjects speak intently in front of the camera, with full knowledge of the forces of disseminated images, their act of recording suggests a different understanding of mediated resistance in the era of hypermediality.

The production and dissemination of urban horror require a medium that opens sensory channels and circulates accumulated affect. The forces of resistance refer not simply to the change in the aesthetic style of horror (i.e., the transition from body-centered horror to the diffusion of horror), but to the fundamental change in the meaning of the image and of image-making practices in the era of hypermediality, when instantly transmitted sights and sounds of neoliberal post-socialism saturate technologically enhanced media cultures. The time period this book examines corresponds to major shifts in the geopolitical relations in Sinophone Asia after the putative end of the Cold War and to a transnational media revolution. From the invention of the Video Home System (vHS) in the late 1970s that destroyed the Asian film markets due to the prevalence of piracy, to the ubiquity of digital recording technologies in the 1990s that changed the logic of recording from reproduction to intervention and manipulation, the era of neoliberal post-socialism coincides with a time of radical transformations in the meaning of the image.[43]

While it is possible to examine the post–Cold War era as the era of mass protests, democratization, human rights movements, and the recent Occupy movements across the region, these forces of resistance cannot be fully understood without considering the fact that we have entered the era of hypermediality, when the fundamental definition of revolution is determined by the mediated meanings of images and sounds.[44] The revolution—as the physical gathering of protesting bodies—has undergone a dramatic transformation. The conventional logic of capture that relies on the notion of an original and the reproduction of mimetic copies has been subverted. The revolution can no longer be understood as the sequential movement from a preconstituted event to its capture on media technology but should instead be interpreted as precisely the *effect* of the image. As Rey Chow argues in the theorization of transmedial entanglements, reality in the contemporary world of hypermediality should be treated as the mobile assemblage and movements across multiple entangled media and cultural platforms. The traditional correspondent relationship between the original and the copy has collapsed, calling for a new metaphor for theoretical thinking in the twenty-first century. Chow writes, "Rather than reality being caught in the sense of being contained, detained, or retained in the copy-image (understood as a repository), it is now the machinic act or event of capture, with its capacity for further partitioning (that is, for generating additional copies and images ad infinitum), that sets reality in motion, that invents or makes reality, as it were."[45] The cinematic dissemination of urban horror probes, therefore, not how the realities of social protests are represented in films but rather how the speculative futures of the image help create mobile realities wherein lie the forces of resistance.

The result of the speed and intensity of the production and circulation of the image, as Chow describes, is "the collapse of the time lag between the world and its capture."[46] A new notion of reality emerged: reality is made *for* the image rather than the image's representing a preexisting reality. This notion highlights how little we know about the potential futures of the image, which is an approximate term for the transmedial and multisensory spectrum of perception that suggests a possible revolution of the sensible world. From Walter Benjamin's discussion of the waning of the aura in the age of mechanical reproduction to Jean Baudrillard's theorization of the precession of simulacra where the signs of the real substitute for the real, the image in the tradition of Marxist criticism has been turned into a site for symptomizing commodity fetishism and value abstraction.[47] While it is well established that the image is moving further away from reality and has lost its representational power, the theoretical debates that center on mimesis and antimimesis have reached a limit. The challenge that confronts the contemporary world as newer technologies of image capture and distribution continue to accelerate image reproduction and circulation is no longer the question of what is true or false. Rather, as the notion of a totalizing reality crumbles, the more urgent task is to acknowledge that the image has become *the condition of reality, before reality can be real.* A new logic of technologized visuality has emerged, where images are meant and required to produce new realities, perceptual frames, and the distribution of the sensible world. Visuality has become the constitutive condition of feelings, sensations, political domination, and public dissent that are premised upon speculations about the afterlife and futures of the image.

Like Rancière, I ask if there is another way to understand the relationship between aesthetics and politics, following decades of reading aesthetics as the reflection of politics. When the two are put in a hierarchical relationship (i.e., politics creates aesthetics), how does one reimagine a different political landscape and system? How does one create Lefebvre's differential space? Rancière opens up both aesthetics and politics for questioning. "Politics," in his usage, "revolves around what is seen and what can be said about it, around who has the ability to see and the talent to speak, around the properties of spaces and the possibilities of time."[48] For Rancière, politics refers to the frame of the sensible world that separates the legible from the illegible, a frame that is constituted and determined by hierarchical power relations in the existing world. Resisting and reframing politics, Rancière's aesthetics is infused with revolutionary potentialities. Rather than a set of generic practices, aesthetics refers to the mode of *dis-sensus,* a term he uses to evoke the fracturing of social hierarchy, a process of reordering the senses, and the redistribution of the sensible world. Aesthetics is the revolution of the sensible world and the locus of the forces of resistance. The elusiveness of urban horror as emergent aesthetic forms draws upon the envisioned power of aesthetics. Regardless of the actions, inactions, and social movements they produce, cinema's rehearsal of public sentiments presents a new affective landscape that is actively revising the meaning of reality.

Although I use the term *film* to invoke the medium specificity of cinema, the ambiguity of what film or cinema is referring to when film is becoming digital offers, in fact, an opportunity to retheorize the question of medium specificity and mediation. The slippage among film, video, cinema, and multisensory image asks a different kind of question that suggests the affective sociality of what is approximated as film. The term is evocative of a dispersed and contingent network of circulation, constituting a mode of visuality that extends beyond the contents of the film—a reality that is set in motion, connecting cinema to social movements, feminism, and political protests and giving rise to more social futurities that this book traces.

Chapters

Urban Horror begins with a historical study of the factory space—the quintessential figure in both capitalist and socialist mass dreams of industrial modernity—in cinematic representations. While theorizing the factory as a Foucauldian heterotopic space—an *othered* space that delineates a history of marginalization and reflects modernity's contingent imaginaries of economic centers and peripheries—chapter 1 traces the factory's marginalized significance in socialist and post-socialist Chinese cinema.[49] Addressing the cultural obsession with factory ruins in the global post-socialist era, the chapter historicizes the factory gate as a persisting cinematic technology that demonstrated the dichotomy between socialism and capitalism during the Cold War and framed post-socialism as a specific global imaginary in the aftermath of the Cold War. Departing from the conventional nostalgic approach to factory ruins in the post-socialist era, the chapter illustrates through a collection of factory films—including the Lumière brothers' first actuality film, the first and the last PRC factory films, and contemporary post-socialist factory ruin films—the enduring persistence of the factory gate in assigning socialist and capitalist values to the factory interior, wherein lies the space of work and production. Arguing that the post-socialist nostalgia for the socialist glorification of labor is nostalgia without origin, the chapter performs a socialist cognitive mapping based on two factory films released in the PRC in 1949 and 1976.[50] As they bracket the socialist era's visual spectrum, these Chinese factory films reveal not how socialism as an industrial system of production is seen but the many contradictions and impasses in a system constructed on the attempt to reverse capitalism, another antirepresentational system. The result is the infinite abyss of mirror reflections, a mise-en-abîme where the notion of the original is paralyzed. Given that socialism was never realized and lies beyond representation, the question that post-socialist factory ruin films pose is never a matter of socialism's disappearance. As global post-socialism continues to reinvent its own socialist past—reanimating the past as imagined from the present's perspective—we are confronted with the factory gate as a persisting mechanism of revelation and concealment that regulates the divide between the visible and the invisible world.[51] Noting the contrast between the hypervisibility of the ruinous socialist-era factory and the oppressive invisibility of new factory cities in China's special economic zones, the first chapter traces the factory's displacement in the mass dream of industrial modernity, which I argue is not the result of de-industrialization (or the disappearance of factories) but comes from the emergent neoliberal post-socialist regime of visibility that masks the global migration of production sites from developed countries to the special economic zones of Asia.

The second chapter examines the evocation of urban horror from a post-socialist feminist perspective, where I observe the emergence of *intimate dystopias* that critique the spectacle of Chinese post-socialist and masculinist phantasmagorias of the interior in filmmaker Li Shaohong's commercial blockbuster films on romance, love, and domesticity, produced in the 2000s.[52] Emerging from decades of state feminism, where gender as a social category was violently subordinated under class interests, the imaginary of the post- in the post-socialist era further subjects femininity to the commodifying forces of the market, contrary to the common narrative of a post-socialist liberation of gender and sexuality.[53] Rather than taking feminism as a transhistorical and universal category, this chapter excavates the nuanced and complex meanings of femininity in order to theorize a space for post-socialist (nonstate) Chinese feminism.[54] Drawing on Li's ambivalent relationship with socialist (state) and post-socialist (market) femininities in a set of films about women and China's megatropolis, the chapter focuses on the 2000s as a significant decade of transition, when film as a medium became a commercial commodity after China's accession to the World Trade Organization.[55] In films that introduce an urbanscape centered on the everyday, the intimate spaces of gendered domestic life, and the post-socialist logic of interior design in urban apartments and lofts, the urban is deconstructed from within. Urbanization is cynically visualized as a spectacle of commodified interiors that give the illusion of living in a box in the theater of the world.[56] Adding a gendered twist to Benjamin's Marxist critique of the phantasmagorias of the interior, Li's feminist interior portrays a post-socialist masculinist urban (bodies-cities) network, where women are seen as displaced, homeless, and disappeared—physically, psychologically, and symbolically.[57] In the struggle for space, both the body and the city are portrayed as intimate dystopias, where the most familiar things become the most estranging sites of horror.[58]

Chapter 3 addresses the rise of urban horror from the changing concept of time that is mediated by post-socialist Chinese documentary films, where an intensive present is seen replacing the traditional chronological succession of time and creating a crisis of memory in the digital age. Focusing on the New Documentary Movement in the PRC that is also a movement of digital filmmaking, I read documentary films and their mediation and production of post-socialist temporalities through digital filmmaking techniques, including ruin gazing, forwarding and reversing, and accelerating and decelerating film speed. In a comparative study of experimental documentaries on post-socialist temporalities in Eastern Europe and China—including the work of Chantal Akerman, Cong Feng, and Huang Weikai—the chapter examines documentary's performativities of time that illustrate the post- as a locus of desires and anxieties, backward and forward glances that create heterogeneous relationships—with their own economy of stasis, velocity, and speed—in relation to the homogeneous and teleological time of Capital. Each representation of time indicates a relationality and positionality toward the post- as a transitional device and foregrounds emergent public sentiments about the neoliberal myth of economic progress.

Contesting the existing spatial imaginary of post-socialism's territoriality—deployed under the guise of neoliberal post-socialism's deterritorialization and reterritorialization—chapter 4 performs a speculative reading of post-socialism in Hong Kong and locates a transnational neoliberal post-socialist history in a formerly nonsocialist region. Reading the Umbrella Movement as a recent rupture of accumulating urban horror, the chapter focuses on post-1997 Hong Kong cinema to locate the public sentiments that are rehearsing perceptions and reactions to Chinese post-socialist zoning technologies that transform Hong Kong into a political and economic zone of exception.[59] Existent before the protesters occupy the streets of Hong Kong in 2014, the relationship between human bodies and Hong Kong as a part of the expanding archipelagoes of special economic zones in South China is already undergoing a crisis in films that centralize the imaginary of a city-without-bodies—a way of seeing Hong Kong as an abstracted urban space where the human body becomes increasingly unimaginable. Speculating a way of rereading post-1997 Hong Kong cinema that is characterized by the narrative of decline as filmmakers emigrate to China, the chapter draws connections between Hong Kong cinema as where the sentiment of urban horror conjures new aesthetic forms and the Umbrella Movement that actualized the futurity of the image. Detailing zoning and the creation of zones of exception as the primary characteristic of neoliberal post-socialist urbanization, the chapter paves the way for future studies on the infrastructural revolutions that create not yet legible affective and urban post-socialist landscapes beyond the Chinese border.

The last chapter of the book explores the work of the Malaysian Taiwanese filmmaker Tsai Ming-liang and the migration of film to the space of art museums and experiential performance art. In the work of a filmmaker who consistently focuses on marginalized and precaritized people and animals, abandoned buildings, and disappearing objects, the question posed by Tsai's phenomenological cinema is the ethics of representing precarity and precaritized bodies through the institutions of art that are created by and therefore complicit in the neoliberal financial system. As Tsai's films and installation art render the experience of precarity—the condition of being assigned the status of nonbeing according to the economic rationality of neoliberalism that considers people and life disposable—a consumable experience of art, how do we think about aesthetic practices and the forces of resistance in the neoliberal environment that sponsors and produces visions and voices of critique? Moving beyond the acknowledgment of complicity, the chapter poses a more urgent question that confronts contemporary filmmakers and artists: How does one rethink the future of the image, where the future is seemingly controlled by the system it critiques? Through Tsai's filmmaking practice, chapter 5 complicates the ethics of representing precarity in the era of global complicity.

A Note on Romanization

The post-socialist PRC and Sinophone world is not homogeneous, as this book illustrates. The heterogeneity of Sinophone cultures is partially reflected in the different romanization systems used in the PRC, Hong Kong, and Taiwan. For consistency, all film titles and most references are romanized using the pinyin system. However, for the names of Taiwanese and Hong Kong filmmakers, writers, performers, and certain references, I have tried to follow the romanization systems used in these specific regions.

.

1

Cartographies of Socialism and Post-Socialism

The Factory Gate and the Threshold of the Visible World

The Afterlife of the Factory Gate

Two male riders casually chat on a slow-moving motorbike. Through a tracking shot, the camera moves in a parallel motion, revealing and following the movement of the human faces against a background of changing landscapes. The human-centered composition soon gives way to the film's nonhuman protagonist: the ruins of an industrial landscape, where the characters' dwindled size is utilized to accentuate the scale and enormity of monumental pipelines and train tracks that belong to a socialist-era steel factory. The visual emphasis lies not only on the sprawling industrial zone that exceeds the frame's limit but also on its dilapidated state as the metals rust away and the workers are out of sight. Showing a local band performing a melancholic Russian-Chinese song for a funeral in front of the factory's smokestacks at the film's opening, Zhang Meng's *The Piano in a Factory* (*Gang de qin*, 2010) presents a multisensory and experiential ambience, inviting the viewers to cross over a temporal and spatial threshold, and arriving at the realm of imagined nostalgia.[1] In a post-socialist nostalgia film that discovers the socialist industrial landscape—where socialism recedes into the infinite abyss of reinvention—the ruinous remains of industrial socialism become an object of mourning, evoking and producing feelings of loss, desire, and sadness from the perspective of a temporality beyond socialism. However, as the ruins of socialist factories are transformed into cinematic canvases of imagined nostalgia, their new visibility stands in contrast to the invisibility of post-socialist factories and the real sites of labor that are clustered in China's special economic zones. Rather than a sign of a disappearing industrial past, the visibility and invisibility of the space of labor proposes a cinematic history of the factory in mediating the conceptions of work, labor, and body beyond a single era and creating a cartography of the visible and invisible worlds under the economic rationality of socialism and neoliberal post-socialism.

Mediating the definition of work and leisure, production and consumption, and labor and rest, the factory is the quintessential figure in both capitalist and socialist mass dreams of industrial modernity. As the ruinous factory becomes increasingly prominent in the globally imagined post-socialist era—most common in the performative nostalgia of post-socialist cinema—a paradox emerges from the hypervisibility of the socialist-era factory ruins and the invisibility of newly emerged factory cities in the Chinese special economic zones. The contrast contradicts the Eurocentric idea of global deindustrialization that obfuscates the migration of manufacturing sites from the developed world to the PRC's special economic zones; it also highlights the factory's persistence as a mediating device that manages the visibility of specific types of spaces that are created in industrial modernity. Whereas the ruination of socialist-era factories becomes a prominent visual spectacle in post-socialist cinema, the sites of real labor in the post-socialist era are in contrast violently pushed outside the spectrum of visibility. The factory—most specifically the factory gate that creates the imaginary of an interior space-time of production and an exterior space-time of consumption—is deployed as a viewing mechanism where selective contents about the space of labor are revealed and concealed. Thus this chapter presents a cinematic history that traces the afterlife of the factory gate in films produced under capitalism, socialism, and post-socialism. The purpose is to unravel a value-assignment system that tenaciously masks the space of labor—a site of tension where human labor as life and as a thing comes into conflict. As different modes of the factory's visibility are deployed, distinct imaginaries of socialism, post-socialism, and the neoliberal post-X are consolidated, probing the role of cinema in creating the visual and conceptual frames of these global systems.

The first camera in the history of cinema was pointed at a factory, and, as Rancière says, referring to Louis Lumière's actuality film *Workers Leaving* the *Lumière Factory* (*La Sortie de l'Usine Lumière à Lyon*, 1895), "Cinema has never ceased replaying the same scenario [of workers leaving the space and time of labor]." The factory gate is a persistent figure of history that continues to frame the human perception of industrialization, whether capitalist or socialist. In the film, workers are seen leaving the gate of the Lumière factory in Lyon, France. In a single take lasting forty-five seconds, the camera stays in front of the factory gate, witnessing the gate's opening, followed by workers (mostly female) exiting in swift and occasionally exaggerated movements (see figures 1.1 and 1.2). According to Rancière in his discussion of persistent figures of history that exist across time and space (i.e., figures that exist beyond the confines of individual texts and reappear in a variety of contexts), the factory gate in Lumière's film represents one of the most important residual records of cinema's relationship to the economic rationalities of European capitalism. The scene of workers leaving the factory replays, with inexplicable persistence, in films made under the capitalist mode of production and consumption. As Rancière describes it, the scene leaves behind a lasting imprint that determined "the fate of cinema, defining the threshold of what it should or should not see."[2] The factory gate is not only a physical architectural object but also a persisting visual threshold that separates the interior of the factory from the exterior. In the distinction between the space and time of production and consumption, the gate as a threshold gives meaning to the capitalist extraction of labor power in an interior that is protected from view. The scene of people hurrying away, as if impelled by an invisible force, is further explored in the German filmmaker Harun Farocki's documentary of a similar title, *Workers Leaving the Factory* (*Arbeiter verlassen die Fabrik*, 1995). Citing the recurrence of the factory gate in mediating the productive interior and consumptive exterior, the film recounts a history of cinema based on collected footage in twentieth-century Euro-American cinemas, showing workers leaving and running away from a space that is kept invisible, evoking an unapproachable site of industrial horror.

First imagined as a space of exploitation, petty crime, and gang activities that gave rise to labor strikes and domestic protests in early twentieth-century European and Soviet cinemas, the gate as the threshold of the visible remains present in the history of cinema, becoming a liminal site where violent disputes unfold.[3] The gate—constructed upon the difference between the inside and the outside—regulates and maintains an unequal circulation of information, therefore creating an asymmetry of knowledge and restricting the freedom to move.[4] A threshold that belongs neither inside nor outside, it is a space plagued by the constant unfolding of dramas and extreme

FIGURE 1.1. In *Workers Leaving the Lumière Factory* (1895), workers exit the factory gate in swift movements.

FIGURE 1.2. The factory gate in *Workers Leaving the Lumière Factory* (1895) mediates the imaginary of a factory interior space-time of production and an exterior space-time of consumption.

forms of violence. In the era of the international communist uprising in the early twentieth century, dramas that took place at the factory gate led to strikes and revolution, spreading revolutionary fervor well beyond the factory itself. Since the establishment of the People's Republic of China in 1949, the imaginary of the revolution entered the factory gate and visualized the factory's interior, where revolutionaries continue the perpetual struggle to increase productivity and ward off the residues of bourgeois class consciousness. While in competition with capitalist industrial modernity, socialist-era factory films confronted specific dilemmas as they looked for a visual language to construct a socialist industrial future that would feature a different conceptualization of labor and industrialism. In one of the first Chinese factory films, Xu Ke's *Resplendent Light* (*Guangmang wanzhang*, 1949), released shortly before the official establishment of the PRC, the camera descends from a sweeping panoramic aerial shot of an industrial landscape overlooking factory smokestacks and warehouses to the street level, where cars, electric trams, and people overflow the intersections of an industrial town in northeast China (see figures 1.3 and 1.4). The camera then enters the interior of a dilapidated power plant, where workers tirelessly labor to restore lost electricity to the region. So the revolution continues—not only against capitalist bourgeois consciousness but also against the existing limits of production in China, where a technological revolution is urgently needed.

If capitalism is a system of abstraction that is beyond representability, what are the approaches of seeing socialism—a system linked to the negation of the abstraction and opaqueness of capitalism? Rather than directly labeling the new visibility of socialism and the aesthetics of socialist realism *as* the equivalence of socialism, the question that Chinese factory films leave behind is an archive of gaps, impasses, and limits that are recorded in the task of rendering socialism in concrete visual terms. The visibility of the factory's interior contains traces of historical limits and conceptual contradictions that have never been resolved. The dilemmas in seeing socialism have less to do with China's late entry into mass-scale industrialization or the relatively few works of proletarian literature and film and more to do with the ambiguous relationship between the ideals of communism and the abstracting system of socialist industrialism.[5] The impasse, as this chapter illustrates through two factory films that bracket the socialist era—Xu Ke's *Resplendent Light* and Dong Kena's *Fiery Youth* (*Qingchun sihuo*, 1976)—persists in the representations of the factory interior. These films highlight two constellations of social imaginaries that mark the beginning and end of Chinese socialism, beginning with the mass dream of a socialist industrial modernity and ending

FIGURE 1.3. Xu Ke's *Resplendent Light* (1949) recodes the city from a space of consumption to a space of production.

FIGURE 1.4. In Xu Ke's *Resplendent Light* (1949), the camera descends from a sweeping panoramic aerial shot of an industrial landscape overlooking factory smokestacks and warehouses to the street level.

with unceasing class struggle. They record cinematic residues that are not reducible to genre development but rather produce unexplored questions on the cultural techniques of seeing socialism.[6]

As China enters the era of the post-, socialist-era factories have become sites for ruin gazing. In a variety of nonfiction and fiction films—Wang Bing's *Tie Xi Qu: West of the Tracks* (2003), Jia Zhangke's *24 City* (*Ershisi cheng ji*, 2008), and Zhang Meng's *The Piano in a Factory*—socialist-era factories are deteriorating and falling into oblivion. Yet the factory gate persists and continues to mediate the cultural representations of socialism and capitalism. Though it is commonly assumed that factories are no longer relevant in the era of the post-, the persistence of the gate challenges the common narratives of post-socialism and post-industrialism that dismiss the cultural, political, and economic significance of factory space. As chapter 3 explores in further detail, ruins give the impression of raw materials to be gazed upon. Yet the way we look at ruins is not raw but rather framed by a long tradition of ruin gazing. In Wang Bing's *West of the Tracks*—a nine-hour documentary about factory workers facing imminent unemployment in China's last remaining state-funded factory districts in the city of Shenyang—the factory gate is presented as a prolonged spectacle of temporal intensity. The camera is positioned at the head of a slow-moving train, and the act of entering the factory gate is performed as a phenomenological experience of slow time travel. As the camera passes through a snow-covered industrial landscape, the long duration of the scene reveals the scale of industrial ruins. In a sequence lasting eight minutes, the camera acts as a sensory organ, a pair of eyes to salvage a disappearing landscape that is identified in a subtitle: "1999, Shenyang Smelting Factory. Built in 1934. At one time, the factory employed 13,000 workers." The camera enters the factory gate and visualizes the interior, this time to reveal the ruination of socialism, conceptualized as a landscape of male bodies, whose physical state and daily struggles reverse the typical glorification of laboring bodies. Entrance through the gate frames the perception of a landscape composed of workers' deteriorating bodies, which provides the medium (the visual stand-in) for seeing post-socialism; in the meantime socialism recedes into spectral nostalgia for an anticipated industrial modernity that was never complete in the first place. Both Jia Zhangke's *24 City* and Zhang Meng's *The Piano in a Factory* begin with the ritual of entering the factory gate, a practice that continues to be deployed in the era of the post-. Contrary to the films' theme of the socialist-era factory's ruination and disappearance, the factory gate as the threshold of the visible world proliferates and establishes its role in mediating the imaginary of the post- as a visible frame that conceals.

Not confined to literary or cinematic imagination, the gate also exists in the fundamental textures of everyday life and in post-socialist urban settings where the creation and preservation of socialist space delineate relations with the past, present, and future. In the case of preservation—an event presumed to be about the preservation of the past—the trend of recycling socialist-era factories for the purpose of creating art and consumption zones in post-socialist China suggests an architectural future anterior, where the anticipation of the post- conditions the present memory of the past. To trace the afterlife of the factory gate, an architectural space such as Beijing 798—the Dashanzi Art District in the suburb of Beijing—provides a case study for understanding the future of socialist-era factories in the present. Celebrated today as the biggest international art district in post-socialist China, Beijing 798 was formerly a high-tech war industry and electronic components factory zone built with East German and Soviet technologies.[7] Occupied in the 1990s by a group of avant-garde artists looking for cheap rent, the factory zone was at the center of a political struggle against the Beijing municipal government and its master plan to gentrify the area for a new science and industrial park.[8] Transformed into a sprawling art district, Beijing 798 has become a mixed-purpose commercial zone where art studios, galleries, boutiques, and trendy restaurants create a spatial narrative about post-socialist art in the era of marketization. For visitors to Beijing 798 today, touring the art district is a packaged experience of art consumption and also of post-socialism—consuming it as a visual spectacle. Whereas former factory warehouses and production units are converted to art exhibition spaces, the art zone is presented as a visual and architectural commodity interlaced with carefully planned skywalks that provide an elevated vantage point for a panoramic view of factory ruins (see figures 1.5 and 1.6). The malling and museumification of socialist-era relics take place with an unmatched velocity in post-socialist China. However, contrary to the narrative of loss and displacement, Beijing 798 indicates the active afterlife of the factory space in shaping the scripted meanings of the post-.

The factory gate persists and, in this case, provides a post-socialist phantasmagoria of the factory interior as an inviting space for the imaginary of neoliberal consumption, while the condition of labor in China's proliferating special economic zones remains guarded from view. In recent years, Beijing 798 has acquired international recognition and has been visited by many foreign dignitaries, from high-ranking government officials to celebrities and

FIGURE 1.5. The skywalks in Beijing 798 provide an elevated vantage point for the panoramic view of factory ruins.

FIGURE 1.6. Touring Beijing 798 is part of a packaged experience of art consumption and of post-socialism.

members of royalty. In an essay documenting 798's international fame, the architects Neville Mars and Martijn de Waal comment on the official visit of President Adolf Ogi of the Swiss Confederation on the fiftieth anniversary of the establishment of diplomatic relations between the two countries: "The Swiss President visited the Factory because it had once again become a symbol. An emblem that both looked ahead to a new future, while at the same time reminding visitors of the past . . . and a site that provided the city with a new cultural identity. In its short existence as an art center, Factory 798 has grown into an icon for the new modern urban China."[9] Hidden in the naturalized narrative of the rebirth of Beijing 798 and discourses about the freedom of art, one discovers a more complex process of creating visual and architectural representations of the post- in China. A site of political resistance sanctioned by the state, Beijing 798 mediates a utopic representation of the post- as the thriving coexistence of socialism and a market economy; it has become an instrument for remapping post-socialist China in the new global economy. However, the future it mediates through the symbolic opening of the socialist-era factory gate is predicated upon a condition: that it provide a representation of the past that is commensurate with the global imaginary of a post-socialist future where the Communist Revolution has been relinquished to make room for a strategic transition to capitalism. From the 1949 industrial town in *Resplendent Light* that transmits electricity as it promotes communism throughout the country to the commodified landscape of factory ruins in Beijing 798, the factory as an architectural and cultural space has undergone significant changes. While the factory is gradually pushed to the margins of post-socialist society, its ruination suggests a process of violent displacement that gives rise to a new social order and spatial arrangement based on a rehierarchized class consciousness.

The factory is the quintessential *industrial heterotopia*, a real and phantasmatic site whose function in society shifts throughout time. And with each shift, the factory punctuates historical junctures that represent the inversion of existing power structures. A Foucauldian analysis of factory films and their historical transformations in PRC film history demonstrates the continuation of the factory's role in delineating the boundaries between socialism and post-socialism. In Foucault's classic essay "Of Other Spaces" ("Des Espaces Autres"), the title evokes the fantastical and intangible dimension of space and explores, through the "other," alienated spaces that gradually fall out of sight. Drawing attention to cemeteries, psychiatric hospitals, and prisons—spaces that are architecturally and culturally pushed to society's margins—the essay reads "other/ed spaces" not for their imminent disappearance but as a new regime of in/visibility. Representing shifts in the order of knowledge, the shifting of the heterotopic factory space leaves behind historical traces of ways of seeing socialism and post-socialism, both cultural realms that are constructed in relation to ways of seeing capitalism.

The figure of the factory in the mass dreams of industrial and post-industrial modernity presents a case where the visible does not reveal but creates a new mechanism of concealment. If we consider the relationship between cultural representation and the systems of capitalism and socialism, a gap is noticeable where the existing mode of representation is unable to match both systems of alienating abstraction. Instead of mimetic representations, capitalism and socialism share the history of leaving behind visible *stand-ins* from abstracting systems that are beyond representability, creating distinct modalities of visibility and opacity.[10]

In the examination of the post- as a global imaginary that manages a spectrum of visibility in the post-socialist world, stand-ins offer objects of study that mediate the specific conceptions of neoliberal post-socialism and capitalism: representations of factory space reveal the conceptions of labor; images of expressways and infrastructure become the language for making visible the opacity of circulation; and the verticality of skyscrapers represents the nonhuman scale of capitalist accumulation. Like fossil remains, they are forms of vision—visual forms—that reveal historical assumptions about the systems of opacity they attempt to capture, while raising questions about the *ways of seeing* capitalism, socialism, and the post-X neoliberal world. Not merely a matter of aesthetic style, these ways of seeing mark the boundaries and territories of visibility and invisibility demanded by each regime. While violently guarding established fields of vision, they also reveal a system's definitions of body, gender, labor, work, leisure, consumption, time, and space in a record of an optical unconscious that continues to regulate the representations of socialism and capitalism in the era of the post-. However, as stand-ins that are conjured to represent abstract systems, these visual ruins also document their own limits of representation, leaving behind traces of impasse and records of contradiction in the way socialism and its difference from capitalism is conceptualized. One of these permanent contradictions lies in the protected space of production inside the factory gate, where socialist and capitalist representations of work and labor create seemingly incommensurable divergences.

In Chinese socialist films that are created to confront the abstraction and opacity of capitalism, the representation of factory space—the site and conditions of work, production, and labor—calls for a socialist cognitive mapping that mirrors Fredric Jameson's method of capitalist cognitive mapping, referring to a process of unraveling an individual cultural text's desire to see, represent, and grasp the antirepresentational totality of capitalism.[11] In literary and cinematic representations of socialist industrial modernity, the factory interior that is obfuscated from view in the capitalist optical unconscious becomes a site that requires extensive construction. Exploring the relationship between socialism and industrialism, the factory brings into view the contradictions and unrepresentability of a system that mirrors the dilemmas of representing Capital. While proposing a vision of negation—a way of seeing a new world through the abolition of capitalist social forms—the representations of socialism in Chinese visual culture should be critically problematized as visions that are labeled "socialism" rather than portraying socialism itself. They reveal, through an analysis of seeing socialism from the perspective of the present, disparities in the conceptions of socialism as a cultural site for imagining Capital's other, whether this is a duplicate or a romanticized alternative. True visions of a communist future may not have arrived, but the anticipation of a different future continues to produce new kinds of visibility and invisibility.

Seeing Socialism: Socialist Cognitive Mapping

Cinema has never ceased replaying the scenario of workers leaving the factory. However, Rancière's comment about one of the first actualities films made in rapidly industrializing Europe has less to do with speculating about cinema's mythical origins than identifying an emergent aesthetics of visuality—an aesthetic form of Engels's industrial horror—where the relation between cinematic aesthetics (as a repeatable framework of the visible world) and the antirepresentational process of capitalist industrialization may be observed.[12] To explore the entwined relationality between socialism and capitalism and the aesthetic forms their entanglement engenders in Chinese socialist film cultures, we must look closer at *Workers Leaving the Lumière Factory*. In the film's beginning, workers gather behind the gate as it opens. The factory interior functions as a container whose contents are suddenly released and emptied out. The rapid outflow of bodies passing through the gate gives a visual language to the process of compression and the synchronization of individual movements, as they become stand-ins for the abstract concepts of flow and circulation in an opaque system. Commenting on the first factory film, Harun Farocki unravels the production of a capitalist visual rhetoric:

The work structure synchronizes the workers, the factory gates group them, and this process of compression produces the image of a work force. As may be realized or brought to mind by the portrayal, the people passing through the gates evidently have something fundamental in common. Images are closely related to concepts, thus this film becomes a rhetorical figure. One finds it used in documentaries, in industrial and propaganda films, often with music and/or words as backing, the image being given a textual meaning such as "the exploited," "the industrial proletariat," "the workers of the first," or "the society of the masses."[13]

In this early film in which cinema functioned mainly as a technological attraction, the film's appeal lies in its ability to render movement in images. The workers' bodies are carefully choreographed, which can be detected in the distinct direction of their exit to the right and left of the factory gate, leaving no one in another's path, and in the presence of the camera that compels the continuous movement of the body, where a woman's tug at a coworker's skirt receives no reaction. More than the physicality of the body's movement, the camera captures something else: the invisible forces that put workers' bodies in a synchronized flow of uninterrupted movement, compelling them to leave rather than gather at the factory, which is a potential site for strike, resistance, and political uprising. Without depictions of the factory's sign or its architectural space, *Workers Leaving the Lumière Factory* is less a representational record of the space of industrial capitalism than a cartography of capitalism's spatial logic maintained by a new distribution of visible and invisible worlds. The movement of the bodies leaving the factory gate and entering the space of leisure and consumption will be reversed in the socialist representation of the factory, where the imaginary of a socialist industrial future begins in a factory of light (an electricity power plant) in socialist China, probing the connections between invisible, industrial light and the opacity of socialism.

THE SOCIALIST LIGHT OF EMANCIPATION:
RESPLENDENT LIGHT (1949)
Light occupies a unique role in the global socialist imagination, as it evokes the expanding global network of industrialized lighting powered by electricity. In November 1920, the leader of Soviet Russia Vladimir Lenin made this iconic statement: "Communism is equal to Soviet power plus the electrification of the entire country" (*Kommunizm est' sovetskaia vlast' plius ele-*

ktrifikatsiia vsei strany). Still written above Moscow's central electric station, Lenin's words launched the future path for the State Commission for Electrification of Russia and established that Soviet industrialization would be built on transforming and appropriating the technological foundations of capitalism.[14] However, as Jonathan Coopersmith notes in his historical study of Russia's electrification, electricity production in Russia remained comparatively low in contrast to Euro-American nations, and "electricity production dropped sharply and did not gain pre-Revolutionary levels until the mid-1920s."[15] When Lenin spoke in 1920, his statement was profoundly paradoxical and contradicted the idea that the electrification of Russia was introduced as part of the revolution. From electrotherapy to cure disease to the construction of hydroelectric dams, the lack of electricity in everyday life strengthened its role in the socialist imagination of an industrial future.[16]

The global history of light and energy is a history of capitalist imperialism, colonialism, industrialization, and war. Appearing first on the European continent, the technologies of light, combined with the industrialization of power, arrived in Shanghai's foreign concessions in 1879.[17] In 1882 the first small-scale power plant (the Shanghai Electric Company) was established with capital investment raised by three British businessmen—R. W. Little, W. S. Westmore, and C. W. Dyce—marking the beginning of the electricity industry in China.[18] In a war for profit, power plants became a competitive business among China's colonizers, as plants proliferated throughout colonial and semicolonial cities from Hong Kong to Tianjin and Dalian.[19] In the Japan-occupied Northeast, the establishment of the South Manchurian Railway Company (Mantetsu) in 1906 propelled a history of wartime monopoly, capitalist imperialism, and forced labor.[20] On the eve of the PRC's establishment and the final battles with the Guomindang Army, electricity equipment and infrastructure became a contested target of control and a symbol for victory.[21] In Shanghai, electricity workers created the slogan "To Welcome Shanghai's Liberation with Uninterrupted Electricity!"[22] The anticipated socialist future spread through electric light, evoking electricity's revolutionary potential in the construction of a new China.

Set in Japan's former industrial colony in the Northeast, the center of electric colonialism, Xu Ke's *Resplendent Light* reclaims light as a symbol of global socialism and the Chinese socialist industrial city. The opening credits appear over prominent close-ups of industrial power grids, introducing the socialist dream of instantaneous connectivity through the symbolic light of communism. *Resplendent Light* depicts an industrial crisis in pre-liberation

1947, told as a flashback of a model worker, Zhou Mingying. Duplicating the original opening sequence, where the camera descends from a panoramic aerial view of the industrial city to a busy street intersection, the flashback reveals extensive damage to the city's electricity infrastructure, from shattered power grids to dilapidated street lights. Caught in the Chinese Civil War, the city has lost its source of light and awaits the workers' collaborative efforts to restore power and to combat wartime espionage. The moment of crisis provides a context for exploring the workers' passion for their work, while offering a site for experimenting with the limits of affective and physical labor and a testing ground for the representation of socialist labor.

In *Resplendent Light*, the worker's cinematic body dramatizes work but also performs strenuous physical labor to help construct the future possibilities of socialist labor. The body becomes a stand-in for the invisible forces that compel the workers to work, making visible the laboring bodies that were violently suppressed in a prior mode of representation. Yet negating the opacity of capitalism summons a new modality of abstraction, where socialism as a mode of production is reduced to the body's physical endurance—working long hours and under hostile conditions—leaving the distinction between socialism and capitalism ambiguous. In a film where light and electricity are imagined as the socialist technology of emancipation, the recoding process inevitably conceals the former technique of exploitation under the guise of socialism. The contradiction culminates in the film's final scene, wherein restored light shines through the city-in-waiting. However, moments before the restoration, the male protagonist enters a fully functional coal furnace to fix a jam in the machinery. With the furnace heated to hundreds of degrees Celsius, the harsh conditions are presented as a visible index of the workers' physical and affective labor. To enhance the cinematic effect of testing the body's limit, the sequence introduces alternating shots of workers inside the furnace's interior and close-ups of a ticking pocket watch, creating an industrial melodrama that highlights the endurance of the human body as it performs the spectacle of socialist labor.

Defined as instruments for building a socialist future, the technology and equipment for generating electricity acquired a new social meaning in *Resplendent Light*. The setting of northeast China in the immediate aftermath of World War II evokes the recent atrocity in the former Japanese colony: the electrification of the Northeast is imbued with a violent history of semicolonialism when people and nature were reduced to passive objects.[23] Primarily concerned with postwar recovery, the film focuses on a representation of 1947 that is already detached from Japanese colonial history. After visually recoding the city from a space of consumption to a space of production, the film reappropriates technology by masking and erasing the association between electrification and the social technology of colonialism that is based on the Japanese colonizers' discovery of a way of ordering the labor and natural resources of northeast China into standing reserves.[24] In a meeting of factory workers, the workers' union outlines a regional crisis of unemployment and economic stagnation resulting from the Guomindang Army's destruction of essential equipment. The male protagonist, Zhou Mingying, gives a passionate speech, analogizing the electric power plant to a train engine that will lead the revitalization of industries throughout the region. Linking electricity to factories and factories to work for unemployed workers, Mingying's speech arouses the vision of a networked society where electricity is the foundation for socialist industrial modernity.

In Martin Heidegger's seminal essay "The Question Concerning Technology," a distinction is made between technology and the essence of technology. Moving away from a definition of technology as an instrument or a means to an end, Heidegger draws attention to technology as a mode of revealing. Naming this concept "Ge-stell" (translated as enframing), Heidegger defines the essence of technology: "Enframing means the gathering together of that setting-upon which sets upon man, i.e., challenges him forth, to reveal the real, in the mode of ordering, as standing-reserve. Enframing means that way of revealing which holds sway in the essence of modern technology and which is itself nothing technological." As Heidegger theorizes, the modern world is constructed upon particular modes of ordering the world in terms of standing reserves, and it is through the recognition and realization of these modes of ordering and framing the world that human existence is defined. As a film that deals with the relationships among technology, electricity, and socialism, *Resplendent Light* overtly celebrates an industrial socialist future, concealing a former way of ordering the world into the orderable, or what Heidegger calls a former way of "revealing." Without challenging the enframing of the world, the new socialist regime masks it by blurring the division between factory and family spaces and creating a contiguous work space and a temporality that extends beyond the eight-hour workday. A survey of the film's architectural space reveals the relocation of traditional domestic space to the factory's interior, where workers fight, work, strategize, and laugh together. In the process of recoding the technology of semicolonialism as the technology of emancipation, the film's depiction of the workers' passion masks a former way of labor extraction. In Heidegger's words, the modern world is organized in cycles of revealing and concealment: "The challenging Enframing not only conceals a former way of revealing, bringing-forth, but it conceals revealing itself and with it that wherein unconcealment, i.e., truth, comes to pass."[25] In the process of creating the socialist industrial city—a recoding process that transformed the city's definition from the space of consumption to the space of production—the space of production infinitely expands, with the goal of reaching the highest level of productivity.

As an early film of the socialist era, *Resplendent Light* enters the factory gate and bears the task of creating China's working class in an industrial space of production. Wrestling with the relationship between human and machine, work and nonwork, and socialist and capitalist electric light, the film illustrates the complexities of representing socialism and the emergent tools for its conceptualization and visualization. The vision of an illuminated China, symbolizing the triumph of communism, utilizes electricity's mystical qualities that defy empirical observation by the human eye. To envision it as the life of communism requires "the very synthesis of matter and mystique that electricity itself represented."[26] *Resplendent Light* leaves behind traces of a socialist cognitive mapping, wherein the immateriality of electricity alludes to a nonperceptual spatial totality that in turn calls for a new rhetoric of seeing and sensing socialism—a task that requires a remapping of the relationships among socialism, urbanization, and industrialization.

THE TRANSMEDIAL DREAM OF INDUSTRIAL SOCIALISM: *FIERY YOUTH* (1976)

Since *Resplendent Light*, representations of factory space during the socialist era have documented shifting visions of socialist industrial modernity. Considering China's history as an agrarian empire, visions of Chinese socialism are constructed upon the negotiated relationships between the rural and the urban as they continue to be redefined. In Marx's original vision, the success of the proletarian revolution depended on the combination of agriculture with manufacturing industries that would gradually blur the distinction between town and country. The socialist city imagines a different kind of urbanism that would surpass the model of urbanization in the capitalist system, and opens up the "urban" as a canvas of the future. Through systemization, expansion, and the architectural construction of the socialist experience of collectivism, the socialist urban experience was at the center of socialist industrialization.[27] Commenting on urban planning in the Soviet Union, the architect Mihai Craciun writes:

To reinforce Karl Marx's assertion that the success of the proletariat's struggle depended on the existence of large industrial cities, urbanism became the statistical expression of communist ideology, a science assigned to organize vast numbers. Urban planning was reduced to devising formulae for repetition, coherence, and prefabrication. The Vesnin brothers' 1920 prototype of a superblock, designed to infuse metropolitan density in half-rural Moscow, resurfaced after World War II as the *microrayon*—the base unit of the socialist city, guaranteeing predetermined density. Soviet academics drafted a blueprint of the Cold War socialist city, carbon-copied throughout the USSR, and later adapted in other communist countries.[28]

Although China was under the influence of the Soviet model in the first decade after the establishment of the PRC, the country's vast agrarian population and wide rural-urban divide made China's conditions of socialist industrialization quite different. Rather than focusing on intensive urban industrialization, Mao's vision for socialist industrialization resided in the countryside.[29] Indeed one reason coastal factories were relocated to remote mountainous areas was to remove the urban connotations of factories.[30] As Lefebvre observes, urbanization and industrialization are tied together rather than separate phenomena or successive historical stages. The urban problematic presents a global phenomenon, and urban reality may be defined as "a 'superstructure' on the surface of the economic structure, whether capitalist or socialist."[31] Therefore the Chinese vision of industrialization without urbanization suggests a point of divergence in global socialism, complicating the representation of Chinese industrial socialism.

Set in a former industrial metropolitan region, *Resplendent Light* features a mostly interior setting, where the camera stays within the factory compound, leaving spaces outside the factory to the imagination. However, in Dong Kena's *Fiery Youth* (1976), one of the last factory films produced at the end of the Cultural Revolution, a continuous workers' revolution features a socialist industrial representation imbued with scenic mountain landscapes and the vibrant colors of nature.[32] Contrary to the densely urbanized industrial town where electric trams and cars capture a busy social rhythm in *Resplendent Light*, *Fiery Youth* focuses on the steel factory's mechanized interior as well as landscapes of mountains, rivers, waves, clouds, and bamboo forests and nature's changing seasons, from cherry blossoms to snow-covered trees. Seamlessly integrated in the spatial fabric between a steel factory's industrial infrastructure and a thriving natural landscape, *Fiery Youth* is not merely a direct representation of Maanshan in Anhui province, one of China's major steel-making cities. Rather, the film's mise-en-scène provides clues for reading a socialist cartography wherein the relations between socialist industrialization and urbanization are remapped, producing the film's unique transmedial dream of industrial socialism.

The film begins with the fiery images of steelmaking. Heat and sparks of fire flood the darkened screen—a distant echo of the socialist industrial light that has become a stand-in for seeing socialism. The camera's position stays initially at the factory gate as workers freely traverse the threshold of visibility, before revealing a mechanized interior landscape with an automatic assembly line. Work and labor as represented in *Fiery Youth* emphasize the workers' operation of heavy machinery by using electric wiring and complex control panels, a mode of representation that is distinct from the postsocialist imagination of socialist labor, which focused on intimate physical contact with tools and objects of production. Adopting a narrative structure that depicts an industrial crisis demanding a solution (similar to *Resplendent Light*), *Fiery Youth* centers on the relentless efforts of a female worker, Liang Dongxia, to create an automated production line for making steel rolls that are urgently needed in the country's expanding infrastructure of oil pipelines. Seen leaving behind complex drawings of electrical designs on a scenic snow-covered walking path, Dongxia is introduced as someone with the technical ability to engineer complex electrical systems and as a female worker whose labor in the factory is defined as the fight against politically incorrect class consciousness. As Dongxia conducts tests and experiments, her efforts are interrupted by sabotage and revenge from competitive fellow workers. The socialist definition of work in late Cultural Revolution films typically refers not to physical labor but to the work of thought reeducation to produce the correct political consciousness.[33] Thus the crisis is resolved because of a technological breakthrough and the defeat of bourgeois consciousness among the workers.

Whereas the narrative of *Fiery Youth* is constructed upon a perpetual workers' revolution that aims to produce politically correct proletariat consciousness, the film's acoustic visuality opens up a cinematic dimension of transmedial fantasy, a cultural site of the socialist political unconscious. If capitalism as a system of commodification leaves behind imprints in the aesthetic models reproduced under the system, traces left behind by a socialist industrial production system also probe the relationship between cultural forms and the economic-political system. Rather than producing direct representations of systems of totality, cultural productions contain memory traces that test the limits of our knowledge of both aesthetic regimes and the modes of production that shape them.[34] In the deliberate attempt to represent the mass dream of socialist industrialization, *Fiery Youth* depicts a self-contained society that never ventures outside the factory compound, except on the rare occasion of a workers' excursion to nearby scenes of nature. The space of the socialist industrial modernity is localized here, leaving the geopolitics and global space of industrialization ambiguous. Questions related to the future spatiality of Chinese industrialization are not addressed, including the industries' relations to agricultural towns that unconditionally supply labor, food, and other resources to industrial centers.[35] The concept of industrialization without urbanization creates a rhetoric that obfuscates the ongoing process of industrial urbanization and leaves behind pictorial paradoxes.

In the film's socialist cognitive mapping, nature is seen as a space and temporality of rest and rejuvenation, separated from the space of production. After working long hours in the factory on the design of the new automated assembly line, Dongxia and her coworkers go on a field trip, where colorful scenes of nature contrast with the monotonous industrial landscape. Without depicting any scenes of travel, the film shows the workers' arrival in nature, where they compose poetry, breathe in fresh air, and rest their feet in the cold river water. The contrast between work and leisure is mapped onto the divide between industrial and natural landscapes. The factory film creates its own representation of the city and the countryside. Following a long shot of the steel plant's silhouette, surrounded by prominent electricity transmission towers, the excursion sequence begins with an abrupt transition to dramatic clouds in the sky, where rays of sunlight seep through, like a powerful but veiled presence. These images are summoned to visualize a revolutionary theme song played moments before in the previous sequence, whose lyrics pay tribute to Mao. To celebrate the hope (*xiwang*) Mao bestows upon the workers, the song is addressed to "Dear Chairman Mao." Meanwhile the film's visual track shows a series of panoramic shots of pictorial landscapes that evoke the sublime vastness and depth of nature. From the glittering surfaces of rivers to the powerful surges of turbulent waves, from ancient trees to ageless mountains, images of a majestic earth powerfully enhance the scales of appreciation for Mao. Filling the acoustic track, the song functions as a bridge that takes the viewers back to a now animated industrial landscape, imbuing it with forces of life and energy. Drawing similarities between the industrial and natural landscapes, *Fiery Youth* reveals a theory of the Chinese socialist landscape, where the differences between nature and industry are blurred, creating a new frame of visibility that shows the socialist imaginary of industrial modernity.

Remapping the place of nature with splendid cherry blossoms and mountains that surround the factory, the film's depiction of the industrial landscape transforms the forces of nature—the surge of the waves, the coverage of the sun, and the cycle of changing seasons—into a language representing socialist labor. In his "Economic and Philosophical Manuscripts," Marx details the concept of alienation as a framework for critiquing the capitalist abstraction of human labor and nature by making the distinction between species-being and species-life. He writes, "Estranged labor not only 1) estranges nature from man and 2) estranges man from himself, from his own active function, from his vital activity; because of this it also estranges man from his *species*. It turns his *species-life* into a means for his individual life."[36] Emphasizing the objectification of labor's product, Marx's formulation of species-life provides a despondent view of the collapse of relationality, interconnectivity, community, and species-life itself. In *Fiery Youth*, the film's depiction of workers' physical and spiritual wandering in a majestically stylized nature probes the relationships among nature, socialist industrialization, and the representation of labor shortly before China's economic reforms. In scenes that juxtapose the sublimity of nature and Dongxia's labor—as she tours the factory compound, reads and studies, and conducts experiments on machinery— her labor is visualized as comparable to the rhythmic percussion of the river's waves. Nature stands in for the limitless possibilities that Mao bestows upon the workers and also becomes a visual index for the abstract concept of labor. Refetishized as species-being, Dongxia's labor is quantified in the image of nature, giving the immateriality of her work a magnitude and scale.

Nature's vibrant colors create sensory stimuli that are both hypnotic and instrumental. While contributing to the acoustic-visual spectacle that accompanies the workers' song to Chairman Mao, the colors evoke a distant sublimity full of the future possibilities of the Chinese industrial revolution. Situated at the borderline between fantasy and reality, revolutionary realism and romanticism, the musical sequence features one of several transmedial representations of the socialist industrial future, complicating the film's technique of socialist cognitive mapping.[37] As the workers' song plays in the background, interweaving the majestic images of nature and the lyrics' celebratory tributes to Mao, the camera cuts to the details of a painting featuring a beaming Mao surrounded by a group of male mine workers. The camera gradually zooms out, revealing the mise-en-scène that frames the painting, which is displayed not in the interior of an exhibition space but against the silhouette of the industrial compound (see figure 1.7). Creating a transmedial dream of socialist industrialism, the painting of this harmonious human landscape is inserted in front of the nonhuman landscape of industrial infrastructure.

In the industrial mass dream that requires multiple layers of mediation, as the film resorts to a two-dimensional representational space, the cinematic vision turns into a site of rupture, where uneven surfaces and textures retain fissures and ellipses that illustrate the dream's inherent contradictions. As Dongxia and her fellow workers strive for improved mechanical automation to advance productivity, the future relationship between machines and human labor remains unclear. On the surface, the painting provides a pictorial representation of industrialism's future possibility, where the Chinese proletarians continue to be the center of the Chinese industrial revolution. Nonetheless the painting also potentially suggests the opposite: that human labor has become a relic of a technologically advanced industrial phase, turning labor into an object of loss that the painting mourns and preserves. Complicating the task of seeing socialism, transmedial representation recurs in the film, in moments when the momentum for the continuous class struggle stalls. To renew the future-oriented vision of industrial development, the film crosses media boundaries and relocates the value of human labor in propaganda paintings that glorify workers' laboring bodies. As Dongxia walks along the factory's train tracks, ruminating over the bitter struggle between opposing forces in the factory, she sees a large-scale painting depicting two male workers performing strenuous physical labor (see figure 1.8). The image takes her back to the past, and she remembers a colleague, describing his sense of responsibility and his desire to turn his blood into crude oil and his blood vessels into oil pipelines during the time of crisis. The image of physical labor functions as a source of inspiration for the future, but also a reminder of labor's displacement in the present. The film's transmedial deployment of painting as a medium for constructing the socialist industrial future opens up a space for critical analysis, where socialism's nostalgia for and anticipation of labor—and the implications of different futures for the working class—are put on display.

The task of seeing socialism creates layered patterns: the mass dream of socialist industrialism moves from one medium to another, leaving each one incomplete and fragmentary, while opening up gaps in socialist cognitive mapping where industrial socialism's antirepresentability creates distinct modes of visibility and invisibility. As the camera enters the factory gate and reveals the hidden landscape within, the question of whether seeing

FIGURE 1.7. Creating a transmedial dream of socialist industrialism: a painting featuring a beaming Mao surrounded by a group of male mine workers is displayed against the silhouette of the industrial compound in Dong Kena's *Fiery Youth* (1976).

socialism means negating the abstraction and opacity of capitalism arises. What does the negated vision entail? As illustrated in *Resplendent Light* and *Fiery Youth*, two films that bracket the visibility of the socialist factory, the negation of the capitalist interior creates a new system of revelation and concealment. The depiction of socialist labor retains and at times magnifies the alienation of workers' species-life. And while rhetorically separate in the PRC's official discourses, industrialization and urbanization continue to develop along parallel lines. Ending the film with the victory of the proletarian class consciousness, the final scene reveals the completion of automation. Stacked rows of steel rolls become the factory landscape, as train carts packed with the finished products are seen leaving the storage facility and heading toward an unspecified destination. Like the workers leaving the factory, the movement of the train seems compelled by an invisible force in

FIGURE 1.8. In *Fiery Youth* (1976) the image of physical labor functions as a source of inspiration for the future, but also a reminder of labor's displacement in the present.

the larger logistical scheme of circulation. Captured by the cinematic unconscious, the urban imagination in *Fiery Youth* expands while its legibility remains in question. The factory is part of a sprawling urban infrastructural network, a dark geography of socialism and an invisibility that is violently protected.

Like capitalism, socialism is a system of social relations that are based on intricately linked rules and laws derived from the processes of production, consumption, exchange, and circulation. Instead of being displaced by socialism, capitalism provides the preconditions for the conceptualization and practice of socialism, while at the same time propelling the search for a radical alternative. However, as Alberto Toscano and Jeff Kinkle write, "The problem of cognitive mapping in socialist transition turns out to be even more complex, if markedly different, than those thrown up by capitalism's distinctive modalities of opacity and invisibility."[38] The desire for a visuality that negates the abstract domination of Capital creates a vision of negation built upon a negative vision. The socialist mass dream of industrialization ends in complete automation in *Fiery Youth* but leaves the role of the workers in the newly mechanized system up in the air. The last scene of the film begins with an image of Dongxia working in front of a massive control panel. As proof of full automation, an exterior shot reveals the movement of mechanical cranes in a crowded storage lot where rows of steel rolls are being stacked and prepared for shipment. Devoid of any human figure, the industrial landscape dominates the frame. The movement of the cranes transitions to the movement of a freight train heading toward the camera, revealing the origin of its departure while disguising its potential destination. The image of an automated socialist industrial landscape is soon joined by a distant shot of Dongxia and her coworkers standing on the rooftop of a factory building. Elevated and removed from the site of production, the workers are reduced to indistinguishable bodies in a space that the socialist factory interior neither includes nor excludes. The film's revolutionary theme song overwhelms the soundtrack, drowning out Dongxia's voice as she waves a final salute to Chairman Mao. The camera pauses for a few seconds on her body as she maintains the same posture. Then the film abruptly ends, leaving behind an image of self-restraint in a worker's body that is positioned in midair, a body that participates in no perceivable future or past. Rife with contradictions, the socialist representations of bodies in the factory space and of the factory space itself capture socialist industrialism's incompleteness—that is the origin of post-socialist nostalgia.

"Has state socialism produced a space of its own?" Lefebvre asks in the context of critiquing the production of space as a historical process in the development of capitalism. Has socialism been able to generate a different space following the revolutionary period? If space is a process rather than a fixed object, the production of a socialist space involves a set of procedures where nature, labor, technology, and knowledge are entered into reproducible relations. Critically assessing the possibility for the socialist production of space, Lefebvre continues, "Where can an architectural production be found today that might be described as 'socialist'—or even as *new* when contrasted with the corresponding efforts of capitalist planning?"[39] While eluding a direct answer to the speculative criticisms of socialist space's difference, Lefebvre concludes, "There is no easy answer to the question of 'socialism's' space; much more careful thought is called for here. It may be that the revolutionary period, the period of intense change, merely establishes the preconditions for a new space, and that the realization of that space calls for a rather longer period—for a period of calm."[40] The Chinese socialist factory—as an architectural and representational space—is the embodiment of a set of preconditions that anticipate differences. However, as Lefebvre suggests, there is a distinction between precondition and realization. The production of socialist space is a process that still lies in the future and has not yet begun. By considering the socialist production of space as a future possibility, Lefebvre's reading brings into question the existing spaces that are currently labeled "socialist."

From the ruination of industrial factories to the nostalgia of romanticized labor, socialism is seen in decay and pushed to the margins in post-socialist visual culture. Nonetheless, to follow the thread of Lefebvre's argument, socialism exists as a set of preconditions for a differential space that remains unrealized. It is a specter that haunts the negated representation of capitalism, and in the time and space of post-socialist China it refers to an emergent cultural field that continues to mediate the relationship between socialism and capitalism. In other words, the socialism seen in decay is the spectral residue of a past vision and an imaginary of the post- that calls for a remapping of the factory gate.

Industrial Heterotopias: Relocating the Factory Gate

The condition of being post-, a state-controlled transition from socialism to market-oriented socialism, has involved the strategic redeployment of factory space. As the center of economic development is reoriented to special economic zones, traditional manufacturing factories that relied on state funding are displaced to the margins.[41] Compared to agricultural land that was once the symbol of feudalism and an urban space that needed a socialist transformation, representations of the factory—as a new industrial space that requires comparatively less historical revisionism—have become the quintessential image of the socialist future. The factory interior has provided a screen of projection, where proletarian class consciousness is formed and socialist technologies advanced.[42] However, as new manufacturing plants in the special economic zones replace socialist-era industrial centers, representations of factory space again reveal ruinous industrial and post-industrial landscapes discovered inside socialist factories. Post-socialist China's industrialization continues yet becomes a violently guarded scene in the darkened geography of state-led market socialism.[43] The factory interiors in the special economic zones that are fueling the post-socialist economy are closed to visibility, whereas the interiors of socialist-era factories are transformed into a cultural space of nostalgia. The new visibility of ruinous socialist industrialism creates a grid of revelation and concealment that exceeds the romanticized notion of nostalgia. Chinese industrialization and urbanization are ongoing transnational processes that are remaking the post-socialist geography of industrial urbanism. The factory gate persists and continues to mediate the imaginaries of industrialism, postindustrialism, urbanization, socialism, and capitalism. As China remaps itself in the geopolitics of the global world system, the relations between interiorities and exteriorities undergo reorientation—and reframe the visibility of post-socialist spaces of production.

Equipped with a police army, surveillance cameras, and protective gates, contemporary factories are increasingly militarized. Farocki's *Workers Leaving the Factory* initiates a new direction of thinking as it traces the dystopic technological advancements in securing the factory gate. To enhance the protection of property, various kinds of fortification equipment (e.g., automated roadblocks, fences, and gates) were developed alongside the advanced technologies of production in the factory interior. In anticipation of violent protests, the gate restricts the flow of movement at the entrance, imposing limits on the spectrum of visibility. In China's state-sanctioned economic zones of exception, where direct foreign investments are reshaping the landscape of production, the prevalence of workers' suicides in factories highlights the unequal distribution of information between laborers and managers. Indeed the factory gate has resurfaced as a site of labor movement and violent protest. In the Taiwan-invested Foxconn City, the number of suicides has grown alongside rising numbers of protests. As the electronics manufacturer gradually expanded the scale of its production from south China's special economic zones to central and northern China, the factory interior that supplies the global demand for Apple products required additional protection from the local Chinese police force against protesters.[44]

In Jia Zhangke's *A Touch of Sin* (*Tian zhuding*, 2013), a film that consists of four vignettes showing individual acts of violent revenge against social injustice, a factory worker named Xiaohui in a Taiwan-owned factory city jumps from his dorm room to his death. Making clear allusions to Foxconn City, the film creates a fictional representation of a young adult worker drifting from one job to another, always in search of better working conditions and higher wages. In this condition of precarity, the Chinese proletariat has been replaced by a new class called the "precariat," whose livelihood is determined by the socialist market system that distributes vulnerability rather than financial wealth.[45] As Athena Athanasiou says in a conversation with Judith Butler on the topic of dispossession, "In designating the politically induced condition in which certain people and groups of people become differentially exposed to injury, violence, poverty, indebtedness, and death, 'precarity' describes exactly the lives of those whose 'proper place is non-being.' This is indeed related to socially assigned disposability (a condition which proves fundamental to the neoliberal regime) as well as to various modalities of valuelessness, such as social death, abandonment, impoverishment, state and individual racism, fascism, homophobia, [and] sexual assault."[46] In a film that is based on a collection of real-life incidents that Jia gathered from Weibo (one of the biggest social media platforms in China) in the early 2010s, disparate violent outbursts lead to vengeful injuries inflicted on others and the self, and these are juxtaposed in the film's narrative space. While each strand portrays a specific case of social injustice—including governmental corruption, sexual violence, and labor exploitation—together the strands gesture toward the totality of a system that exceeds the representational limit of a singular incident. The cause of Xiaohui's suicide is both known and unknown. By showing his body hitting the ground, the film spectacularizes the body, creating a gap between the excessive visibility of the human wounds and the invisible systems of subjection that escape representability. The visibility of this violence highlights its opacity rather than its communicability. The rhythmic movement of the factory's production line continues without interruption. Belonging neither inside nor outside, the factory gate reappears in the post-socialist era as a site of extreme danger. Regulating the distinctions between the post-socialist mode of production and its predecessor, the gate opens and closes, and in so doing mediates the visibility of labor at the site of production.[47]

In the era of the post-, the factory interior remains visible and has become one of the primary cultural sites where the transition from socialism to post-socialism is negotiated and visualized. As the real sites of production in new manufacturing cities are displaced to the margins of the visible spectrum, the interiors of socialist-era factories reemerge as the central landscape in seeing post-socialism. Rather than conveying the direct image of socialism, post-socialist factory interiors are geopolitical imaginaries that reinvent ways of seeing socialism in the era of the post-. While remapping China in the post-socialist world, ways of seeing socialist-era factories call for a critical reassessment of the cultural constructions that are identified as socialism. Post-socialist nostalgia satisfies a contemporary cultural need.[48]

The need to remember socialism signifies the demand for an alternative public space where collective dissatisfactions with the present may find a form of expression; it also answers the global desire for seeing socialism in specific modalities of representation. Whereas socialism remains a set of preconditions—and its realization proceeds in a path indistinguishable from capitalist modes of production—*socialism* more accurately refers to an empty signifier that nonetheless determines emergent aesthetic forms.

Therefore the incomplete mass dreams of socialist industrialism as represented in *Resplendent Light* and *Fiery Youth*—films that bracket the socialist era—indicate the necessity of reexamining post-socialist nostalgia as a nostalgia without origin, where cultural practices perpetually reinvent the locations and memories of an origin. In contrast to the violence-prone factory interiors of *A Touch of Sin*, the socialist-era steel factory in *The Piano in a Factory* lies silently in a state of ruin. Depicting the efforts of a divorced father and former steel factory worker, Chen Guilin, making a grand piano by hand for his daughter, the film uses the ruinous steel factory—with exposed pipes, giant furnaces, and smokestacks—to provide an architectural language that stages nostalgic longings for socialism. In the middle of a custody battle with his ex-wife, whose new boyfriend makes money by selling fake drugs and serves as a symbol of market forces, Guilin embarks upon a post-socialist industrial mass dream to make a piano from scratch. When translated into Chinese, the word *piano* consists of the Chinese characters for *steel* and *zither*. While evoking the connection between the modern piano and the Industrial Revolution that transformed the musical instrument into its modern form, the idea of making a piano in a destitute socialist-era steel factory embodies not only a uniquely post-socialist industrial dream but also the cultural need to reconstruct socialist labor in the present. Committed to making a single piano for his daughter's piano lessons, Guilin recruits laid-off workers who are doing odd jobs in town. Emphasizing the specialized skills of each worker, he assembles people in a way that is analogous to assembling individual parts in an intricate machine. Thereafter the abandoned factory comes alive. The daily rhythm of going to work, eating together during breaks, and having production strategy meetings returns, bringing back the time of communal living and shared social temporality. However, the film's emphasis on the communal experience of production relies on a specific post-socialist reconstruction of the socialist definition of labor. Through a landscape of hands—a series of images showing the movements of human hands working in harmony with tools and machines—the making of a piano is turned into a visual symphony that reanimates the abandoned factory interior. Intimately touching and stroking both the tools and the products, the hands-in-labor are a post-socialist landscape of humanism, where factory production is reimagined as a collection of individual craftsmanship. The emphasis on individual distinction is a reactive response to the modalities of valuelessness and disposability that led to the factory's closure. But this focus also reproduces a logic of concealment that erases the tension between worker-centered humanism and the mechanical post-humanism inherited from the socialist era.

The imagined labor in *The Piano in a Factory* represents a nostalgia without origin. While depicting the state-led displacement of socialist-era factories, the factory interior becomes a space for exhibiting romanticized physical labor. Revealed alongside a colorful and passionate flamenco performance, the finished piano is actualized through the doubling of the workers' bodies. The juxtaposition of physical labor and musical spectacle creates a visual analogy that compares the laboring body to the dancing and performing body, replacing the violent alienation imposed on workers' bodies in the factory assembly lines, where the body is fragmented into individual parts that must repeat specific tasks. The film ends with a shot of the daughter playing the piano, but there is a note of melancholy. As the camera slowly retreats from the factory interior, the post-socialist industrial dream of making a piano reaches its end. Featuring no political struggle or proletarian revolution—a common feature of socialist-era factory films—the post-socialist film dreams of neither labor movement nor political protest in the factory interior. Depicting sentimental memories in the factory compound, including elaborate plans to memorialize the factory's iconic but soon-to-be-demolished smokestacks, the camera in *The Piano in a Factory* eventually gestures toward a peaceful retreat.

The factory in the film is architecturally ruinous—workers are seen making the piano amid piles of debris, caved-in rooftops, and broken windows—and its location and original purpose are left undisclosed. With no sign of the factory's industrial power and importance in the past or the present, the film also withholds any indication of the workers' power, as their daily life is confined to the factory town plagued by unemployment. The object of their industrial dream—a piano for a child's musical lessons—obfuscates the economic and political importance of industrial factories in state-led socialism and post-socialism. Transforming physical labor into musical dance performances, the film suppresses the potential visual and acoustic cues that may allude to or trigger workers' uprisings, even as sporadic protests in the special economic zones of exception occurred during the film's production.[49] Visible only as a ruinous landscape, the factory interior becomes a blind spot in the field of vision—its presence further disguised in the overexposed visibility of the film's nostalgic dream.

Toward a Different Space: From Foucault to Lefebvre

The factory gate persists in the era of the post-. However, a gradually narrowing spectrum of legibility is being mapped onto the visibility of the factory interior, calling for new ways of seeing, sensing, and experiencing this marginalized site that is prone to violent protests and domestic class wars. Cao Fei's *Whose Utopia* (2006) and Jia Zhangke's *24 City* (2008) are two experimental documentaries that challenge the geopolitics of seeing the factory interior. Abandoning the dichotomized factory imaginary as the site of either overpowering abuse or romanticized nostalgia, the factory space is represented as precisely the unrepresentable and is opened up for the creation of something radically different—what Lefebvre defines as a heterotopic space.[50] Whereas Foucault theorizes heterotopia as othered spaces in society—spaces that undergo different processes of marginalization, reflecting modernity's invisible forces of violence that perpetually create new centers and peripheries—Lefebvre approaches heterotopia as a *different place* imbued with the potential for an urban revolution.

Rather than focusing on the process of displacement, Lefebvre's theorization of heterotopia poses the question of how to rethink the factory interior as a site of resistance. Calling heterotopic space a "different place" and an "other place," Lefebvre writes, "What is it that makes such a place different? Its *heterotopy*: a difference that marks it by situating it (situating itself) with respect to the initial place. This difference can extend from a highly marked contrast all the way to conflict, to the extent that the occupants of a place are taken into consideration." Emphasizing the urban as a contradictory space whose visible dimensions also represent blind spots in the field of vision, Lefebvre's heterotopy does not refer to a consciously designed difference. As illustrated in socialist factory films, the literal representation of the factory interior as a different place perpetuates the Heideggerian technologies of enframing while masking them as alternative visions. Instead of a conscious plan of subversion that may require years to materialize, heterotopy refers to everyday senses, experiences, and encounters capable of creating moments of irruptions, where the possibility of a different space may be momentarily grasped. For Lefebvre, the urban problematic is a "highly complex field of tensions, a virtuality, a possible-impossible that attracts the accomplished, an ever-renewed and always demanding presence-absence." There is a gap between what the eyes can see and the abstract logic of space that coordinates and reproduces systems of movement and stasis. Associating the urban with the condition of blindness, Lefebvre observes, "Blindness consists in the fact that we cannot see the shape of the urban, the vectors and tensions inherent in this field, its logic and dialectical movement, its immanent demands. We see only things, operations, objects (functional and/or signifying in a fully accomplished way)."[51] The urban has always been a visual paradox, where what is visible is already the end point of a cumulative process. Lefebvre's heterotopy suggests a way of moving beyond the plentitude of the visible, so that we can reconsider ways of approaching hidden virtuality.

Published shortly after the May 1968 protests in France, Lefebvre's theorization of a "different" space is clearly in conversation with Foucault's description of heterotopic space written shortly before the uprising.[52] Whereas Foucault's heterotopia evokes a wide range of othered spaces that touch on phenomenology, crisis, rites of passage, and more, Lefebvre pursues a more systematically critical approach to the production of space, showing patterns that deviate from the standard norm of urban development. However, concerning the question of how a different space is produced, Lefebvre's idea becomes elusive and suggestive, most notable in the distinction he makes between "habiting" and "habitat." He writes:

> Toward the end of the nineteenth century, urban thought (if it can be characterized as such), strongly and unconsciously reductive, pushed the term "habiting" aside, literally enclosed it within parentheses. It opted instead for "habitat," a simplified function, which limited the "human being" to a handful of basic acts: eating, sleeping, and reproducing. . . . Habitat, as ideology and practice, repulsed or buried habiting in the unconscious. Before habitat became commonplace, habiting was an age-old practice, poorly expressed, poorly articulated linguistically or conceptually, seen sometimes as degraded, but always concrete, that is, simultaneously functional, multifunctional, and transfunctional. . . . These include the diversity of ways of living, urban types, patterns, cultural models, and values associated with the modalities and modulations of everyday life. Habitat was imposed from above as the application of a homogeneous global and quantitative space, a requirement that "lived experience" allow itself to be enclosed in boxes, cages, or "dwelling machines."[53]

Distinguishing habitat from habiting—a key concept that alludes to the modalities of living, sensing, and discovering experiences in everyday life that are not yet commensurate with the patterns, rhythms, and practices imposed by the treatment of space as habitat—Lefebvre locates heterotopia in spontaneous moments of irruptions, when "disparate heterotopic groups suddenly see, if only for a fleeting moment, the possibilities of collective action to create something radically different."[54] The urban revolution lies in the discovery of something different in the most normalized spaces. Even in one of the most contentious and scripted spaces, the factory interior, strategies of resistance lie in the practice of retracing recurring patterns and representations.

In Cao Fei's *Whose Utopia*, a twenty-minute experimental documentary video, the interior of the OSRAM Lighting Factory in Foshan in the Pearl River Delta is arranged in three parts.[55] The question "Whose utopia?" is explored through three distinct ways of seeing and not seeing the factory interior. The gap among these distinct views subverts the existing modalities of representing the factory interior and transforms the factory into a site where difference may be explored and represented as beyond representable. Part I ("Imagination of Product") presents a factory interior made of machines, assembly lines, and automated mechanical movements. Evoking the view of the product, the factory interior is first seen as a landscape of machines at work with no humans in sight. As the camera moves up and down the assembly line, where lightbulbs receive various kinds of processing treatments—heating, cooling, fire, water, and electrical currents— the products appear as an identical mass. Their rapid movement through the assembly line does not allow for any identification. The role of the human in this process is left in question, until the second half of part I reveals the human labor involved in assembling, inspecting, and packaging the lighting equipment. However, the rapid succession of shots treats the workers as the machines' extended hands, each busily engaged in repetitive movements. Suspending the narrative of glorification or exploitation, the focus on the object's movement from raw material to molding, inspection, and packaging radically challenges the definitions of factory space in both capitalist and socialist modes of production. Although the film leaves the products after they arrive at the factory's storage facility, the journey they will undertake beyond the factory gate hints at a transnational route of production and distribution that delineates a map of post-socialist global trade. Passed from the hands of machines to humans, lying in boxes and awaiting shipment to disparate parts of the world, these nonhuman objects become agents for facilitating an experience that is incommensurable in existing frameworks. What they will encounter beyond the factory gate is left to the imagination. Through the embodied views of the lightbulbs—a representation of the unrepresentable mediated through the life of inanimate objects—the factory is recentered as a site for sense production, a utopia embedded in a space of everyday life.[56]

However, as the video's title suggests, the space of utopia is a site of struggle and a right that needs to be reclaimed. Part II ("Factory Fairytale") and part III ("My Future Is Not a Dream") explore the potentialities and limits of seeing the workers' bodies in the factory's mechanized interior landscape. Performing ballet and other kinds of dances, factory workers introduce a new visibility of the body that conflicts with the assembly line's perpetual forward movement. A diverse group of workers, varying in gender and age, move their bodies (and fingers, which the camera's close-ups emphasize) in spontaneous patterns. As the workers perform against the bleak background of stacked boxes, machinery in perpetual operation, and a landscape of laboring bodies, the performance is not portrayed as empowerment or dissidence. Leaving no traces and evoking no perceptible responses from other factory workers, the dances create momentary interruptions that make perceptible the invisible rhythms of work that subject the body to certain postures and repetitive movements. In dance the body is engaged in another kind of production, and the labor it performs defies the standard notion of productivity. Closing part II with the caption "You cry and say 'Fairytale is a lie,'" the video sends a message to workers to beware the fairytale of economic progress and fictitious capital. A camera positioned in front of two microphones facing rows of empty seats invites the articulation of a collective voice. The emptiness of the room leaves to the imagination the potential for future gatherings, while carefully avoiding the visual rhetoric of socialist realism that transformed the factory into a site of perpetual political struggle.

Following the dance that defies the profit-driven notion of productivity, part III introduces a landscape of human faces with photographic portraits of individual workers—a practice that recurs in Jia Zhangke's post-socialist factory film *24 City*. Whereas *Whose Utopia* is set in south China's special economic zones, where workers' visibility is carefully guarded, *24 City* depicts a socialist-era factory in Chengdu, the capital of Sichuan province, that was demolished to make room for 24 City, a luxury apartment complex. The factory gate returns to frame the disappearing space of socialist production. As the camera surveils the front of the factory gate—a position ingrained in viewers ever since Lumière's *Workers Leaving the Factory*—workers are seen again as a synchronized mass, but they are now entering, rather than leaving, the factory. The ceremony of crossing the threshold of the gate is complete. Originally a state-owned military equipment factory, Factory 420 housed workers who were relocated from Shenyang in northeast China to Chengdu in the southwest in 1958, which was common practice during the Cold War.[57] As China's state-led neoliberalism dispensed with its responsibilities in former industrial centers, Factory 420 represents an enclave of a severed generation, haunted by cumulative layers of displacement. Interwoven with interviews performed by professional actors and factory workers, 24 City presents a landscape of human faces, with long takes at close range creating a photographic portrait of each interviewee.[58] Rather than trying to produce portraits of the disappearing human subjects, the film's photographic portraits experiment with the face as a Lefebvrian heterotopic space for seeing and sensing "something different." As the film's subjects look straight into the camera but without any verbal externalizations of thoughts and memories, the docudrama is punctuated with long pockets of silence that transform the face into a new terrain of meaning and that render existing channels of communication inadequate.[59]

In 24 City, the multilayered experience of displacement—first from the Northeast to the Southwest, then the factory's imminent closure—attests to the cumulative consequences as the state shifts toward industrialization. The workers' experience of displacement in formerly state-owned factories echoes the untold stories of a new kind of domestic displacement as rural migrant workers are recruited to work in the special economic zones. Nonetheless 24 City and Whose Utopia are not about the reportage of specific workers' histories but the rediscovery of the face as a new factory landscape. In the camera's photographic still shots, the face becomes increasingly abstract. The camera's prolonged gaze interrupts the face's assigned meanings, what Gilles Deleuze calls the three poles of the face; these faces cease to be individualizing (distinguishing or characterizing each person), socializing (manifesting a social role), or relational (ensuring not only communication between two people but also, in a single person, the internal agreement between his character and his role). The photographic still shots interrupt the normative narrative progression and give rise to a new space and time, an "any space whatever" that Deleuze theorizes as a space for the irruption of differences and discontinuities through cinematic techniques.[60] Akin to close-ups, which Deleuze theorizes as the mutation of movement, the photographic still shots make the background fade away and transform the workers' bodies and faces into an indecipherable void that is open to radical new meanings. The camera's prolonged gaze at once constructs the workers' presence and effaces this presence. The landscape of faces conveys the excessiveness of irreducible experiences that can exist only as the gap between the visible and the meaningful. Releasing the workers' faces from the scripts that narrate their meaning, *Whose Utopia* and *24 City* merge the factory interiors in China's special economic zones and in socialist-era industrial centers and propose an inverse visuality, where the direction of the gaze is reversed. The workers perform the act of looking through the camera lens, beyond the factory gate, and confront a new landscape produced under Chinese post-socialism's neoliberal strategies.

IN TRACING THE HISTORICAL vantage point of the factory gate and the relational exteriorities and interiorities it mediates, we find not only the persistence of the gate as the enduring threshold of the visible world but also the factory's gradual displacement from the center of capitalist and socialist mass dreams of industrial futures to the invisible margins of a supposed post-industrial world. Since the post- has always already been a geopolitical imaginary mediating how global relations are perceived, its gesture toward the end of an era is often a technique of concealment for new profit-driven transnational networks that demand the reterritorialization of existing borders. After the term *post-industrial* was popularized in the 1970s, industrialization continued in a regime of concealment in the proliferating economic zones of exception that are rewriting the urban history of China and its neighboring regions.

The factory gate is a site of openings and closings. Examining only fragments of the post-socialist urban experience, this analysis illustrates the system of assigning "socialist" and "capitalist" values to the factory interior. Occupying a significant space in the mass dreams of socialist and capitalist economic development, the factory nonetheless provides only a partial view of post-socialist China's urban transformations. Following the workers' gaze toward spaces that lie beyond factories, industrial centers, and special economic zones, the next chapter examines the spaces of everyday life and sites of domesticity, where the imaginaries of post-socialist intimacy conjure new species of sites that expose the intricate networks of gendered displacement in China's thriving megacities.

2

The Post- in Post-Socialist Femininity

In the ending sequence of Li Shaohong's *Baober in Love* (*Lian'ai zhong de baobei*, 2004), the camera follows the male protagonist Liu Zhi's gaze along a trail of blood toward the lifeless body of his lover. Baober, the woman in love whose tumultuous emotions have been mapped (through computer-generated special effects) onto the equally chaotic urbanscape of pre-Olympic Beijing, sits frigidly on the stairs of her factory converted loft, her slit belly bloodied and exposed (figure 2.1). Diagnosed with the psychological symptom of an imagined pregnancy, Baober performs a final act of self-destruction with a note of triumph. Proudly gazing at her lover, she firmly insists, "I told you. She is here [inside my body]." Her self-mutilation is a proclamation of defiance against aggressive pathologization; it also probes the recoded meanings of the body in the imaginary of post-socialist femininity. The post- is a geopolitical and temporal imaginary that manages the threshold of the visible world. Excavating the post- involves the recognition of an emergent structure of meaning production and the exploration of distinctive modalities in which the new spectrum of visibility is anchored. The post- is mediated through a variety of temporal and spatial

FIGURE 2.1. An image of the self-destructive body in Li Shaohong's *Baober in Love* (2004), in which the filmmaker explores the intangible reality of women's perpetual displacement in post-socialist China.

representations and becomes perceivable through the conjuring of specific bodies, sites, memories, and temporalities. Whereas chapter 1 uncovered the afterlife of the factory gate and its role in mediating the global imaginaries of socialism and post-socialism, this chapter explores the post- as a cultural site for reimagining the gendered body by examining the changing articulations of post-socialist femininity and masculinity in the era of market commodification.

Released in 2004, *Baober in Love* represents a unique historical juncture, situated in a cultural landscape radically reshaped by the aftermath of China's admission to the World Trade Organization and the anticipation of the 2008 Summer Olympic Games in Beijing. What began as a lighthearted Chinese adaptation of Jean-Pierre Jeunet's French romantic comedy *Amélie* (*Le fabuleux destin d'Amélie Poulain*, 2001) brings into view a Chinese woman filmmaker's emphasis on an imagined pregnancy—an imaginary space associated with femininity that does not yet have, and will probably never have, a correlate in social recognition.[1] This imaginary space redraws the boundary between femininity and masculinity and gestures toward a utopian *outside*—a space marked by the desire for a virtual time and futurity untouched by the combined forces of socialist and capitalist patriarchy. As Elizabeth Grosz explicates in her reading of Plato's and Thomas More's conceptions of utopias, *utopia* refers not to the projection of the future but to the rehearsal of a virtual future based on the conditions of the past and the present.[2] Baober's imagined pregnancy and her ultimate self-destruction put the question of embodiment at the forefront in the filmmaker's reimagining of post-socialist femininity and futurity. The film links embodiment and a utopic dystopia, leaving room for speculations on a number of issues: What is the importance of the body in imagining the post-socialist present and future? And in what sense can utopia be understood as embodied?[3]

In the post-socialist film market, where urban romance is an increasingly popular genre, *Baober in Love*'s citation of the French blockbuster suggests Li's experimentation with film as a market commodity, but also her complex remapping of post-socialist Chinese femininity in the limiting spectrum of women's bodies and visibility in a globally commodified network.[4] This analysis takes cinema as a record of post-socialist gender negotiations where bourgeois heteronormativity reemerges as the field of recoding gender identities.[5] In a post-socialist woman's body, the post- becomes a complex site of a geopolitical and temporal imaginary, where bodies are infinitely experimented on, transposed, and superimposed. The case of Baober illuminates a post-socialist cultural field of gender recoding that is currently undertheorized. Taking up the state of gestation that eludes attention in classical Marxist texts, Li's commercial venture proposes the philosophical need to rethink the ethics of a proper feminine subject in the continuous project of Chinese feminism; it also documents a filmmaker's negotiation with the changing definition of *femininity* in a socialist market economy.

The 2000s marked a moment of transition and crisis in the cultural industries of East Asia. Starting in the early 1990s, East Asian countries, including South Korea and Taiwan, were pressured into lifting their protective tariff systems against foreign-imported films in various free trade agreements.[6] After China's accession to the WTO, the PRC film industry underwent a fundamental restructuring as the ruins of the state-sponsored film production system gave way to new market-oriented schemes of production. Although PRC films were still under the protection of a quota system, the presence of Hollywood competitors induced a sense of crisis, resulting in dramatic geopolitical shifts in the conception of Chinese cinema.[7] In this crisis mode, a new Chinese blockbuster consciousness emerged as filmmakers and production companies catered to an emerging class of global Chinese audiences. The global geopolitics of film production shifted from catering to a Hollywood-centered global audience to a China-centered reserve of potential viewers.[8] Exceeding numbers in Europe and the United States combined, potential film consumers in the PRC and Sinophone regions exert a powerful influence on the imaginary of post-socialist Chinese cinema.

Li Shaohong is one of the Fifth Generation filmmakers who graduated from the Beijing Film Academy—a cohort that includes Zhang Yimou, Chen Kaige, and Tian Zhuangzhuang—but her production experience in television and film suggests a different genealogy of post-socialist Chinese cinema. Contrary to her contemporaries' focus on China's rural landscape in the 1980s and 1990s, and later the stylized martial arts films of the 2000s, Li's focus has been on Chinese women who are subject to an enduring system of violence—through the extraction of their labor, the exploitation of their bodies, and cultures of misogyny—that has persisted from the socialist era to the present. From the gruesome murder of women by a former film projectionist in *The Case of the Silver Snake* (*Yinshe moushaàn*, 1988) to the female prostitutes who live through the socialist abolition of prostitution in *Blush* (*Hongfen*, 1995), Li's early films are filled with the haunting presence of women in different modes of perpetual displacement.[9] Yet the 2000s marked a period of transition for Li and her generation of filmmakers. The post- in post-socialist filmmaking was no longer a conceptual horizon for artistic experimentation but a rapidly shifting structure where market forces reshape the definitions and styles of post-socialist aesthetics.[10]

It was amid a changing cultural, aesthetic, and political-economic landscape that Li debuted three feature films set in post-socialist urban China, in which she blends genre conventions with experimentation, and heterosexual romance with horror. Here horror is explored as the phenomenological experiences of gendered embodiments—through the camera's alignment with the female gaze, the gendered viewing positions it implies, and the sensory urban experiences it evokes—that are created from the films' unique collection of illegible (not yet legible) urban spaces and imaginaries, where the sights, sounds, and embodied senses of gender violence are rehearsed and replayed. Depicting female characters whose lives in China's metropolitan centers inevitably end in death and sexual-economic exploitation, Li's films from the 2000s, including *Baober in Love, Stolen Life* (*Shengsi jie*, 2005), and *The Door* (*Men*, 2007), contribute to a unique gendered landscape where the legacies of Mao-era state feminism are considered alongside a global media network that circulates and reproduces commodified femininity. Alluding to a cinematic architectural feminism, the films' settings probe the relationship between post-socialist urban imaginaries and post-socialist femininity. Li's urban cinema goes beyond the traditional model of searching for a city's "true" representation and emphasizes the unrepresentability of the urban. Like post-socialist femininity, the post-socialist city is being recoded from the space of production to the space of consumption.[11] The post- in the post-socialist city gestures toward a process of becoming where the anticipation of the future shapes present perceptions. As Li's films reimagine post-socialist women's visibility, the gendered body seeps into urban imaginaries of Chinese metropolises, creating expanded spaces of consumption and unrestrained desires in a continuum of bodies and cities—an embodied landscape.[12] Set in metropolitan Beijing and Chongqing, the films provide a backdrop where post-socialist femininity is staged, dramatized, and experimented with in some of China's most rapidly developing centers of consumer culture. Prominently featuring spaces of post-socialist consumption—department stores, luxury apartments, and shopping centers—Li's experimentation with post-socialist femininity is intertwined with the spatial imaginaries of global neoliberalism, where the body is subject to the colonizing forces of consumerism. The linkage between bodies and cities thus evokes a cinematic history of the production of gendered space and the locus of the filmmaker's Marxist-feminist critiques of neoliberal post-socialism.

Illegible, elusive, and prone to disappearance, the self-destructive and violently exploited female bodies in Li's films are new visible-and-incomprehensible presences that defy the images of socialist and commodified femininity. Infinitely receding in the mirror reflections of societal desires and anxieties, femininity and masculinity are bounded relations that shift according to the constellations of social forces that map onto the materiality of the body. Tracing the evolution of femininity in modern Chinese history reveals a range of incommensurable feminine bodies. Beginning with male performances of *qing* femininity in eighteenth- and nineteenth-century Chinese theater, femininity has evolved through distinct stages of discontinuous development. Defined as the "natural expression of female sexual physiology," Republican-era femininity put the feminine body on display as an assemblage of natural attributes and commodified consumer products. In the globally circulating imaginary of capitalist-colonial modernity, early twentieth-century Chinese femininity—in the quintessential image of the modern girl—emerged from the transnational circulation of women's images and products in the European, American, and Japanese empires.[13] To be a modern woman meant being feminine in specific ways that connected femininity to emergent consumer behaviors and cultures. However, as a mutable space that is structurally maintained and strategically deployed, femininity shifted from commodified beauty to laboring bodies of liberated working women during the transition to socialist nation-building. Shifting from the commodified femininity of consumption, socialist femininity was recoded as productive femininity, where the official rhetoric of libera-tion obfuscated the induction of women's labor power into socialist nation-building projects. In Tani Barlow's transnational history of Chinese femi-ninities, socialist femininity is defined by a woman's "compassionate service to society through labor and social service to the dispossessed." However, when China entered the era of economic reform, post-socialist femininity was "recoded as money."[14] The history of changing definitions of feminin-ity highlights the concept as a contested site of meaning production. In the post-socialist era, it also opens up questions of how gender identities are called upon to mediate the cultural imaginary of China's transition from socialism to post-socialism—a notion conditioned by the geopolitics of the Cold War and post–Cold War world.

Through the transnational circulation of media cultures, post-socialist femininity that is increasingly defined by a capitalist commodity culture de-notes a cultural field where corporate interests mediate every definition of femininity. *Baober in Love* may be easily dismissed as an example of re-coding post-socialist femininity according to the logic of global capitalism—a feminine subject position demanded by the global film industry and neo-liberalism. However, the problem with this critique is the presupposition of a linear economic developmental model that determines the recoded fate of femininity. If we let go of the assumption that commodified femininity is the inevitable end point, we see that Baober's self-destructive body probes a space of discontinuity and nonsynchronicity while constructing a non-participatory site where the post- in post-socialist femininity is negotiated, radically reimagined, and opened up for questioning.

In the era of intensifying market development, the temporal imaginary of teleological economic development leads to the resurgence of market forces in shaping new definitions of the body. However, as the conception of femininity engenders new speculations in the era of economic reform—where femininity is subject to the commodifying forces of the market—a totalizing and gen-eralized definition of post-socialist femininity as capitalist and commodified femininity forecloses the possibility of examining the post- as an active cul-tural field for remaking the future(s) of femininity. In contrast to the notion of a globally commodified femininity that originates in capitalist countries and then is exported to China, post-socialist femininity consists of a wide spectrum of post-socialist experimentations with the body, whereby different bodies are conjured according to different imaginaries of the post-. Demonstrating vary-ing degrees of resistance to and compliance with the presumed finality of commodified femininity, cultural representations of post-socialist feminine bodies open up a corporeal landscape where the body is already a theory of perception.[15] As Merleau-Ponty says, "Our own body is in the world as the heart is in the organism: it keeps the visible spectacle constantly alive, it breathes life into it and sustains it inwardly, and with it forms a system."[16] The body consists of systems of meaning production and sensory orientation that are masked in the assumption that bodies are passive biological entities awaiting external stimuli. Treating the body as a theory of perception from which meaning-making systems arise, I read Li's urban films as unique feminist blockbusters, where the conflicts between commodified femininity and a *different* post-socialist femininity seep into the films' representations of embodiment.

Embedded in this reading is a gender history of the "future anterior"— the principal methodology in Barlow's monumental work tracing an intellectual history of women as the subject in Chinese feminism(s). Whereas the post- may invite sweeping conclusions about the inevitable commodification of post-socialist femininity, the post- and its assertion of a different future—its departure from socialist femininity—also created a range of *other* femininities in the present that await excavation. Barlow describes the future anteriority as a methodology that deconstructs assumptions of the "real": "A history written to highlight future anteriority is not particularly concerned with what women *are*, that is what women *must have been before, given what women really are*. . . . Emphasizing future anteriority shifts attention away from ideal typical or representative women per se to writing and thinking focused on decoding women and their proposed future role."[17] The self-destructive body of Li's female character is not meant to represent the lived reality of urban women but to illuminate the body as the agent for imagining different post-socialist futures. Turning the body into a site of action, the destruction of the body creates a rift in the presumed transition from socialist to post-socialist definitions of femininity and opens up a space for other types of bodily performativity.

Post-socialist femininity, although increasingly defined in terms of capital, has also produced bodies and spaces of resistance. Connecting bodies to narrative plots of displacement, Li's urban-themed films visualize China's rapidly expanding urban centers as interconnected networks of circulation. Though women are on the move, their simultaneous immobility and entrapment paradoxically complicate the capitalist logic of circulation as free, open, and transparent and call for further investigation of the existing power structures that systematically regulate movement and displacement in the city. Imagining Beijing and Chongqing as sites of murder and exploitation, Li's films open up uncharted territory of feminist urban geography by connecting the problematic of the body to the urban fabric. As a complex network that brings together economic transactions and social relations, the city represents an expansive site of a gender-recoding system operating through housing distribution, property ownership, and consumer purchasing power.[18] Depicting the homeless, outcasts, and disappeared women, Li's films about romance in the city center on female bodies and characters that are displaced on multiple levels. The extent of women's displacement ranges from the literal destruction of their homes during citywide gentrification to alienation from their biological bodies and the invisible but systematic expulsion of women from expensive urban centers—unless they are in compliance with the post-socialist femininity demanded by the institutions of neoliberal heteronormativity, including conjugal marriage.[19]

The annihilation of Baober's body is not an isolated fantasy but a moment of disruption in an expanding urban network built to secure the smooth transmission of assets, legal rights, and power according to the combined logic of Confucian patriarchy and neoliberal heteronormativity. Women's displacement and erasure in the symbolic realm is an ongoing problem throughout history. But in the context of post-socialist China's intensifying urbanization, female displacement materializes in unique urban imaginaries. To fully explicate the cinematic archive of embodied urbanscapes of dispossession, the next section presents a collection of intimate dystopias, theorized as a series of expanding dreams of the interior that connect spatial imaginaries of the body to post-socialist domestic home spaces that are rarely recognized as an integral part of urbanization. In an attempt to map out an interconnected urban fabric that is driving women toward dispossession, the focus on bodies, homes, and cities provides a way to deconstruct a new urban network built upon the commodifying powers of the interior-design and architectural industries as they manufacture various "dreams of the interior" that supply the phantasmatic but nonetheless real basis of post-socialist urban living.

Manufacturing Dreams of the Interior

Since China adopted free-market economic reform policies in the late 1970s, dreams of modern living have proliferated. Interior- and furniture-design industries flourished, and elaborately decorated intimate public spaces such as cafés, teahouses, and karaoke bars emerged. The interior is the primary locus of capital investment and also one of the most significant sites giving shape to the mass dream of urban modernity, thus leading to what Walter Benjamin calls the phantasmagorias of the interior. Drawing from the urban model of nineteenth-century Paris, Benjamin offers phantasmagorias of the interior as a way of reading interior space not as a physical location but as the psychological state of living in a competitive capitalist society. He writes, "The private person who squares his accounts with reality in his office demands that the interior be maintained in his illusions. This need is all the more pressing since he has no intention of extending his commercial considerations into social ones. In shaping his private environment he represses both. From this spring the phantasmagorias of the interior. For the private individual the private environment represents the universe. In it he gathers remote places and the past. His drawing room is a box in the world theater."[20] Turning the drawing room into a private phantasmatic spectacle, the phantasmagorias of the interior reflect the psychical landscape of modern living as a complex process of boundary making and reterritorialization. However, the passage reveals a hidden drama of gendered paranoia amid the sense of celebrated self-empowerment. The more individuals invest in the creation of a private universe, the more they are living, as reality, the illusion that disguises the alienation of their labor power with the dream of consumption and ownership. In twenty-first-century China, phantasmagorias of the interior spring from the intense economic and emotional investments associated with reclaiming individuality and private space. Yet such phantasmagorias of the interior "with Chinese characteristics" breach the theoretical setting of the drawing room, encompassing a wide range of societal symptoms and nesting conceptually onto various urban topoi and subjects. While post-socialist China dreams of elaborate interior decorations and a space of home and intimacy, Li's films draw on popular trends of home decor to crudely highlight women's homelessness and displacement. The dream of the interior is not a romanticized concept that celebrates urban modernity; it is a critical lens that deconstructs cultural and architectural imaginations of the home as the site that recodes post-socialist femininity according to the commodifying logic of neoliberal post-socialism.

Replacing the Parisian arcade and the department store from Benjamin's analysis of European modernity, Li's films, which target urban audiences in China, take place in a selection of quotidian locations in Chinese cities, including a luxury loft that was converted from a socialist-era factory, construction sites, Western-style townhouses, and an underground basement city. Contrary to Benjamin's Parisian city viewed from the perspective of a strolling flâneur, Li's cities consist of sights and scenes of alienation (and self-alienation) from the perspective of urban female nomads, bringing into view women's precariousness under multiple patriarchal systems of dispossession. Under post-socialism—a historical catachresis and an ideological vacuum that nonetheless produces concrete realities—patriarchal values of Confucianism and global capitalism merge and strengthen each other, making property and home ownership in urban China the privilege of male heirs.[21] Although many Chinese citizens face a lack of affordable housing and the possibility of homelessness, these structural problems have a disproportionate impact on single, divorced, and lesbian women.[22]

Women's precariousness is not a new problem. The hypervisibility of women as manual laborers, soldiers, and active participants in the public realm during the socialist era should be carefully contextualized. In her gender history of Chinese women's liberation from 1949 to 1966, the seventeen-year period that established the Chinese socialist system and its ideologies, Dong Limin cautions that "gender equality" needs to be situated in China's long and violent history of revolution, during which time "women were never accorded a clearly gendered revolutionary identity or role; neither was women's liberation ever the sole objective of women's movements."[23] On the topic of gender equality, Mao said, "In order to build a great socialist society it is of the utmost importance to arouse the broad masses of women to join in productive activity. Men and women must receive equal pay for equal work in production. Genuine equality between the sexes can only be realized in the process of the socialist transformation of society as a whole."[24] Beneath the scheme of gender equality, this passage reveals the fetishization of the language of gender emancipation as a tool for the state apparatus to extract labor power. Socialist femininity as a subject position was in turn defined by the public services a woman could provide rather than a signifier of difference to be recognized in equality. Although the transition from socialist to post-socialist times continues to create narratives of women's liberation or oppression—depending upon one's analytical perspective—the historical movement of time results not in forward motion but in perpetual cycles of stasis.

During times of intensifying deterritorialization and reterritorialization in post-socialist China, a woman's imagined reproduction—a gesture toward claiming her own space—demands a specific gender history of space. As market forces transform Chinese cities into new spaces of consumption, different spatial nexuses that channel and direct the flow of consumerist desires and capital are replacing the city that was coded as the site of production during the socialist era. As suggested by Li's cinematic works, the space of the home emerges as the most significant site of manufacturing and materializing new dreams of consumer culture. In characters' paranoid obsession with the everyday practice of interior decoration and home improvement projects, the home is alienating and incompatible with the men and women who occupy it. The examination of domestic space thus problematizes the consumerist rituals of decoration while deconstructing the home as not only a physical dwelling space (a house) but also an expansive social mechanism that monitors, regulates, and produces the subject positions required for the unobstructed flow of commodified desires.[25]

As points of mediation that connect the body to the city, imaginaries of the home are an integral dimension of urbanization. Challenging the dichotomous divide between public and private space, Li's dystopic urban cinema considers the home a mechanism that maintains this illusory divide. Relying heavily on the representations of heterosexual love and sexuality, the films portray gender relationships through the metaphors of patriarchal masculinity and oppressed femininity. However, the notable essentialism in Li's architectural feminism highlights a defining characteristic of feminist thought in the post-socialist era. Between early twentieth-century Chinese feminist theory and post-socialist feminist discourses, there are observable continuities and discontinuities with a gender theory based on the discourses of evolution and heterosexuality in nature, resulting in a social theory that interprets gender roles as the extension of presumably natural sexual differences.[26] An examination of Li's films is not only relevant to the work of historicizing the meaning of post-socialist femininity but crucial for thinking about the nuanced histories of Chinese feminism(s). Following the socialist era, which de-emphasized the significance of biological sexual difference, the woman's biological body and its role in heterosexual relationships resurface in the era of the post-, when the boundaries between gender roles are retested and redrawn. Opposed to the idea of market feminism—the belief that China's economic reforms will achieve gender equality by offering women more opportunities and greater powers of consumption—Li's films present scenarios of intimate dystopias where women, property ownership, and women's space in the symbolic realm become intricately intertwined.[27] Li's collection of intimate dystopias portrays the encroachment of market socialism's commodifying powers, resulting in women's perpetual state of displacement.

A Valentine's Day Gone Awry:
Deconstructing the Home in *Baober in Love*

In the post-socialist film market, where urban romance with a strong female lead is an increasingly popular genre, *Baober in Love*'s citation of the French blockbuster suggests not only Li's experimentation with film as a market commodity but also her complex remapping of post-socialist Chinese femininity in the limiting spectrum of women's visibility in a globally commodified media network. As an unofficial adaptation of the French blockbuster, *Baober in Love* documents a record of transformation. Produced with a blockbuster consciousness, the film is notable for its bold and experimental use of computer-generated imagery (CGI) that Li acquired in Paris. While Beijing is transformed into the embodied site of Baober's urban experience, the city is lighted up in magical light shows, and its urbanscape recomposed through the film's elliptical selection of mysterious and disconnected locations, such as a surreal seaside, a library in a Chinese courtyard home, and a basketball court for the physically disabled. Released in time for the Western Valentine's Day, the film bewildered audiences and critics, who described it as "confusing," "not as expected," "[something that] should not be played on Valentine's Day," and "horrific."[28] Such responses provide clues to the film's opening of a new sensory channel that overwhelms the existing framework of interpretation. While the film speculates that the market value of *Amélie* was found in a globalized and commodified French femininity, the female protagonist Baober gradually brings the French Amélie into the body of a post-socialist Chinese woman, turning this body into a site of experimentation and a lens to examine what the post- entails in post-socialist Chinese femininity. Ultimately Baober's self-destructive body suggests the violent shedding of an acquired shell—a phantom body that is both desired and rejected.

Li's exploration of post-socialist femininity begins with a sight and site of trauma in Baober's childhood. As Baober hesitatingly recites "My Birth," an essay she has been assigned to write and read in front of her class, the camera floats across several disjunctive episodes, including her discovery as a newborn in a trash mound, a metaphor that links Beijing's pre-Olympic urban transformation and the birth of post-socialist femininity. Through an elliptical cut, little Baober is seen chased by the shadow of a black cat and rushed out of school with a herd of her panicking classmates. The scene of panic transitions to a demolition site in the city. As people and heavy demolition equipment rush through, Baober stands screaming in the center of the frame. The camera reveals her surroundings through a circular pan, wherein

FIGURE 2.2. In *Baober in Love* (2004), Baober screams against a paradoxical ruin-scape featuring a mise-en-scène of pre-Olympic Beijing's simultaneous rebirth and destruction.

the rooftop of her family house is violently torn open, and the ruinscape gives rise to Beijing's new skyline, filled with skyscrapers and high-speed expressways (see figure 2.2). A girl's birth in Beijing is presented as a spectacle of trauma. Her story of birth intertwines with the city's large-scale demolition projects, extending women's displacement from the body to the city. Viewed as the original site of trauma, the multisensory image of urban demolition is replayed with a compulsion to repeat. In an attempt to give a specific and legible context to a woman's psychological and physical state of displacement, the opening scene illustrates the production of gendered urban horror—a new affect that is discovered at the moment when the *new* logic of post-socialist Chinese urbanism abruptly arrives, leaving no time and space for ruminating the evolved structure of gender violence. Setting the film in pre-Olympic Beijing, which put post-socialism on global display, *Baober in Love* searches for an architectural rhetoric of expulsion and homelessness that is echoed in the city's post-socialist transformation.

Unsurprisingly, the ruinscape in post-socialist Beijing bears little resemblance to the sunny and colorful streets of Parisian Montmartre in *Amélie*, and the chronicle of a Chinese woman challenges her French blockbuster prototype. The cinematic assemblage of Amélie-in-a-Chinese-body relies on an elliptical narrative structure, where the tale of Baober's life is presented in disjunctive fragments that allow for the coexistence of incommensurable personality traits and experiences. Li's exploration of post-socialist femininity is built on speculations of a feminist spectacle's potential market value, which leave behind traces of experimentations and negotiations. In addition to the young Baober in an iconic red dress and short hair, multiple Baobers exist as the camera freely switches between the perspectives of Baober in childhood and as a young woman who wears big wigs and disguises her feminine figure with androgynous clothing. Unique but not distinctive, the character Baober easily blends into Beijing's metropolitan setting and could be any young woman living in the city, thus representing a new generation of female urbanites born during China's years of economic reform. Whereas the opening sequence shows the destruction of a Chinese-style brick house—a symbol of home and the bygone socialist past—an array of post-socialist imaginaries of the home are introduced in the film as Baober and her male lover, Liu Zhi, roam the city for a new place of residence. The intensification of their relationship brings forth new dreams of the interior, involving a settled address and designer furniture. However, with the ability to see things that no one else does—like Amélie, who is capable of transforming Montmartre and its people by focusing on details that no one else notices—Baober perceives that Beijing's homescape and the dream of a bourgeois interior objectify female bodies in the domestic space, putting an embodied femininity in permanent expulsion. Conveying the horror of displacement through space, each of the lovers' new residences transforms into a schizophrenic battle zone where one's fantasy of domestic ownership turns into the other's nightmare of dispossession. The post-socialist interior landscape of the home, as one of the main loci of consolidating consumer desires that connect the body to the city, is violently inverted and overthrown.

In Karatani Kojin's definition of an "inversion" that takes place before a cultural form becomes legible, he describes a process that "transforms our mode of perception . . . [which] does not take place either inside or outside of us, but is an inversion of a semiotic configuration."[29] Through the change of perception, new systems of legibility are formed, while their "origins" are suppressed as soon as they are produced. In Li's representation of Beijing, Baober's erratic associations of images and spaces create a spectacle of the city that is at the limit of legibility. However, it is precisely at this moment that a prior representational order of the city as connected networks of consumption and private ownership is exposed, creating a sense of violation and the cinematic evocation of embodied horror. Contributing to a contested notion of the post-, Baober sees the pre-Olympic Beijing as a city oblivious to its history of gentrification and the new class- and gender-based stratification. Discovering the home as an emergent representational space before it becomes a repeatable convention, the film performs different deconstructions of homes as they are represented in a variety of post-socialist urban dwelling places.

The first notable deconstruction of the home takes place in a VHS video containing recorded footage of Liu Zhi's autobiographical confession of life's discontents that Baober finds and edits. Fast-forwarding and rewinding, pausing and replaying, Baober is fascinated with the video, which contains the visible evidence for Zhi's sarcasm about making every decision according to the expectations of post-socialist bourgeois masculinity. Working long hours to fulfill the dream of living an affluent urban life, Zhi becomes disillusioned and begins an extensive commentary on the furniture he owns. Listing in detail each piece of designer furniture, Zhi reveals a philosophy of furniture that critiques the lifestyle of overconsumption and waste.

In an essay titled "The Philosophy of Furniture," Edgar Allan Poe comments on one of the inspirations of horror: a badly decorated room. Considering decoration a form of art, Poe expresses special contempt for the American interior, which is a "mere parade of costly appurtenances" and a false "aristocracy of dollars."[30] As an uninvited messenger for Zhi, Baober delivers his philosophy of furniture as she barges into his luxury penthouse and screens the video in front of Zhi's wife. To illustrate Zhi's critique of his own living space, the penthouse sequence employs a split screen (see figures 2.3 and 2.4). One screen shows an apartment view through Baober's perspective; the other repeats the same detail from Zhi's video footage. "This is the penthouse that my wife has chosen," says Zhi in the video. "She enjoys a refined lifestyle and spends a lot of time selecting and buying furniture." Cut to pieces and fragmented by the split screen, Zhi's apartment undergoes a critical dissection. From the Maldives-imported toilet that features wave sounds when flushed to the designer glass staircase, the luxurious apartment is shaded in dark colors and grays and made to resemble a living tomb devoid of color, vitality, and life. Adding to the ambience of lifelessness, Ran Ran, Zhi's wife, wears a white facial mask and bathrobe in the scene, making her nearly indistinguishable from the interior setting. As Baober busily opens closets and peeps into drawers to bring out objects of childhood memories that do not belong, her discoveries accentuate the perception of the luxury apartment as an alienating prison. While holding a small pet dog—a symbol of post-socialist private ownership—Ran Ran is indistinguishable from the

FIGURE 2.3. Split screen in *Baober in Love* (2004): the cinematic dissection of the Chinese phantasmagorias of the interior.

FIGURE 2.4. Split screen in *Baober in Love* (2004): one screen shows an apartment from Baober's perspective; the other repeats the same detail from Zhi's video footage.

designer furniture that fills her home. The picture-perfect apartment—a replica of the dream house showcased in interior design magazines—resembles a terrifying site of domestication. In gendered phantasmagorias of the interior, the post-socialist man is the traditional financial provider, and femininity is a commodity for purchase, exchange, and display.

At its core, the phantasmagoria of the interior is part of a vision machine of power, manufacturing the illusion of privacy and private space and reproducing spatial arrangements to secure the smooth transmission of post-socialist consumer desires. A home is equipped with windowpanes, thresholds, keyholes, and television screens, all of which are framing devices that transform an ordinary household into a social machine that regulates the seen and the unseen. As Beatriz Colomina suggests, modern housing is not simply the separation between the interior and the exterior; a house functions by the viewing mechanisms it produces. Through windows and doors, an exterior view is domesticated and framed so that subjects in the house are not only "actors" who play the part of the seen but also "spectators" who see and control what they see.[31] Proposing the term *domestic voyeurism*, which situates the domestic house in the center of a private panopticon, Colomina explores the house as a three-dimensional viewing mechanism that gives the illusion of an omnipotent view, as external landscapes are interiorized. Yet to enjoy the full view of the domesticated landscape—for example, through the penthouse skylight that overlooks Beijing's cityscape—the body needs to occupy domestic roles and viewing positions that in turn subject it to systems of control. By setting up a picture-perfect home copied straight out of China's newly popular interior design magazines, Ran Ran slips into the body of commodified femininity, replicating a spatial imaginary that transforms the home from a domesticated site to a site of domestication.

Since the 1990s the number of interior design magazines in China has significantly increased.[32] Along with the recent establishment of decor-related internet platforms and the arrival of multinational design and home furnishing corporations, phantasmagorias of the interior have become a fundamental driving force of societal and interpersonal change. In a study of the relationship between gender and home ownership, especially in major metropolitan centers such as Beijing and Shanghai, the sociologist Deborah Davis observes that a new array of home decor magazines is giving shape to popular post-socialist imaginations of privacy, home, and domestic life. Whereas interior design and home decor were minimized in the socialist era, the dream of owning and constructing a private home reached a new level of intensity in the post-socialist era.[33] After the dissolution of socialist communes and housing systems, joint ownership or tenancy is now exceptional, and men are typically the sole owner or renter on housing deeds and leases.[34] However, the right to property ownership also means a new social definition of masculinity, one that is built upon the exchange of labor for a home. Zhi's luxury penthouse represents a simultaneously desirable and alienating post-socialist dream of the interior. At the same time that the male protagonist demonstrates purchasing power in this dream house, he is interpellated as a participating subject in an expanding consumer society and caught in the perpetual cycle of work and consumption. While the capitalist dream of the interior shapes post-socialist masculinity and femininity, what remains unexamined is the possibility of disruption, as dramatized in the factory loft and the final home space deconstructed in *Baober in Love*.

THE FACTORY LOFT

The factory loft, Zhi and Baober's choice of residence, reflects a new trend in Beijing's real estate market that extends capitalist urbanization to the ruins of socialist-era factories; it also symbolizes the complex relationship between socialism and post-socialism. In Beijing, the factory loft represents a unique architectural phenomenon closely associated with post-socialist urban gentrification. The idea of converting socialist-era factories into private dwellings and work spaces is exemplified by the Beijing 798 art zone. As discussed in chapter 1, Beijing 798 was formerly a high-tech war-industry and electronics factory zone built with East German and Soviet technologies, celebrated today as the biggest international art zone in China.[35] At the time of *Baober in Love*'s release, 798 was turning into the embodiment of the post- in post-socialism, representing the triumph of art and the transformation of a space of socialism into a neoliberal shopping mall. Yet precisely at the space where histories are disjoined and rejoined, the commodified factory turns into an outlet of the film's sensory experimentations, dramatizing (through special effects) the sounds, sights, and haptic visuality of Baober's experience of urban dispossession.

Framing landscapes and bodies, housing design is not only a part of the phantasmatic theater of the interior but also a social mechanism that reproduces the hegemonic dominance of an existing social hierarchy. Following Baober and Zhi's elopement, the two quickly form a romantic bond as they roam the city—chasing each other in the subway, resting on the bus, and kissing in a magicalized construction site that is visually enhanced by computer animation. Appearing and disappearing at will, Baober's presence in the first half of the film consists of elliptical sequences showing her interactions with other socially marginalized subjects, including Beijing's senior citizens and the physically disabled. Playing no significant role in the narrative, these sequences—set in a dusty library in a small Chinese courtyard house and a basketball court for the physically disabled—present a cityscape of Beijing that is disjunctive and incomprehensible. Frequently visiting these spaces that are without identity, Baober is seen as a free-spirited flâneuse whose view of the city digresses from recognizable landmarks. Her spatial itinerary challenges the conventional understanding of homelessness and disrupts the imaginary of the home as a capitalist commodity. Her movement in the city proposes unique spatial practices that are not legible in the abstracting system of capitalism, where movement and circulation are based on logistical calculations of efficiency and profit.

Upon the lovers' move into the factory loft, the loft's empty interior evokes a philosophical problem and highlights a divergence in the lovers' views of space. Specifically, each interprets the emptiness of the space differently. Whereas Zhi views it literally as an empty space to be filled, Baober treats it as a space full of absent presences. In the film's final deconstruction of home space, the factory—the site that embodies the mass dream of socialist industrialization—is transformed into a private domestic dwelling. The spatial transformation paves the way to a dramatic sequence in which the act of interior decoration is comparable to the destructive violence of war. But underneath the visual spectacle, the scene that mediates gendered urban horror probes the uneasy and presumably clear-cut distinction between socialism and post-socialism, especially through the eyes of the film's female protagonist. Originally an open space laden with heavy equipment, the factory loft requires the addition of many household items to turn it into a livable space. Creating an extended shopping list, Zhi imagines the home in terms of material objects, the ownership of which completes the imagined domestic space based on the market logic of consumption.

Although Baober voices her disinterest in the idea of filling the space with objects, the capitalist dream of the interior—when combined with the traditional patriarchal claim on property—transforms the home into a site for securing the homogeneous imagination of a post-socialist domestic space. In a visual spectacle with special effects—one of several instances where gender violence is visualized with blockbuster consciousness—Zhi leads an encroaching army of interior decorators and contractors to transform the loft into a properly domestic space (see figure 2.5). Interspersed with flashbacks that show Baober's traumatic memories of Beijing's urban gentrification, the sequence compares the accumulation of furniture in the loft to a war zone,

FIGURE 2.5. Zhi in *Baober in Love* (2004) leads an encroaching army of interior decorators and contractors to transform the loft into a properly domestic space.

showing bookshelves and chests dropping from the sky like bombs, ready to crush the petite female protagonist. As Baober is gradually cornered in a losing battle for space, the sequence ends with a fantastical scene. The camera circles around the suffocating Baober, who escapes the loft by magically flying out of the window. Discovered sleeping under sheets of newspaper on the street in the next scene, Baober has fled from the picture-perfect home built according to the logic of capitalist consumption. Her spectacular departure marks a moment of disruption in the imagination of heterosexual romance and the coding process of post-socialist femininity.

As discussed previously, the discourse on gender equality and the discourse on the social construction of femininity in the socialist era are linked to the process of fetishizing the language of liberation for the purpose of creating more labor power in the socialist nation-building project. Therefore, when combined with the realities of intense urbanization and homelessness in the post-socialist era, the question of femininity may be articulated only by borrowing a nonlinguistic visual vocabulary that opens up a channel for the gendered and lived reality of post-socialism. One of the most important issues raised in Li's urban cinema is the expansiveness of the consumerist dream of the interior. In the dissection of post-socialist heterosexual relationships, the deconstruction of home spaces highlights the significance of the home in creating and maintaining gender and class hierarchies, while at the same time anchoring individual bodies in the hierarchical order of post-socialist urban society.

The Door, Conspiracy Theory, and the Male Interior Decorator

In one of Li's subsequent films, *The Door*, the violence associated with post-socialist masculinity—exemplified by the male interior decorator—is accentuated as a post-socialist symptom causing murderous desires. A psychological thriller, *The Door* features a male urbanite, Jiang Zhongtian, who puts together various clues—the timetable of the subway, a text message his girlfriend sends—in a suspected conspiracy theory against him. Facing potential unemployment, he begins to experience a different relationship with the city. Everything that is visible, audible, and perceivable is no longer what it seems. The door and windows of his apartment—normally used to shut out the outside world—turn into an extensive system of surveillance, through which people continue to peep in and monitor his life. He alone knows the truth about the double personalities hidden beneath friendly smiles and about the nature of his disappeared girlfriend, whom he suspects of being a gold digger. Remapped by Zhongtian's paranoia, Chongqing appears in dizzying displays of high-rise apartment windows—a feature that echoes Alfred Hitchcock's murder mystery drama *Rear Window* (1954), in which a wheelchair-bound photographer becomes convinced he has witnessed a murder from his apartment window. The world turns into a collection of Zhongtian's sensory perceptions of a post-socialist city: competitive, alienating, and capitalistic. Unable to compete with friends who are successful entrepreneurs, Zhongtian transfers his frustrations to home-improvement projects, playing the role of an interior decorator.

A tribute to thriller master Hitchcock and a partial adaptation of Poe's nineteenth-century short story "The Black Cat," *The Door* shows the male protagonist standing listlessly in front of his newly decorated wall. Touching and smoothing over the flower-patterned blue wallpaper, he caresses the wall in a moment of crisis when his girlfriend goes missing. As the film reveals, her dead body lies concealed behind the apartment wall—a site of trauma in the space of intimacy they once shared (figure 2.6). Changing the setting of Poe's story to the Chinese megacity Chongqing, *The Door* transforms the post-socialist city into a haunted site of murder. The film works meticulously with the apartment setting, from door to window, from peephole to light switch. Every corner and detail of the apartment is turned into a potential object of violent aggression. Behind closed doors, every object and amenity implies a history of violence. The intimate space the lovers shared is revealed to be a high-rise graveyard.

Released in 2007, *The Door* is one of Li's experiments with the blockbuster form, bringing to view a filmmaking pattern that tests the compat-

FIGURE 2.6. Pouring cement, plastering, painting, and ritualistically hanging wallpaper, the male protagonist in *The Door* (2007) devotes himself to interior decoration, underscoring the post-socialist phantasmagorias of the interior that are prone to gender violence.

ibility between the market value of blockbuster elements and the exploration of post-socialist masculinity and femininity. Pouring cement, plastering, painting, and ritualistically hanging wallpaper, Zhongtian devotes himself to interior decoration, underscoring the darkened phantasmagorias of the interior and the significance of the post-socialist home in mediating gendered fantasies and consumer desires. The opposite of a haven of privacy or safety, Zhongtian's bourgeois apartment employs the visual rhetoric of a dystopic dream of the interior where the act of decorating is linked to the violence of murder. Seeing the city as a conglomerate of closed doors, *The Door* hyperbolizes the male protagonist's obsession with interior decoration in an effort to symptomize a consumerist fantasy that turns deadly. The post-socialist home, rather than being a neutral space, is exposed as an urban imaginary—a productive site where the unobstructed flow of consumer desires is given a concrete form of expression. The act of decorating places the protagonist into an affective relationship with the city he lives in, dramatizing the illusion of ownership and the man's further entrapment in the commodified dream of the interior.

Committing murder and burying his secret inside his apartment wall, Zhongtian disposes of (or preserves) his lover's body, revealing an imaginary of the home as the object of both desire and fear. A comparison between Poe's "The Black Cat" and Li's *The Door* illustrates a desiring guilt complex in which the home functions as the instrument of both concealment and revelation. In Poe's story, a man tortures and kills his black cat, Pluto, and later, perhaps out of temporary remorse and guilt, adopts an almost identical cat with the exception of a large white patch on the new cat's chest. After the cat nearly trips him while he is walking down to the cellar, the enraged man wants to kill again. Stopped by his wife, the man murders the wife instead and buries her body in the wall of their cellar. Thinking that he has committed the perfect crime, the man, along with the police, is shocked to hear the sound of a cat wailing from the wall, and to the narrator's horror, the corpse of his wife is discovered with the black cat standing on top of her head.[36] Designing horror through architecture, Poe spatializes the searing and relentless return of guilt by giving it an intimate setting that lies directly beneath consciousness.

Li's *The Door* further accentuates this guilt complex through the male protagonist's compulsive and neurotic work of pasting, tearing down, and repasting wallpaper in his apartment. Depicting Chongqing's metro trains that pass by the apartment with nerve-wracking punctuality, the film highlights gender violence as a haunting presence that regularly seeps into the man's (un)consciousness. Like a silent alarm of the gruesome murder, the ubiquitous sound of the train penetrates all parts of the megacity, delivering subliminal messages to the murderer who forgets his crime. The postsocialist city that is characterized by infrastructural development—depicted in the image of train tracks, expressways, and the Yangtze River cableway (Chang Jiang suodao)—transforms into a gendered landscape of paranoia and alienation. Li's compulsive interior decorator uncovers a history of gender violence that is visible but incomprehensible. Buried in the most intimate setting of the home, the knowledge of atrocity seeps through everyday household problems. Mold, water leakage, and electrical surges form a network of urban dysfunctions circulating in post-socialist Chinese cities.

In addition to borrowing cinematic styles and literary motifs from Hitchcock and Poe, *The Door* is also a film adaptation of *Sanchakou* (*Crossroads*) that centers on a story of revenge and embezzlement by the popular Chinese horror story writer Zhou Dedong. *The Door* thus experiments with a range of commodifiable generic instruments of suspense and horror circulating in both domestic and global markets. Not a conventional horror film, *The Door* illustrates the influence of market forces in the portrayal of gender violence against women. Continuing her experimental citational practice in post-WTO filmmaking, Li portrays violence against women in a way that builds upon a blockbuster consciousness wherein film technologies and styles are tested for their market value. Driven by the desire to cross borders and to explore specific genres—especially horror, action, and thriller genres, where male filmmakers dominate—Li includes a Hollywood-style action sequence that is choreographed by the Hong Kong stunt coordinator Bruce Law. Featuring a high-speed car chase and physical fights, the film moves through some of the most arduous geographical locations in Chongqing, from mountain roads to the elevated Nanjing-Yangtze River bridge that was then under construction.[37] The performance of post-socialist misogyny is also a testing ground for commercial filmmaking, creating uneven textures and directions that contain traces of the negotiation with market forces.

As the last film Li made in the 2000s, *The Door* captures a Chongqing resident in crisis. Yet it is a crisis of paranoia that reanimates the city, highlighting its transportation networks, communication systems, and the door as a new post-socialist imaginary and architectural language. This then opens up new pathways, connections, and histories that are not otherwise discernible. The male interior decorator is the inheritor of sensory channels that lead to violent aggression. As the familiar city is turned upside down by the male protagonist's development of a conspiracy theory, speculations about his lover's infidelity expose paranoid thoughts in a losing battle against a new class of post-socialist men, whose masculinity is recoded as the capitalist accumulation of wealth. Powerless against the changing tide of time, Zhongtian engages in a reactive remasculinization of the self, identifying and eliminating the female body as the cause of the threat. From Li's perspective, the imaginary of the post- in post-socialist masculinity reveals a capitalist social hierarchy that redefines heterosexual intimacy. Immersed in the belief that his romantic relationship has been lost to the commodifying system, Zhongtian joins the system himself. While whispering manipulative instructions that are disguised as words of comfort to the body, the interior decorator slowly wraps his lover in a transparent plastic bag. No longer capable of movement, the body stands petrified—its feminine beauty immaculately preserved—like a carefully packaged commercial doll. Turned into an inanimate object, the corpse turns into a screen space where frustrated masculinity is exteriorized and projected onto the female body that, even in death, looks miraculously beautiful, with pale skin, red-painted lips, and long eyelashes (see figure 2.7).

FIGURE 2.7. The miraculously preserved and beautified female corpse in *The Door* (2007).

As a horror film that draws inspiration from a variety of literary and cinematic sources, *The Door* has more than one monster. The male aggressor plays only a supporting role, his paranoia and anxiety alluding to a greater monstrosity that escapes recognition—namely, the commodified feminine beauty that the film compares to undead corpses. However, as the film's audio track replays the scene of the murder—in which only the male protagonist's voice is heard during a monologue of manipulative instructions given to a corpse—the beautified corpse differs from the dangerous and seductive femme fatale. Whereas the film begins with the soundtrack of the murder, the female lover Wen Xin's screen presence suggests a paradoxical self-negation, with the audience unsure whether or not the woman on screen is the appearance of a ghostly spirit. A wandering ghost who is occasionally summoned, Wen Xin is set adrift in a culture of commodified femininity, belonging nowhere and finding no voice of her own. The corpse is one representation of women's displacement that preoccupies Li's cinematic imagination. In a culture of objectification, where female bodies appear as manipulable corpse-objects, a closer examination of Li's female characters reveals a body landscape that complicates the homogenized spectrum of visible bodies in the era of the post- and proposes the retheorization of postsocialist femininity.

Intimate Dystopias 93

Rearticulating Post-Socialist Bodies

In *Stolen Life*, released shortly after *Baober in Love* and before *The Door*, a young female college student, Yanni, falls in love with Muyu. Aspiring to an independent life in Beijing, she decides to quit school and moves in with the man she loves, only to discover that Muyu is using her, and other women in the city, to produce babies that he sells in China's black market for human trafficking. In a narrative that repeats the theme of sexual-economic exploitation, *Stolen Life* calls attention to women's bodies as a significant site in the interrelated spatial imaginaries sustaining the smooth transmission of urban patriarchy. Yanni's pregnancy, rather than disrupting the flow of capitalist desires, turns into a commodity that further subjects female bodies to the commodifying logic of the free-market economy. The film shows the physical transformation of Yanni from an androgynously dressed teenager who hides her hair in woven hats and her body in oversized sweaters to a pregnant woman stranded in her bed.

Set in Beijing's subterranean city—the interconnected basements under residential apartments—the confined and claustrophobic room where the lovers reside provides an architectural metaphor for Yanni's exploited pregnancy. Equipped with a locksmith, a tailor, a kiosk, and delivery services, the underground city is the residence of China's floating population, many of whom travel from rural areas to search for jobs in the city.[38] In contrast to Baober, who wanders aimlessly like a flâneuse in the city, Yanni is confined to the basement, part of a vertical architectural metaphor, displaying a view of bustling city life from its very bottom. Brought to Room 216, believing she is entering into a romantic relationship, Yanni unknowingly subjects her body to an economic transaction system that treats women's bodies as machines capable of producing valuable commodities. Although the growth of the fetus remains hidden from view, the environment surrounding Yanni undergoes noticeable changes. As a film that complements *Baober in Love*, *Stolen Life* portrays the domestic interior as a decaying tomb. In an extended sequence on Yanni's life in the basement, she narrates her experience living in an urban cave completely isolated from the bustling life of Beijing. In a nightmarish phantasmagoria of the interior, the confined and pregnant Yanni lives under a white mosquito net, surrounded by decaying food left by Muyu. After her sole connection with the outside world—a television that transmits only blurred images—breaks down, she becomes further withdrawn. Adding to her isolation, additional misfortunes, such as the basement's frequent blackouts, hunger, and simply boredom, mummify her into a living corpse unable to venture out of her bed (see figure 2.8). As her living conditions worsen,

FIGURE 2.8. The pregnant Yanni surrounded by rotten food in the subterranean basement city in *Stolen Life* (2005).

the film becomes a record of the gruesome exploitation of a young woman's compromises in the name of love. Yanni's body, more than the bleak living conditions of Room 216, represents a site of gendered urban horror—related not to the physical deterioration of the young woman but to the alienation of her pregnant body that is gradually stripped away from her.

Connecting displacement, alienation, and homelessness from the space of the home to the space of the body, *Stolen Life* presents the despondent alienation of female bodies that questions the fundamental significance of the body. In a series of films that replay feminine displacement in different settings and among different social classes, Li poses a question that is left unanswered: what to do with the body that is subject to infinite alienation and recoding, a perpetual surface of inscription for intersecting systems of power. As the site of extreme alienation—a space of abstraction, nonbelonging, and intimate dystopia—what does one do with the body in the era of the post-? In other words, what are the strategies of reclaiming the body, as it is subject to the forces of socialism and post-socialism?

Among Li's films from the 2000s, two openly engage with female pregnancy and the transformation of the female body as a site for articulating gender differences. As Wang Lingzhen observes, feminism in the post-Mao era pursues a different mode of analysis than feminism in the United States and the West in general.[39] Whereas US-based feminism advocates the examination of the intersections of gender, class, and race, post-Mao Chinese feminism emphasizes gender as a distinct category of analysis, following decades of state-sponsored feminism during the socialist era. In a historical context wherein the language of feminism was co-opted by the state, the focus on female pregnancy rethinks the relationship between body and visual language and the possibility of a strategically essentialist feminine language through the biological female body. In the case of *Baober in Love*, Baober embarks on her own construction project following the magical-realist spectacle at the factory loft as she dreams and lives the fantasy of pregnancy. The doctor diagnoses her pregnancy as the symptom of a psychological pathology and denies its physical basis. However, Baober's psychological pregnancy can be read as the collapse of the mind-body dualism, showing their interrelation. Opening a channel to the psychical construction of femininity through the imaginary construction of a space inside Baober's body, the psychological pregnancy turns into a productive claim on space through the act of multiplication and doubling. Yet the only method of proving the pregnancy is a paradoxical act of self-destruction: the female protagonist slits open her belly in the final scene, while gazing at her lover and murmuring her insistence on the child's presence.

To further understand the act of doubling, Baober's psychological pregnancy can be read in relation to Freud's classic essay "The 'Uncanny.'" Freud begins the text with a survey of the various definitions of the German word *unheimlich* and concludes that the *unheimlich* shares an inexplicable connection with the *heimlich*, things that one already knows and with which one is familiar. Although his definition has had a lasting impact on literary and film criticism, what remains underexplored is the origin of the uncanny "double" and its initial function as a mechanism of self-preservation, an "insurance against the destruction of the ego." Linking the double and Baober's pregnancy, it becomes possible to suggest that Baober's symptom does not refer to a psychological neurosis but to an act of self-preservation—women's self-produced multiplication, doubling, and splitting. By doubling oneself, one is able to assure immortality, although, according to Freud, this act may also turn out to be the "uncanny harbinger of death," if the double is not successfully suppressed in relation to the rest of the ego. This is the space where a special agency, which serves to observe and criticize the self, takes shape in the exercise of censorship. In a familiar citation of the destructive features of paranoia and the delusion of being watched, Freud leaves the analysis of the double on a curious note. Since something that we cannot quite account for happens, the double becomes a thing of terror, contrary to its initial function. He writes, "Our knowledge of pathological mental processes enables us to add that nothing in this more superficial material could account for the urge towards defense which has caused the ego to project that material outward as something foreign to itself."[40]

Rather than concluding that the double is frightening, Freud is most intrigued by the missing link that transforms self-preservation into frightful destruction. Leaving that note unresolved, he goes on to observe not only the fear of the double as a psychological mechanism but its transformation into cultural and sociological taboos. Playing with these taboos, Li experiments with psychological pregnancy as a stage to display self-produced doubling. In a nude scene that caught most of the Chinese media's attention, Baober stands looking at herself in a mirror. What she sees is not a direct reflection of her body but a psychological reinvention of herself as a fully pregnant woman (see figure 2.9). However, the pathologization of her condition turns a self-splitting frenzy into a dangerous and neurotic delusion. In a few shots prior to her self-inflicted violence, Baober is shown struggling to break free from a suffocating cloth wrapped around her face and body. To enhance the sensation of suffocation—the film's evocation of an embodied and gendered urban horror—the ending sequence consists of disjunctive images of Baober and her unborn child floating under water, until, at last, her own skin turns into an unbearable constraint. After chopping off her hair and shaving off her eyebrows, Baober is last seen lying on the staircase of the factory loft. She has cut open her belly. As Zhi looks at her with incredulity, Baober responds with a rather triumphant tone: "I told you. She is here [inside my body]."

The film ends with a paradox: the self-destruction of the biologically sexed body gives rise to a moment of triumphant self-articulation. Acting as if her body belongs to someone else, Baober remains nonchalant toward her wound and deeply enchanted by her act of performance. Playing with doubles and self-splitting, Baober's imagined pregnancy problematizes the interpretation of pregnancy as a biological event or biologism that is inscribed in the heteronormative reproductive system. In her reading of Simone de Beauvoir's "The Mother," which critiques pregnancy and maternity as cultural sites that reproduce society's expectations of women, Gayatri Chakravorty Spivak borrows the language of Marx to describe the subjection of women's bodies to alienation: "It is possible to read Beauvoir's description of the female body in gestation as exactly not biologism. The pregnant body here is species-life rather than species-being, to follow Marx's famous distinction

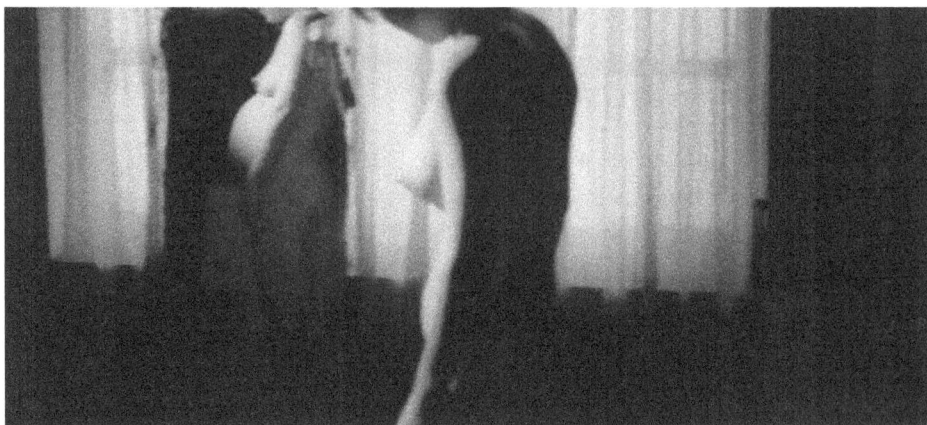

FIGURE 2.9. Baober's phantom body during her psychological pregnancy in *Baober in Love* (2004).

in the *Economic and Philosophical Manuscripts*. It is the site of the wholly other, rather than the man-consolidating other that woman is supposed to be."[41] In the case of Baober, her psychological pregnancy problematizes the assumption that pregnancy is simply a biological event; Spivak suggests a way of reading the pregnancy as a cultural site where specific meanings and functions are assigned to the pregnant body. The psychological pregnancy alludes to what Spivak refers to as "species-life" and the "site of the wholly other"—a conception of a feminine space and temporality that are perceived as lost and require reclaiming. In the same way that the science fiction writer Margaret Atwood challenges the commonly used phrase that describes birth as the "*deliverance* of a baby," the case of Baober suggests a way of looking at pregnancy and birth as the deliveries of "mothers"—mothers who are socially legible only as part of the heteronormative economy of human reproduction.[42] By literally letting go of her physical body, Baober exposes a gender-specific codifying system that alienates women's reproductive labor while disguising it as a biological act.

At a time when post-socialist masculinity and femininity are recoded as money, *Baober in Love* resorts to an imaginary state of gestation, highlighting the contrast between a utopian opening of multiplicity and excess that disrupts the singularity of post-socialist femininity, and a dystopic closure of such possibilities. Baober's self-destructive body makes visible the state of the female body—simultaneously alienating but also the necessary grounds for women's agency. A passage from Beauvoir echoes the film's emphasis on pregnancy: "Pregnancy is above all a drama that is acted out within the woman herself. She feels it as at once an enrichment and an injury; the fetus is a part of her body, and it is a parasite that feeds on it; she possesses it, and she is possessed by it; it represents the future and, carrying it, she feels herself vast as the world; but this very opulence annihilates her, she feels that she herself is no longer anything."[43] What can be explicated from this passage is the conflict between pregnancy as a process of dispossession and a deeply fulfilling and joyful process that every woman longs for. In Beauvoir's spatial imaginary of feminine pregnancy, the intimate interior space where life is conceived is an extension of the social fabric that reproduces, sometimes violently, the historically shifting concepts of femininity. Far from a utopic feminine space growing inside her body, the terrifying hallucinations that Baober and the audience experience—amplified by the sights and sounds that are legible and audible only to Baober—are indicative of the paradoxical fissures in the utopian ideal. Imbued with the overabundance of feelings and emotions, Baober's imagined pregnancy and her weapon of protest already contain the records of her anxiety over the dispossessing forces of the anticipated motherhood. In the end, the construction of a feminine utopia also records a feminine unconscious where existent but not-yet-legible traces of a historical anxiety is imprinted.

Connecting Bodies and Cities:
Toward an Architectural Feminism

Rather than claiming that neoliberal post-socialism has arrived in China, Li's portrayal of intimate dystopias provides the occasion to observe the making of neoliberal post-socialism from below, in the rituals of everyday life, in acts as common as interior decoration where a post-socialist urban future is collectively rehearsed and experienced. Highlighting the anxieties over female subjects' dispossession that connects bodies and cities, *Baober in Love*'s final image of the protagonist's self-annihilation raises critical questions about the neoliberal post-socialist techniques of producing and managing objectified space. As body and city are rendered indistinguishable, what we see in Li's deconstruction of home spaces is twofold. The renditions of "intimate dystopias" are, first, the illustration of post-socialist phantasmagorias of the home as a mass dream mechanism that connects (and implants) human bodies to the imaginary of an urban futurity. Second, as post-socialist dreams of the interior that are sustained by commodity fetishism and consumer culture are reproduced, so are the gendered and classed subject positions and bodily performativities required to complete these dreams. Therefore the nightmarish urbanscape portrayed in Li's works suggests the desires to perform a cinematic dissociation from these projected future roles, resulting in bodies that are self-destructive and prone to disappearance and cityscapes that are fragmentary and *unheimlich* (unhomely).

In the portrayals of contemporary China's intimate everyday landscape, one discovers a mode of seeing and sensing the urban environment not as a fixed entity but as a repeated rehearsal of gender roles and consumer dreams that are guided by the desire for a neoliberal post-socialist future. Dreaming of a "site of the wholly other" and a different futurity, Baober fantasizes a pregnancy that radicalizes the conceptions of post-socialist temporality and space, not in the creation of a City of Women where a new society is conceived as the complete reversal of the current gender norms, but as a mode of dissociation that insists on problematizing the mechanisms and channels of creating the new *ordinary* bodies and cities in everyday life. Since the idea of the ordinary shifts in different historical moments and contexts, this chapter provides a reading of Li's architectural feminism, where post-socialist bodies and cities are treated not as the products of neoliberal post-socialism but as the mediating mechanisms that are essential in creating the current iteration of a market-oriented world.

3

The Post- as Media Time

Documentary Experiments
and the Rhetoric of Ruin Gazing

Temporal Experience in the Era of the Post-

What does time mean in the era of the post-? What mediates and produces the experiences and perceptions of time as newer media technologies are introduced? Since this book addresses the post- as a temporal imaginary that reinvents the concept of space in the present, it becomes pertinent to ask how different conceptions of time that are associated with the post- are produced and transmitted in the era of hypermediality. As new human senses, sensations, and experiences of time are now technologically produced and rendered reproducible, urban horror is given a new dimension—namely, the exposure of temporal experiences to technological and industrial manipulations, where time is mediated and has a specific aesthetic rhetoric that remains concealed. Here the cinematic transmission of urban horror as a public sentiment opens up a new field of inquiry on the relationship between digital technology and the transformations of human (and post-human) temporal experiences, in a case where the dissemination of technologically mediated time has created ramifying effects that are actively shaping the legibility of the present. Taking up documentary as the main subject—a genre and practice of filmmaking that has a special claim on the access to reality—

this chapter presents an archaeology of post-socialist temporalities and their cinematic representations and asks how post-socialist time is mediated and produced in a digital media environment.

As mentioned in the introduction, the time period this book examines corresponds to shifts in the geopolitical relations between East and West after the Cold War and to an era of new media revolution. Rather than focusing on scenes of police brutality, environmental pollution, or other familiar tropes of post-socialist degradation, the question posed by Chinese documentary in this inquiry has less to do with the oftentimes scripted documentary horror demanded by the global market and is more relevant to the experimentations with new temporal experiences that are embedded in the techniques of filming *reality*, including the cinematic aesthetics of instantaneity, contingency, and the transmission of real time. From documentary techniques that are deployed to create the aesthetic effects of time (e.g., shaky camera movement that produces the experience of instantaneity, fast-forwarding and rewinding, and the acceleration and deceleration of film speed) a new question emerges, where the genre's notable desire for reality generates a wide variety of technologically mediated temporalities wherein exist the heterogeneous relationships and attitudes toward the rationalized time of Capital. Exploring the post- as media time and mediated time, the following analysis focuses on a set of experimental documentaries that, in their attempt to make time in the era of hypermediality visible and representable, details a history of post-socialist temporalities that defy or collaborate with the singularity and homogeneity of capitalism's conception of rationalized time.

To begin, a recent Chinese documentary that was circulating at international film festivals and on university campuses reveals the production of post-socialist time as culturally and technologically mediated. Cong Feng's two-part digital experiment *Stratum 1: The Visitors* (*Diceng 1: Laike*, 2012) features a familiar scene in post-socialist Chinese documentaries: bulldozers, demolition, and urban ruins. As Abé Mark Nornes observes, "There are three inevitabilities in Chinese independent documentary: demolition, Christianity, and the slaughter of animals great and small. This is only a slight exaggeration."[1] Nornes's candid remarks highlight the role of globally circulating Chinese documentaries in providing the frames for seeing, sensing, and experiencing the realities of post-socialist China, raising questions about these frames of legibility that are produced in the era of digital technology and during a globally imagined post-socialist time.

Set in the suburbs of Beijing, *Stratum* documents the demolition of residential buildings, presented in two parts that accentuate the relations and tensions between human memory and machinic surveillance footage. In a striking ending sequence to part A, the filmmaker deploys the technique of ruin-in-reverse, where scattered rubble is seen as coming alive, resuscitated, rather than destroyed by the arm of the hydraulic breaker. On the surface, the film documents a typical demolition, an event happening across post-socialist China. Yet the careful experimentation with urban ruins—from the choice of an object of disappearance to the reversal of the demolition—suggests an irrefutable desire to capture and retain time, to represent time as multilayered and heterogeneous, and to experiment with urban horror as a cinematic temporal experience in order to challenge the progression of an intensifying and homogeneous present time. The question that Cong's documentary experiment poses is not what the film can tell us about the realities of Chinese urbanization but how the replay of urban ruination and the urban form constitute a time-making machine—producing, mediating, and visualizing post-socialist temporalities, wherein a spectrum of tensions, desires, and anxieties are put on display.

My analysis explores documentary time—documentary's representation of time—that opens an archive of temporalities for historical excavation. Particularly relevant to this discussion is a set of films created under the global post-socialist condition—Chantal Akerman's *D'Est/From the East* (1993), Huang Weikai's *Disorder* (2009), and Cong Feng's *Stratum* (2012)—where the future-oriented anticipation of the post- produced different cinematic forms of the present, revealing records of time that are often concealed in the films' visible contents. Rethinking the Chinese independent documentary movement that began in the 1990s and its relationship to digital technologies, this discussion foregrounds an emergent environment of hypermediality that is creating new forms of temporal representations.[2] Treating the post- not as a descriptive term but as a frame of legibility, these films are representative works of the post–Cold War global market that respond to the desire and demand for *seeing* post-ness, a task that requires the reorchestration of time, including the notion of chronological time (past, present, and future) and its relation to socialist and capitalist time, as well as the technological notions of speed and instantaneity that Paul Virilio uses to describe the "globalized expansion of the present."[3] The common ground shared among these documentary experiments lies not in the post-socialist realities of the Eastern bloc or China but in three documentarians' approaches to the representation of time in the aftermath of the Cold War.

Recorded in these experiments are recurring urban spaces and the rhetoric of ruin gazing.

The Repetition of Waiting: Chantal Akerman's *D'Est*

Nothing really happens in the Belgian filmmaker Chantal Akerman's experimental documentary *D'Est* (*From the East*, 1993).[4] Based on footage filmed in 1992 and early 1993—during the immediate aftermath of the dissolution of the Eastern bloc—*D'Est* is a record of the filmmaker's itinerant journey from East Germany across Poland and the Baltics to Moscow. Without any discernible narrative, events, points of view, or intent, the film is made up of long takes that gaze intensely at seemingly disparate snapshots of Eastern bloc countries. Like a psychological drift effortlessly moving between domestic and public spaces, the camera at first lingers on extended long takes that show a lone tree, scenes of domestic life, and human faces with subtle expressions. It then transitions to another rhythmic mode of capture, with laterally moving tracking shots of an urban street and long lines of people waiting. The filmmaker declares that *D'Est* is the result of the urgent need to make a film "while there's still time" (*tant qu'il en est encore temps*). But Jonathan Crary speculates that Akerman's statement more specifically refers to the attempt to preserve a milieu where "there is still a world of time-in-common, a world sustained by a collective inhabiting and sharing of time and its rhythms," before the time of Capital arrives with annihilating force.[5] For Akerman, as for many of her contemporaries, the collapse of the Eastern bloc meant the imminent arrival of global capitalism in a territory marked as capitalism's antithetical *other*. It meant the end of history and the start of ruin gazing, before the actual process of ruination even began.

The film's setup gives the impression of a documentary intent on preservation, but this slowly fades away in the dry and repetitive scenes of waiting. Moving in slow lateral motion, without pause or interruption, the camera reveals neither the origin nor the end of the long lines of people—an everyday routine that occupies much of the film. As if these people were arranged by an invisible force, the film's portrayal of lines and people-in-waiting is unconcerned with what they are waiting for or what their destinations may be. It is the *waiting*—the constellation of social and biological rhythms with the body as a point of synthesis—that fascinates.[6] Capturing an array of moments in waiting, the eventless film challenges the conventional understanding of a documentary event and the telos of narrative cinema. In a film supposedly about the post- in post-communism—the preferred term in the Eastern bloc to designate the end of Communist Party rule—the post- is presented as persistent rhythms, existing in the cycles, rituals, and repetitions of everyday life.[7] For Akerman, making a documentary about the time of "transition" involves a contrary mode of thinking about continuities and residues that contradicts the temporal logic of time as singular, homogeneous, and linearly progressive. Post-socialist time, as suggested by the film, is not the beginning of a new era but an opening to a liminal threshold where conceptions of socialist, post-socialist, late socialist, and capitalist times enter into indivisible relations.

The camera does not move. Yet the prolonged intensity—growing in the alternation between stasis and movement, between long takes at a fixed angle and slow tracking shots—opens a portal to movements occurring beneath the film's visible surface. The rhythms of the film collaborate to delineate a post-socialist world of quotidian routines. These rhythms of everyday life—the pattern and familiarity that escape cognitive attention—highlight the central subject of the documentary. *D'Est* does not insist on identifying the moment of collapse or signs of post-socialist change. Instead, the film's contemplative gaze at "nothing" is a way to silently retrace, through meditative self-deconstruction, the phenomenological process through which meaning arises. Beginning with the relationship between sound and image, *D'Est*'s unique editing method of noncorrespondence, wherein live-recorded sound is assigned to a noncorrespondent image, denaturalizes synchronization and brings to consciousness the forces of interpretive frameworks in creating the post-socialist worlds that the mind wants to see (and hear).[8]

The experiment of *D'Est* provocatively suggests that the post- is not an externally existing reality waiting to be captured but a mediated interpretive framework that determines the spectrum of perceivable knowledge. When viewed under this lens, the documentary—already made with a sense of urgency, made "while there's still time"—gains an additional layer of depth. In contrast to the task of preserving the relics of socialist cultures, *D'Est* is a documentary mirror, made to reflect the desires, anxieties, and anticipations that are characterized as post-socialist. This mirroring introduces a temporal imaginary and a structure that are an integral part of post-socialist documentary reality. As *D'Est* defamiliarizes through long extended takes, the experiment represents a unique direction in post-socialist documentary filmmaking in that it locates reality not in the conventional with*out*, where reality is posited as an externality, but in a contingent with*in*, where reality is made up of desires and anxieties shaped by geopolitical forces.

In the presumed era of post-socialism, the questions that *D'Est* leaves behind—What does it mean to make a documentary during post-socialist time(s)? What does the post- entail?—hint at a line of inquiry that is urgently needed in the present moment, when the documentary form has become the dominant mode of seeing post-socialist worlds.[9] As a documentary about the geopolitics of the visible in the aftermath of the Eastern bloc's disintegration, *D'Est* provides an intimate point of comparison for the subject of this chapter: an archaeology of Chinese post-socialist times as recorded, captured, slowed, accelerated, decelerated, forwarded, and reversed in documentary films that make special claims on post-socialist realities.[10] The intention is not to provide a comprehensive examination of post-socialist documentary practices that emerged in the PRC and the Sinophone world but to open up questions about the transnational imaginary of post-socialist times that exceed the territorial borders of a single nation-state.

D'Est was made in anticipation of a post-socialist time—time that is subject to the homogenizing tendencies of global capitalism, which abstracts lived time into quantifiable units of production and consumption. But as Derrida says of anticipation, it is a paradox that opens the future while nullifying it. In *Echographies of Television*, he says, "Anticipation opens to the future, but at the same time, it neutralizes it. It reduces, presentifies, transforms into memory [*en mémoire*], into the future anterior and, therefore, into a memory [*en souvenir*], that which announces tomorrow as still to come."[11] *D'Est* is not a documentary about the post-socialist present. Instead it introduces a rift in time where the future is lived as a memory and with irreducible particularity. While *in* anticipation, the "future" seeps into the present and becomes something to keep, capture, and archive. *D'Est* is a record of this documentary time. The post-socialist Eastern Europe it captures is the spectral residue of the specific kind of post- that it anticipates, whether this anticipation is for the hegemony of global capitalism, the dissolution of a (counter)system, or the beginning of another kind of controlled society. The daily rhythms it captures—from the repetitive movement of slicing food to the movement of street traffic—are replete with anticipation without end. By depriving the audience of the object of anticipation, *D'Est* exposes the temporal economy of the image taken *in* post-socialist Eastern Europe. It is an image of the future anterior, an archive of the future past. Deconstructing the moments of anticipation as an integral part of her experimental practice, Akerman calls for a critical approach to "post-socialist" visual culture. Instead of recording *real time*, *D'Est* opens the path toward an archaeology of radically diverse post-socialist times. The daily snippets of everyday life put into question the grand narrative of post-socialism as a unified reality. In addition, they illuminate the post- as a locus of desire and anxiety, backward and forward glances that create heterogeneous relationships—with their own economy of stasis, velocity, and speed—in relation to the homogeneous and teleological time of Capital.

In the two decades since Akerman's trip to the East, the geotemporal imaginary associated with the Eastern bloc countries has deterritorialized and reterritorialized a new world map centered on an infrastructurally integrated Eurasia, most recently visible in China's Belt and Road Initiative that began in 2013.[12] A mass dream of geo-economic intercontinental integration, the initiative builds upon geospatial metaphors of economic corridors, land trade routes, and maritime silk roads, connecting China, Mongolia, Russia, Central Asia, Southeast Asia, and India. From the railroads and expressways linking China and Europe to the infrastructure of cable networks for a borderless wireless environment, Belt and Road is an example of how the post- is used to advance the experimental acceleration of speed by the reduction of physical distance and the synchronization of local times. Cities from Rotterdam to Warsaw, from Chongqing to Chengdu, have been turned into dots on a globally connected military and economic logistics route, transforming distance into punctuated time in a synchronized timetable. As Virilio explains, infrastructural expansion—including both hardware and software—has effectively eliminated the distinction between "near" and "far."[13] In an environment of simultaneity, a new perpetual present replaces conventional distinctions among past, present, and future.[14] In a general milieu where the post- is conceived as accelerated time and time in acceleration, Akerman's deconstructive lens shows a record of the future past—an anticipation that shapes the conception of both the present and the past. Rather than presume the homogeneity of a singular post-socialist time, the post- has always already been an imaginary of the future that seeps into the present, creating speed, slowness, forward motion, and backward motion that are integrated into the temporal economy of documentary films. As post-socialist cultures are made widely available, with some instantaneously accessible in global media networks, the speed of transmission obscures the lure of the post- as a contingent social production and a viewing lens used to process the raw information received.

With its special claim on reality, the documentary has become the ubiquitous mode of global filmmaking. In the aftermath of the Cold War, documentary film has also been a significant cultural asset bringing together the near and the far, East and West. The media intimacy it forges has unique value in a post-socialist world that desires to see the ruination of socialism and the emergent condition of the post-. In experimenting with the documentary form, *D'Est* raises fundamental questions about documentary filmmaking in and about the post-socialist bloc: Does documentary mean the media capture of a specific land, nation, and people conceived as socialist or post-socialist? Or is documentary a media composite of digital data, computer algorithms, and mediated information?[15] The questions and problems that *D'Est* leaves behind push the boundaries of documentary filmmaking as defined by national borders. As this chapter demonstrates through Chinese experimental documentaries produced in the 2000s and 2010s, the critical concerns and practices of *D'Est* reverberate across post-socialist worlds, illuminating a wide spectrum of post-socialist temporalities.

The archaeology of post-socialist times opens the possibility of conducting *rhythmanalysis*, rhythm as a mode of analysis on socially produced temporal patterns and the forces of their institutionalization.[16] Proposed by Lefebvre as one of the opacities of urbanization that escape the visible field, the *rhythmanalytical* project tackles the fundamental core of everyday life: the temporal realm of capitalism that extends beyond the working day of factories and manufacturing towns.[17] From natural and mechanical rhythms to repetitions and cyclicalities, the categories considered in rhythmanalysis create awareness of the temporal regimes that constitute everyday life. Extending the discussion of the working day in Marx's *Capital* to the realm of the quotidian, rhythmanalysis probes the social production of time that depends on time's naturalized imperceptibility. "We are only conscious of most of our rhythms when we begin to suffer from some irregularity," Lefebvre writes.[18] Rhythm enters into the lived, but not necessarily the known. In the process of filmmaking, the real record of time may not always coincide with the film's visible content but may lay dormant in the directions, speeds, and rhythms that challenge the limits of perception. As Paul Ricoeur argues in *Memory, History, Forgetting*, time is unthinkable without mediation.[19] The rhythmanalysis of post-socialist time thus requires recognizing the medium and rhetoric of time that have entered into media circulation. The archaeology of post-socialist times therefore depends on tropes that recur in an unconscious loop of repetition and that await the work of excavation.

In an era defined as transitional, where the socialist past and future are both violently cast off, the intensive focus on development in the present leads to the reenchantment of alternative temporalities searching for forms of expression. Seeing ruins from the mirage of post-socialist megacities—

the recurrent trope that replays in Chinese documentary and narrative cinemas—does not necessarily suggest sentimental nostalgia but could indicate the (re)emergence of the urban as a time-making machine for experiencing different imaginaries of post-socialist temporalities as both spectacle and critique. Ruinizing space, gazing at ruins, and then reversing ruin gazing—representations of post-socialist times are warped in their treatment of space, creating temporalities that are seen in flux, instant reply, fast-forward, and slow motion. As China enters into the era of economic reform—with political and economic experiments on a form of neoliberal post-socialism—the intensive focus on the present creates a condition in which ways of seeing post-socialist times also require experimentation. To see and sense time, and to render it legible, involves the establishment of a relationship between the filmmaker and the historical world he or she occupies. The extended long take that Akerman routinely deploys in *D'Est* corresponds to her desire to make a documentary "while there's still time." The long take functions as a retaining device for fleeting time while challenging a cinematic positivism that mistakes the effects of reality for reality itself. For documentarians conducting experiments on ways of seeing post-socialist China, their experiments record rhythms, speeds, and tempos of post-socialist times that constitute a temporal landscape beyond the immediately visible realm. Post-socialist times are not preexisting but are made through exploration, self-fashioning, and becoming. The archaeology traces these moments of becoming post-socialist, which continue to frame the realities we see as post-socialist China.

The case of Akerman's *D'Est*—a film about the post-socialist world made from *the other scene* and by a filmmaker who does not "rightfully" belong—captures the geopolitics of the visible that often remain unspoken or concealed in a world still divided by Cold War imaginaries. Gazing toward the post-socialist East from an equally anticipatory West, *D'Est* forgoes the familiar narratives on the fall of socialism and focuses instead on a concealed system (without a proper name) that legitimates the extinguishment of the past and renders the post- the equivalent of the end. However, the post- that the film anticipates may never arrive. It is posed as a question, interrogating our conception of the idea as it takes shape. Decades have passed since the production of *D'Est*. The anticipation of the post- has not subsided but has become a global media event with documentary impulses. What Akerman really recorded "from the East" continues to haunt the contemporary documentary scene in and about China, where post-socialist realities are routinely produced and distributed in the age of digital media. The production of post-socialist times continues to evolve and calls for a close examination of Chinese documentary experiments.

The Post- as Media Event with Documentary Impulses

Since the early 1990s, China has witnessed the emergence of the independent (*duli*) documentary movement that broadly includes documentary films, cell phone videos, and other productions of digital capture.[20] The term *independent* generally indicates drastic ruptures in the production and distribution processes that locate film and video work outside the traditional state- and market-controlled systems. Since the invention of the digital camcorder and new media platforms for distribution, the documentary movement has been characterized as a technological event in which technology plays a leading role in fundamentally transforming the materialist basis of post-socialist visual culture.[21] Whether characterized as an oppositional practice of artists seeking freedom of expression or a movement led by technological innovation, the spectrum of definitions attributable to independent filmmaking suggests more than a divergence of interests. Rather, it highlights Chinese documentary as an active cultural field where relationships among the state, the market, technology, and art are reshaped to delineate specific imaginaries of the post- in a country on the trajectory toward *becoming* post-socialist.[22]

The post- is a contingent historical construct that leaves behind a trail of desires, anticipations, and disillusions; it is not a static state of being or an a priori condition. In the story of origins attributed to the independent documentary movement, the narrative of radical breakage and newness often obfuscates the lure of the post- as a ready-made tool for periodization with liberating potential. Under the assumption that reality lay beyond reach in the previous socialist regime, the discourse of newness describes an independent filmmaking movement finally opened up for accessibility in the era of the post-. Closely associated with grass-roots actions, the democratization movement, and an emergent public media sphere, the desire to become post- is interwoven with the belief in the image's future potentialities, the transformative power embedded in the image's capacity to reveal the truth. Therefore, as China enters the era of the post-, so does the image's *supposed* truth-claim. Despite fundamental changes in the ways images are captured and produced—seemingly controlled by the individual, digitally captured, and distributed through unofficial channels—the independent documentary movement enters a new web of interdependencies that underlie the production of images. This movement does not necessarily showcase an image culture closer to the truth but rather exemplifies an emergent post-socialist desire for unmediated reality—a concept that arises amid, and is paradoxically necessitated by, an increasingly technologically mediated environment.

The post-—and the desire for unmediated reality—is foremost a media event with documentary impulses. To become post-socialist involves constructing a different relationship between the event of image capture and its signifying process under the socialist condition. But as Nornes suggests, the post-socialist Chinese documentary movement has a relatively short history compared with the documentary practices of Japan and Euro-America, although the development of the former parallels other recent documentary cultures that emerged alongside movements of democratization in post–Cold War Asia. However, without historical precedents for ethical practices and aesthetic styles, Nornes asks, what happens when an independent film culture appears "suddenly in the vacuum created by propagandistic nonfiction media, and then *conceptualize[s]* documentary primarily as an individual, creative process in opposition to an oppressive mass media?"[23] With limited possibilities for public distribution—a phenomenon conceptualized as post-socialist emancipation from the socialist state—the blurred boundary between independent and personal filmmaking results in filmmaking practices that disregard subjects' consent and acknowledgment of the camera. The filmmaker's voyeuristic camera replicates the power structure of the state's surveillance system, extending rather than subverting the hierarchy of power that produces the order of the visible world. The problem with documentary practices that are labeled "post-socialist," "new," or "independent" in China can be attributed to the lack of questioning over *how* these terms function as sites for imagining, producing, and managing "realities" through documentary as a filmmaking practice. The documentary movement is part of the global phenomenon of becoming post-, a process materialized through the changing relationship between reality and image, especially image in the age of multimedia capture.

Reality arises from transmedial entanglements and can no longer be approached through the conventional logic of capture that treats reality as an externally existing and unified whole. Rey Chow reformulates Benjamin's thesis on art in the age of mechanical reproduction into a new theory about the logic of capture, defining the constituents of reality as the relationship between the original and the afterlives of its parts. Chow writes, "By calling attention to the copy-image as an endlessly multipliable and endlessly movable part, *Benjamin has in effect inaugurated a reconfiguration of the conventional logic of capture*: rather than reality being caught in the sense of being contained, detained, or retained in the copy-image (understood as a repository), it is now the machinic act or event of capture, with its capacity for further partitioning (that is, for generating additional copies and images ad infinitum), that sets reality in motion, that invents or makes reality, as it were."[24] In the age of mechanical reproduction, reality is set in motion. Rather than an externally existing whole, reality is the motion of information that travels across media platforms and linguistic and national borders, its movement disguised or illegible. In the context of reading post-socialist Chinese documentaries, Chow's theorization of transmedial entanglements provides an analytical tool to rethink the fundamental rationale of documentary as the infinite process of partition rather than settled reality. The problem that confronts documentarians and critics alike is the relationship between documentary and China. As new digital technology renders the event of capture more easily accessible while effectively eliminating the time lag between production and distribution, this enhanced technical capacity makes China more visible but conceals the optical and ideological mechanisms of its visibility. To document or record (*jilu*) China in the age of hypermediality and digital capture, the documentarian confronts two different types of documentary realities. While one tends toward defining China as the traditional formation of a unified nation, land, and people, another reveals China as mediated information.[25] The relationship between China and documentary continues to evolve, creating a wide spectrum of experiments on China as documentary, where reflections on documentary's truth-claim become part of recorded reality. The Chinese documentaries discussed in this chapter were chosen for their experimentations with these concepts.

In *Ex-Cinema*, Akira Lippit suggests approaching the *ex* in experimental cinema as an "exergue," "a space outside the work, outside the essential body of the work, and yet part of it, even essentially—a part and apart."[26] *Exergue*, a Derridean term that Spivak considers untranslatable in *Of Grammatology*, has a literal meaning in French: "that which is out of the work." Referring to the inscription or abstract placed in front of a text, the Derridean usage of *exergue* subverts the traditional definition of the preface as pre-text placed in front of and outside of the book, which in turn is given the position of authority or origin. An anterior outside that is often posterior in reality, the exergue destabilizes the identity of the book while dislocating its authoritative origin. As Spivak writes in her own preface to Derrida's text, "The preface, by daring to repeat the book and reconstitute it in another register, merely enacts what is already the case: the book's repetitions are always other than the book. There is, in fact, no 'book' other than these ever-different repetitions."[27] In the discussion of experiments that explore the relationship between China and documentary, Derrida's spatial metaphor illuminates experimentation as a conceptualized externality—an exergue, an essential outside that repeats and reproduces itself. To discuss the experimental is to conduct an excavation of the outside(s). Unlike the minor or the marginalized outside situated in relation to the dominant body of texts, the *ex* in the experimental signifies the constant movement in between, beside, and outside an imagined center and the dominant mode of reality it represents.[28] Never an isolated domain, the experimental is a set of relationalities and configurations set in motion that require careful contextualization.

According to Lisa Rofel, one of the most common discourses about post-socialism recounts the story of emancipation. The arrival of post-socialism—a term often conflated with global capitalism and neoliberalism—has created a narrative of liberation, where innate desires suppressed under the socialist regime return following a period of interruption. For Rofel, post-socialism, global capitalism, and neoliberalism do not represent totalizing and unified realities that arrive in China.[29] Rather, they are new imaginary spaces engaged in experimental practices of refashioning China as China rejoins the world economy. Although the independent documentary movement claims that it is outside the official state production and distribution channel, the conceptualized outside is still subsumed under the network of international film festivals and for-profit foreign distributors. Being independent—searching for the outside—thus involves the (un)conscious remapping of *Chinese realities* in the global spectrum of post-socialist China's visibility.

Seeing Urban, Seeing Time:
The Urban as Time-Making Machine

The post- is a site for managing repetitions and variations, continuities and discontinuities, and similarities and differences between the Cold War East and West. It is, essentially, a cultural field where the relationship among past, present, and future is put in flux and undergoes experimentation in anticipation of the post-. In the imaginary of *becoming* (instead of being) post-, heterogeneous representations of the post- appear in different forms of speed, acceleration, deceleration, slowness, or stasis used in documentary films to record the present. As a temporal imaginary that signifies the aftermath and the posterior, the post- implies a structure of time that internalizes radical breakage and forward motion, leaving behind a trail of unassimilable temporal experiments that either symptomize or collaborate with the forward-moving structure. Documentary, with its special claim on lived time and the representation of real time, provides a record of post-socialist time's visual rhythm. Requiring a medium, post-socialist time depends on the conjuring of specific motifs and figures of duration in order to make time visible and accessible. Each representation of time indicates a relationality and positionality toward the post- as a transitional device, and foregrounds emergent desires and anxieties toward the neoliberal myth of economic progress.

One of the most significant motifs in the independent documentary movement deals with China's *becoming* urban. *Post-socialist China* refers to an urbanizing China, and the urban cityscape has historically been a visual medium used to spatialize and represent the accelerated rhythms of modern life and the concept of urban modernity in Chinese film history. For example, Yuan Muzhi translates the rhythm of Shanghai nightlife into a visual-temporal film language through the rapid succession of commercial neon signs in *Scenes of City Life* (*Dushi fengguang*, 1935). Enchanting and dizzying, vibrant neon lights become a symbol for the temporality of cosmopolitan Shanghai, while transforming the city into a twenty-four-hour consumption space that renders traditional concepts of day and night obsolete.[30] Yuan's experimental cityscape, like many early European city films, is obsessed with the camera's upward glances and movements. In *Scenes of City Life* and *Street Angel* (*Malu tianshi*, 1937), the camera lingers on the verticality of skyscrapers and towers, in addition to spaces of transit such as bridges, tunnels, and street intersections.[31] By emphasizing the space of transit, movement, and chaos, Yuan shows time in flux and accelerating. As broader sociological changes took place amid new cycles of work, leisure, and consumption, experiments on how to perceive the urban played a constitutive role in the creation of corresponding temporal experiences seeking new forms of expression.

After China entered the socialist era, imaginaries of the urban continued to mediate time and the conceptualization of social rhythms. The literary and cinematic imaginations of the city changed from the space of consumption to the space of production, and socialist factory towns and cities appeared as industrial production centers.[32] Xu Ke's *Resplendent Light* (1949), discussed in chapter 1, is set in an electricity power plant in the industrial region of northeast China. Delivering light and heat across vast regions, electricity quickly transformed into a symbol of emancipation. Instantaneous and far-reaching, the spread and speed of electric light became a medium for the representation of socialist time. Supporting the mass dream of creating a socialist industrial future by reappropriating the foundations of industrial capitalism, *Resplendent Light* recounts a group of factory workers' relentlessness in their efforts to restore light to the city that the Guomindang Party left in darkness. The socialist light of work and production replaces the capitalist neon light of consumption and leisure, reengineering the work-leisure cycle in the socialist imagination of uninterrupted productivity.[33]

Although urbanization continued throughout the socialist era, the imaginary of the post-socialist relies on the logic of discontinuity, separating the socialist from the post-socialist as the transition from rural to urban, from stasis to accelerated mutability. However, the sensorial and haptic rhythms of modern life seen in early city films have been replaced, as has the time of work and production seen in socialist factory films. In the era of the post-, the urban as the medium of post-socialist times is closely associated with the emergent tradition of ruin gazing—where the sights of ruination, gentrification, disappearance, and destruction create screen events of time that are displayed with different velocities, durations, and rhythms. In the era of economic reform, when intensive urbanization has been condensed into a short time span, urban ruins have effectively become one of the most prominent visual media for experiencing and representing time. From the demise of socialist-era factories portrayed in Wang Bing's *Tie Xi Qu: West of the Tracks* (2003) and Jia Zhanke's *24 City* (2008) to the violence of gentrification in Cao Fei and Ou Ning's *San Yuan Li* (2003), Ou Ning's *Meishi Street* (*Meishi jie*, 2006), J. P. Sniadecki's *Demolition* (2008), and Shu Haolun's *No. 89 Shimen Road* (2010), the number of documentaries featuring China's urban ruination in current global circulation suggests ruin gazing as a distinct visual rhetoric in the representation of post-socialist time. Whereas the speed of change always seems to outpace the speed of film production, the velocity of post-socialist development provides the context for an array of alternative temporalities represented in slow motion, backward movement, and repetitive loops. Each temporality evokes specific experiences of heterogeneous post-socialist times.

As Julia Hell and Andreas Schönle note, "In the era of global media coverage and round-the-clock exposure to visual data, ruins have become ubiquitous. They are images that denote raw reality, yet the way we see them is not raw but framed by a long tradition of ruin gazing." Ruin gazing is an aesthetic and literary tradition used to confront imminent disappearance and death; it is also an evolving visual technology meant to extend human perception to a time and space beyond reach. Since the advent of industrialized time during the development of capitalism, the gaze toward ruins has fractured the singularity of the present, creating the opportunity to leap into heterogeneous temporalities and to speculate on a different future for the past.[34] Through ruin gazing, the conditions of the present are put under intense scrutiny, suggesting the potential for articulating discontent and resistance. Since urbanization continues at an unprecedented speed in post-socialist China, the Chinese documentary scene provides a unique landscape of ruins as experiments with alternative temporalities. Ruination has become a media event on a loop, played and replayed with cumulative intensity and with a varied range of rhythms and speeds. Post-socialist time, rather than being a coherent totality, provides the context for documentary experiments with time and its representations. Each representation conveys a unique relation to the post- as a transitional device connecting the past that is reimagined from the perspective of the future—that is, a reconstructed socialist past and an imagined post-socialist future. To experiment with documentary time is to delineate an outside space, not as the documentary movement's marginalized other but as a relational outside that puts the presumed authority of a singular, homogeneous, and linearly progressive post-socialist time to the test. The direction, duration, and speed of documentary time probe a specific history, calling for an archaeology of post-socialist temporalities.

Strange Loops I: Cong Feng's *Stratum* and Digital Memory

Acoustically and visually, Cong's two-part digital documentary experiment *Stratum 1: The Visitors* consists of "strange loops"—footage of urban demolition looped backward and forward. Divided into two interconnected segments, part A shows a performative recitation of oral history that emphasizes human memories, while part B shows surveillance-style footage that focuses on nonhuman actors and the disappearance of residential buildings.[35] Set in a demolition site in a Beijing suburb, *Stratum* is one of many recent documentaries addressing post-socialist China's intensifying process of urbanization and its anthropological, environmental, and affective residues. Part A begins with a temporally reversed sequence that challenges the authenticity of the indexical image. Against an acoustic background of a ticking clock—a rhythmic tempo that makes indistinguishable time's forward and backward movement—the opening frame gradually reveals a desolate mound of earth where debris is seen being restored to the traumatized landscape. The agents of demolition, including a front-end loader and a human scavenger, appear to labor toward the earth's restoration, despite their work of demolition (see figures 3.1 and 3.2). The same technique of reversal is recycled at the end of

FIGURE 3.1. *Stratum*'s (2012) first ruin-in-reverse at the beginning of part A, showing a front-end loader and human scavenger laboring on a demolition site.

FIGURE 3.2. Debris and ashes are restored to the traumatized landscape in *Stratum* (2012).

part A, featuring Bach's *Goldberg Variations* played in reverse, which shows a hydraulic breaker's dance-like movement while its powerful drill pieces together, rather than breaks apart, the ruins of demolished buildings (see figures 3.3 and 3.4).

Cong's experiment tackles a common subject in the independent documentary movement; the difference lies in the observation of the relationship between post-socialist temporalities and the global obsession with China's urbanization as a media event. In digital recordings and photographs that showcase China's urban transformations, the architectural expansion of megacities and infrastructural growth simultaneously satisfy an undercurrent desire to see the revitalization of capitalism-in-crisis by revealing its success in China, while restoring faith in the economic experiments of neoliberalism and China's market post-socialism.[36] In the documentation of an everyday occurrence split into two parts and rendered as qualitatively different temporal experiences, the real subject of the film departs from the surface visibility of the image and emerges instead from the strange loops between the two parts and in the hyperrealist film's melodramatic inserts of ruin-in-reverse. Circumventing the anthropologic and humanistic focus on the plight of displaced residents, *Stratum*'s meticulous record and dramatization of demolition shines light on the film's nonhuman subjects—the residential buildings that once housed communities and memories—bearing silent witness. As two human actors exchange childhood memories during the final hours of the demolished buildings, the speed of the demolition— accomplished in mere days—dramatically highlights the gap between what could be said and what remains unsaid. The film opens a portal to a temporal imagination, making visible an excess of temporalities.

Facing the same challenge to make a documentary "while there's still time," Cong's two-part record of urban demolition reopens post-socialist documentary's relationship to time. In an image culture searching for visible evidence of post-socialist China's transformation, *Stratum* probes the elusive subject of time, whose representation defies reductive positivism. In Akerman's *D'Est*, the anticipation of the post- exerts a powerful underlying conflict in the temporal economy of the image, between the persisting routines and social rhythms that remain unchanged and the post- as a framework in search of change. Using extended exposure times, the film's long takes linger on the same faces and landscapes, bringing the forces of both temporalities to consciousness. While challenging the traditional narrative structure of origin and end, *D'Est*'s experiment lies in exposing the ever-present temporal structure that conditions our interpretation of the image. The relationship

FIGURE 3.3. *Stratum*'s (2012) second ruin-in-reverse at the end of part A. The dance-like movement of the hydraulic breaker pieces together, rather than breaking apart, the ruins of demolished buildings.

FIGURE 3.4. An acoustic ruin-in-reverse featuring Bach's *Goldberg Variations* played in reverse accompanies the visual spectacle in *Stratum* (2012).

between Akerman, an outsider looking in, and the socialist East is always already temporal. The filmmaker highlights this relationship rather than conceals it. *D'Est* is not reportage on life after socialism but a self-reflexive record of the forces of the post-, the after, and the imminent end. When Cong made his documentary experiment in the 2010s, the filmmaking scene in China had already entered the digital age. While the technology, treatment, aesthetics, and style of time play a predominant role in the new documentary movement, these aspects remain mostly undertheorized.

Experimenting with the conventional observational mode, Cong's documentary on post-socialist time utilizes stratum as a spatial metaphor.[37] Evoking multilayered strata in the accumulated sheets of geological time that lie beneath the surface, stratum as a temporal metaphor seems counterintuitive in a digital environment permeated by the presence of instantaneous real time, a conception of time that depends on the elimination of delay and the synchronization of the actual time during which an event happens and its record.[38] However, as the film's title suggests, the real-time record of demolition is designed to evoke temporal strata where time is unevenly accessible, cumulative, and stratified. The question *Stratum* poses requires an archaeology of time in post-socialist China but also an understanding of the historical circumstance from which the experiment with time arises.

Real time is foremost mediated time and information, a style of post-socialist realism that remains concealed and conveniently exploited in the global documentary market. Critical reflection on real time presents a special issue in the Chinese documentary movement, where the desire for real time—through the aesthetics of *xianchang*—determines the spectrum of sensory experiences and the aesthetic styles of realism in documentary films. *Xianchang*, a term that links *present* and *site*, has been translated in various ways. Luke Robinson compares it to *liveness*, referring to "a state requiring the simultaneous copresence of director, event and audience. . . . It is about the ability to capture or watch something when it happens, where it happens."[39] Angela Zito describes it as "shooting on location, in the now, with a total acceptance of contingency."[40] J. P. Sniadecki compares it to cinema verité, the observational mode, and direct cinema, where "the goal is to record the flow of lived-experience as it unfolds, only rarely including overt self-reflexivity, and almost never turning the gaze of the camera directly back on the filmmaker."[41] In the era of digital filmmaking, when ubiquitous electronic devices of various sizes and image resolutions can generate live records of reality, access to the instantaneous present is an ongoing media phenomenon and a sign of the desire and discontent of being in the intensifying present. With the technique of xianchang—of making documentary in the here and now, with the improved accessibility of portable recording devices—post-socialist documentaries are often noted for their truthful (and unprocessed) representations of reality. However, as Cong's experiment explores, xianchang is an aesthetic style of realism that conveys a specific imaginary of post-socialist time, where time is technologically reproduced as the sensory experience of instantaneity.

To be post- means having the technological and social capacity to be in the here and now, where contingency and the ability to master the unpredictable are both fascinating and anxiety-inducing. The desire to capture contingency has generated a range of documentary experiments that produce different styles and appearances of contingency. From aesthetic styles of nonselective editing and long takes to production experiments that give the camera to the filmed subject, post-socialist documentary practice involves the production of real time as mediated sensory and visual experiences.[42] Cong's documentary is both a part of and apart from experiments on real time. Through the film's two-part structure—the coexistence of human memory and surveillance-style footage—the aesthetic styles of real time are looped into coexistence, creating but also exposing real time as mediated time and a spectacle of the senses. In Mary Ann Doane's definition of real time—the "time of the now, of the 'taking place' of events," with "no gap between the phenomenon and its analysis"—*real* as opposed to unreal time runs in a loop. The notions of a real time and instantaneity are deeply embedded in technological mediation.[43] On the surface, *Stratum* is a documentary about a single demolition event that spans a few days. Making the film during a limited window of time, Cong uses footage of the incremental disappearance of residential buildings, a physical marker of time's progression. However, as the film deploys time experiments throughout—looping, reversing, and repeating the seemingly irreversible progress of destruction—the rationale for the documentary shifts from the recording of an event that assumes a natural scale of time to experimentation on time itself.

Beginning and ending with the reversal of ruination, part A consists of an hour-long conversation between two men, walking and talking around the demolition site, mostly at night, when the pace of demolition slows down. The film subjects, who are not residents of the demolished neighborhood, reminisce about childhood against a background of rubble and debris that serve as emotional triggers. As they search for signs and objects to aid the flow of memory, the film's visual track alternates between still frames and long shots that disjoint the soundtrack of the conversation and elliptically

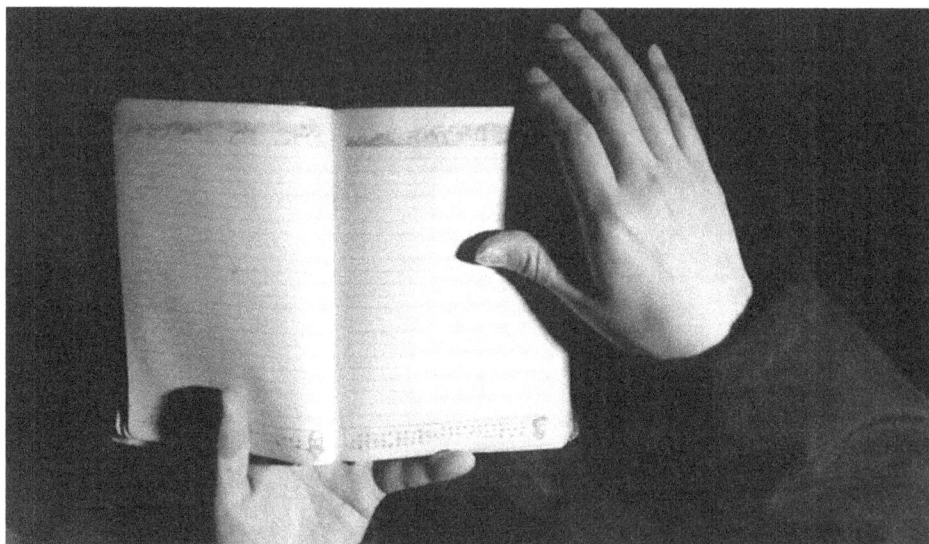

FIGURE 3.5. The animation of ruins in *Stratum*'s (2012) part A, where the repetitive movement of the character's hand turning the pages of a half-empty diary creates a hypnotic rhythm inducing the outflow of personal histories.

conceal the image of the speaking subjects. Casting light on the ruin in dark-ness through the men's flashlight, the camera reveals treasures, such as a scribbled wall painting depicting young lovers and an abandoned diary with half-filled pages. In a long take that shows the close-up of the diary and a character's hand slowly turning its empty pages, the repetitive movement induces memories about the man's mother and creates a hypnotic rhythm that sparks an outflow of personal stories (see figure 3.5). As the men resume their walk up and down the standing buildings and around the demolition site, each encounter with an object opens the door to memories that no lon-ger have physical references. From a childhood romance and a mother's ill-ness to neighborhood gossip, memories flow in a stream of consciousness. The humanizing gaze of the camera transforms any object it meets into a well of histories, assimilating and absorbing the nonhuman landscape into a web of affective relations. Nostalgic and anthropomorphic, the film's visual scheme accumulates through repetition. As the men walk and talk, rubble and debris turn into phantom human organs, animating the still life of inan-imate desolation. The site of ruin turns into the extension of human senses, each rock and exposed piece of concrete equipped with feeling sensors.

Transforming into a screen any surface the camera touches, ruins become animated in the film, giving the land under destruction the scale of human time. Against a desolate background that grows more unrecognizable each day, two human figures whose thoughts permeate the demolition site are consistently present in the film's visual composition. However, as the camera's treatment of the human figures changes from affect-inducing close-ups of faces near the beginning of part A to distant long shots of bodies against mountains of debris that render the humans small, the men's bodies are turned into a medium of time. The reduction of their screen size creates an opening onto the extrahuman dimensions of time, evoking temporal sheets and layers that exceed the anthropocentric scale. In a nighttime scene near the end of part A, the soundtrack of falling debris—sliding rocks, glass, and rubble caused by the characters' downhill movement in the next scene— seeps into the preceding visual frame, where trucks are seen busily working on site. Zooming in and revealing the men's presence in the next frame, the sequence transitions from night to day. The lapse in time is indicated by the change of light and also by the incremental growth in built orogeny, which shows humanity's comparative insignificance.[44] In successive zoom-out shots, the artificial mountain gradually overwhelms the frame. Each shot introduces a new human-to-environment ratio, subverting while re-creating the preexisting scale of time (see figures 3.6 and 3.7). The more prominently the film's visual composition features the artificial stratum, the more different forms of time—layers of temporalities consisting of affect, personal histories, and object attachments—are compiled and compressed. Movable beneath the men's precarious steps, the stratum of debris adds to the depth of time, revising the narrow frame of anthropocentric time.

Trained as a meteorologist, Cong sees the world through ecological metaphors that he superimposes on China's post-socialist urban transformations. Avoiding the cliché image of skyscrapers in an urban jungle, *Stratum* digs beneath the vertical line of the cityscape and exposes the manufactured geological strata, giving the film its title. Compared to the earth's deep geological history, the stratum made of artificial layers of dirt, debris, wire mesh, and concrete is relatively short-lived and prone to imminent disappearance. However, through the film's reverse vertical excavation that reveals the city's composition, the urban stratum evokes the *deep time* (geologic time) of matter and the telluric knowledge of the depth of the past.[45] Recording the tearing down of buildings and the shallow layer of dirt underlying the new ground, *Stratum* unfolds a geological urban history in an era when time is presumed to be depthless. The present prevails,

FIGURE 3.6. Experimenting with the scale of time in *Stratum* (2012), successive zoom-out shots dwindle the human figures while subverting the preexisting scales of time.

FIGURE 3.7. The more prominently *Stratum*'s (2012) visual composition features the artificial stratum, the more layers of temporalities are compiled and compressed.

while traces of the past are buried in intimate but inaccessible proximity. The geological scale of time—time of prehuman, posthuman, or nonhuman scales—is not a device signaling the end of human-centric time in the digital era but a platform that makes multiple scales of time perceivable, including the time of affect and memory, the time of machines, and the time of the planet.

As Virilio wrote in *Open Sky* twenty years before Cong's experiment, we live in an era of intensive present. In the worldwide deployment of present time through telecommunications technology, the present has been globalized and eternalized. The time of chronological succession has evaporated, replaced by an instantaneous and chronoscopic exposure time: there are no longer distinctions among past, present, and future but an *everlasting present* under a new measure of time that is underexposed, exposed, or overexposed.[46] A new scheme of presence emerges, where the legibility of a subject's or object's existence is determined by its exposure time in the present media environment. Made during post-socialist time, *Stratum* experiments with scale in a way that fractures the post- as a unifying temporality and the dominant framework for the film's interpretation. The event of demolition works like a visual paradox—revealing, concealing, and exposing the cultural fascination with ruins as the search for alternative temporalities in the expanding present time.

While the film is premised upon the real time of demolition, *real time* is further deconstructed and stratified into different scales of time, illustrating documentary time's mediated compositions that are concealed under the aesthetic effects of synchronicity. Whereas part A creates a humanistic perception of time through oral history and the sensory experience of walking through a demolition site, part B records the demolition's final stages with the camera placed in the last standing residential building. Shot in the conventional observational mode, part B's footage consists mainly of static long takes of the demolition site, with occasional zoom-ins and zoom-outs that slightly alter the vantage point of the event (see figure 3.8). Evoking the viewing position of the film's nonhuman actor—the last standing residential building—the camera salvages the final activities that can be witnessed from this disappearing vantage point. Alternating between full-scale long shots of the demolished site and close-ups of anonymous humans who labor, fight, and rest on an urban landscape that changes by the second, no particular rationale is given for the selection of the scenes. The transition between shots is similar to the looping footage from surveillance cameras planted throughout the city—a sightless, machinic vision

FIGURE 3.8. Shot in the style of surveillance footage, *Stratum*'s (2012) part B records the demolition as a chronologically unfolding event.

whose assembled omnipotent view exceeds human perception and no longer requires a human subject.[47]

Each part of Cong's experiment documents a typical demolition event. But underneath the visible event we find another documentary that records the widening gap between time that exists in human memory and time as the expanding accumulation of machine-generated records, a temporality of media technology that mimics the logic of capitalist accumulation. Since the invention of film—a technology of celluloid capture—the possibility of limitless production and storage has expanded the capacity to preserve, but has also put the legibility of time into crisis. As Doane says in *The Emergence of Cinematic Time*, "Because film is capable of registering and recording singularities, contingencies—theoretically without limit—it inevitably raises the specter of an archive of noise, linked to issues of legibility, cataloguing, and limitless storage."[48] Filmed in the style of surveillance footage, part B records chronological time through the demolition's progress. Ending part B is a shot of the last remaining part of the building, a step on the ground level—the object-evidence of total destruction that provides the necessary frame and context to the repetitive movements of heavy machinery and workers laboring all day at the site. The extended recording time gives the appearance of documentary realism, but is haunted by the specter of an archive of noise—of having recorded nothing.

Occasionally cutting and alternating the camera angle while maintaining the style of distant observation and staticity, part B records the last stage in the demolition's progress as well as the filmmaker's relationship with a digital archive, a topic of critical reflection that has received relatively little interest in the new documentary movement. Still in the formative stage, the documentary movement is also a movement of digital filmmaking. Coinciding with the expansion of media capitals in the post-socialist era, the digital nonetheless remains a descriptive tool for periodization rather than a way to reexamine the concept and phenomenology of time and memory in a media environment constructed upon infinite digital accumulation. However, as part B's nonselective selection of focal points illustrates, digital documentary filmmaking is about finding an anchor point in time and in the post-socialist visual and documentary economy, which operates according to the rationalizing logic of capitalism and its economization of (screening) time. Part B's nonselective selection is symptomatic of the fascination with and anxiety over the temporality of digital memory, which is at once infinitely expandable but illegible as unmanaged information. In an era when recording has become widely accessible and affordable, Cong's documentary confronts demolition and ruin gazing as digital realities that exceed the conventional frame of a sociological event. Avoiding interviews with displaced subjects or demolition workers—two approaches that underlie other urban demolition documentaries, such as Ou Ning's *Meishi Street* and J. P. Sniadecki's *Demolition—Stratum* redefines post-socialist reality from specific imaginaries of people, land, and nation, to the effects of the digitization of time and the conditions of time's legibility.

As D. N. Rodowick suggests in *The Virtual Life of Film*, the meaning of the image in the digital era has changed from analogical automatism to digital algorithm.[49] The transition of the image's material basis from celluloid to computer codes affects the image's sociological (after)lives, as attested in the association between digital activism and the new Chinese documentary movement. It also affects the less-understood process of perception and meaning-making. Perception hides its organizational activity and creates the illusion of seeing the object as a preexisting and independent entity.[50] While *Stratum* may be perceived as a documentary about demolition, the film's content shows *how* the perceived demolition arises while experimenting with descriptions of the process. The speed of the demolition provides an affective record of the transition from socialism to post-socialism and from celluloid to digital filmmaking. In the era of waning indexicality—whereby the image transforms from the indexical imprint of external reality to computerized information that no longer relies on the same logic of capture—what demands attention is the inability to access and organize digital information in ways that are meaningful.[51] Exceeding the anthropocentric frame of temporality, the emergence of the digital archive poses a new question for documentary filmmaking about medium specificity. Already embedded in the aesthetic styles and contents of documentary, the question of medium specificity remains inseparable from the question of ethics—of how to remember, what to record, and, in the case of *Stratum*, the depth and texture of time as it undergoes intricate changes during post-socialist times.

Unassimilable and unsynchronizable, the film's two-part structure proposes two different approaches to the documentation of an everyday occurrence and shows different interpretations of post-socialism and its times: one existentially phenomenological, another the accumulation of a digital archive. Although qualitatively different, both parts are concerned with the consequences of cultural amnesia. Whether referring to the process of urban gentrification (part A) or the possibility of falling into a digital graveyard in a media-saturated environment (part B), the film's structure forms a dialectic that illuminates the urgent desire to remember and the ephemerality of that remembrance in the expanding digital archive of disappearance.

Strange Loops II: Cinematic and Musical Ruin-in-Reverse

Rather than providing a grand narrative on post-socialist time—an era that has been imagined and periodized throughout the 1980s, 1990s, and 2000s in literary and film studies, with transitions from scar-healing to root-searching, from avant-garde to commodified culture—*Stratum* puts into question the existing lens of history while suggesting a fundamental reevaluation of time and the frames of its legibility.[52] Whereas time remains a phenomenological experience in *Stratum*, the film's evocation of nonhuman scales of time suggests an abstraction, a way of approaching time that is possible only conceptually. Post-socialist time, unlike the human-centric experience of historical events, is given scales, layers, and dimensions that are let loose to speculation. In a documentary event in which the filmmaker and subjects have no personal relationship with the site of demolition, the performance of speculation redefines disappearance as a singular event. As a recurrent and interconnected system, demolition follows capitalism's temporal logic of "rendering past." The demolition site through which *Stratum*'s characters drift is only one dot made visible on a temporal cognitive map that desires to archaeologically excavate the long and stratified history of extinguishment, creating a distinct aesthetics of archaeology.

In Jameson's essay on the temporality of capitalism, a topic not explicitly addressed in Marx's *Capital*, he concludes that the verb *auslöschen*, "to extinguish," holds the key to understanding how Marx conceptualized temporality in the capitalist system.[53] Focusing on the relationship between past and living labor—a reminder that any present act of labor depends on the consumption of past labor—Marx notes that the temporality of capitalism is built upon a systematic process that renders invisible "dead" and "stored" labor from the past. Yet it is in the accumulation of perpetually extinguished pasts that capitalism as a system becomes eternalized. The pasts open onto an unthinkable magnitude of stored labor power that Heidegger would describe as "standing reserve"—a process of *enframing* and revealing the vast potential of the world through what he defines as technology.[54] As capitalism extends itself through cumulative repetition, the temporality of capitalism may be characterized as indistinguishable cycles of production and consumption. The present is kept alive through a system that renders invisible the entirety of the production process, from the labor involved in making specific commodity objects to the extraction of the earth's elements that provide the material basis of today's technologically networked society.

The archaeology of media history, for example, requires a constant reinvention of origins. Perpetually searching for the limit of our current understanding, media history depends on an imaginary outside, a history that begins "before media become media."[55] While the imaginary outside has inspired critical reflections on the history of human intervention, beginning from the extraction of the earth's elements, this search is only a beginning rather than an end. The future of the capitalist system is constructed upon extinguished pasts, where intricate layers may multiply infinitely. However, as pasts are pushed outside the visible and sensible spectrum, the extinguishment's complexity and magnitude remain, in most instances, unthinkable. During times when human-scale categories are rapidly becoming obsolete, new ecological frameworks—anthrobscene, econocene, technocene, *man-thropocene*, and capitalocene—emerge to mend the gaps in archaeological thinking.[56] Nonetheless, what these attempts have made more poignantly visible are the ellipses, some of them forever lost in the stratum of extinguished pasts. The crisis that documentarians confront is not how to fill the depth of time with as many details as possible but how to reveal the excavation's impossibility and the violence of omission—a process that requires a shift from literal representations to conceptual abstractions.

Prior to making *Stratum* in urban Beijing, Cong Feng made several documentaries set in the remote village of Huangyangchuan in Gansu province, north-central China. Featuring landscapes and rhythms of life far from the chaos of China's megatropolis, Cong's trilogy of films—*Religion* (*Xinyang*, 2006), *Doctor Ma's Country Clinic* (*Ma dafu de zhensuo*, 2007), and *The Unfinished History of Life* (*Weiwancheng de shenghuo shi*, 2011)—is given a special title: *Italy in Gansu* (*Gansu de yidali*). As Cong explains in an interview, "Italy" is partially based on the local dialect, where *yidali* means "being together," a phrase that reflects the friendships he built over nearly a decade of living in an area supposedly secluded from the developmentalist temporality of post-socialism.[57] After Cong left the city for China's remote peripheries in the early 2000s, the decade he spent in Gansu produced hours of oral histories of villagers conversing and talking about their everyday life. In *Doctor Ma's Country Clinic*—a nearly four-hour documentary with an additional hundred hours of footage in the filmmaker's archive—the small clinic for villagers' physical health gradually unravels the similitude of the mind and body. In conversations between the doctor and his patients, the dialogue centers on physical symptoms that eventually lead to psychological stress. The assumption of physical illness fails, leaving the cause of the illnesses, which often appear to be minor discomforts such as colds and stomach aches, ambiguous. As the camera sat in the corner of the doctor's office, quietly observing the doctor-patient conversations taking place throughout the day, the footage it collected over a number of years starts to reveal a pattern that escapes the film's literal representation. Consisting almost entirely of villagers' conversations in the doctor's office, with the exception of occasional shots of them working in the fields, the documentary is structurally committed to the observational mode, leaving behind traces of thinking that lack a means of expression.

Following Cong's move to Beijing in the last stages of editing *The Unfinished History of Life*—another four-hour documentary on rural villagers' lives in Gansu—he began to conceptualize an experimental project.[58] The sight of demolition in a city that quickly eradicates and buries existing communities and histories under thin layers of soil resonated with what he desired to film in his Gansu documentaries. In a phenomenon of seeing double, the rocky silhouette of Gansu's scenic mountains begins to merge indistinguishably with the mountain of debris in the Beijing demolition site. The artificial stratum buried beneath new layers of soil provides the rhetoric for what the filmmaker and the villagers are incapable of communicating—

namely, the accumulation of extinguished pasts and the irrecoverable gaps of knowledge that can only be left to the imagination. The oral histories that preoccupied the filmmaker for a decade now seek another documentary language, requiring techniques that go beyond the quantitative accumulation of recording sessions. In a documentary movement initiated by digital filmmaking, the extended duration of documentary film becomes an aesthetic style of reality that calls for its own conceptual abstraction. The project of filming rural life in rapidly developing post-socialist China results in a spiral that loops between the mountainous terrain in Gansu and the debris mountain in Beijing. The excavation of villagers' physical and psychological strata, living in poverty, unemployed, and at the margins of Chinese society, finds a corresponding image in the artificial urban mountain. Quickly formed, reorganized, and removed, the new urban stratum is built upon layers of buried pasts. Projecting the definition of *orogeny*, characters walk against the demolition site's desolate background; the geological term warns of the possibility of massive earthquakes in newly formed urban mountains. The history of the earth sets a precedent that is likely to repeat with unthinkable consequences in the present. The compressed urban stratum calls for new techniques to conduct the archaeology of post-socialist times as a measure against forces of radical erasure.

In addition to the evocation of deep time through the film's geological metaphor, *Stratum* experiments with ruin-in-reverse—a technique of reversing the linear progression of the event that creates the effect of turning back time. Following the opening sequence that reverses the destructive work of a front-end loader, part A concludes with another ruin-in-reverse. Behind a half-demolished building, the extended arm of a long-reach demolition excavator moves in the air, its powerful drill wavering as blocks of bricks and debris fly toward it, restoring and resurrecting shattered pieces of rubble. In the film's soundtrack, the pianist Glenn Gould, one of the most celebrated twentieth-century interpreters of Bach's music, performs the *Goldberg Variations* where some canons in the variations are inverted imitations of a basic form, and as the film reverses the music, it creates an acoustic ruin-in-reverse. As Hell and Schönle note, looking at ruins may give the impression of having access to raw reality, but in fact the view has been framed by a long tradition of ruin gazing.[59] In a media environment saturated with the visible evidence of the socialist world's ruination, Cong's experiment with ruin-in-reverse is a time-image of affect that guides the end of part A to a point of culmination, where the unstoppable progress of demolition is transformed into a variation on life rather than death. Aesthetically mesmerizing and affectively overwhelming, the simple technique of reversal functions like a musical variation that creates different melodies based on the same bass line. Piecing together the shattered body of demolished buildings and creating new life from the movement of variation, the ruin-in-reverse serves as a kind of utopian renewal that is nonetheless a part of cinema's obsession with death and contingency.

Reading early execution films produced by Edison Studios, including *Execution of Czolgosz with Panorama of Auburn Prison* (1901) and *Electrocuting an Elephant* (1903), Doane explicates the lure of death as a film subject. She writes, "Death and the contingent have something in common insofar as both are often situated as that which is unassimilable to meaning. Death would seem to mark the insistence and intractability of the real in representation."[60] In *Electrocuting an Elephant*, set in Coney Island, the subject—an elephant named Topsy—is led to stand on an electrified iron plate. Invisible to the human eye, electricity passes through Topsy's massive body, resulting in lethal effects that are shown in the body's involuntary movements and eventual stasis. The body, whether animal or human (as in the *Execution of Czolgosz*'s electrocution of a prisoner), becomes the medium of electricity's invisible forces. In Cong's *Stratum*, the humanizing gaze of the filmmaker and the characters anthropomorphize inanimate concrete buildings, rendering them animate beings that experience rapid deaths of their own. Like a death experienced twice, the spectacle of ruin-in-reverse unveils the hidden mysteries of destruction and disappearance. In contrast to the utopic dream of resurrection, the technique of reversal treats piles of rubble from buildings as the corpse of the old city. Reversing their death has the effect of making death visible and alive, while each restored piece of concrete is haunted by the temporality of its imminent end.

The reversal of total destruction creates a new variation on the spectacle of death while simultaneously exposing the witnessing of death as the uncomfortable bass line in documentary filmmaking, a way of evoking phenomenological affect that is dependent on the spectacle of horror. Cong's experiment calls into question the general lack of self-reflexivity in approaching the growing archive on post-socialist ruins. Not a subjective technique developed by one documentarian, ruin-in-reverse has a longer presence in the history of film and suggests an evolving visual or acoustic technology—a rhetoric of ruin—that remains mostly concealed. The textures and layers that are buried in the process of visualizing disappearance are met with new or recurring experiments in ruin gazing, which evoke alternative temporalities and convey the inadequacies of the present.

The Rhetoric of Ruin: Glenn Gould, Musical Ruin-in-Reverse, and Transmediality

When theorizing the aesthetics of experimental art, Adorno attributes new experimentation to the artists' recognition that the existing spectrum of knowledge is no longer adequate. He writes, "The violence of the new, for which the name 'experimental' was adopted, is not to be attributed to subjective convictions or the psychological character of the artist. When impulse can no longer find preestablished security in forms or content, productive artists are objectively compelled to experiment."[61] Cong's experiment with ruin-in-reverse is not a subjective choice but is deeply embedded in the post-socialist cultural phenomenon of ruin gazing. Critical of the intensive focus on the present, post-socialist Chinese documentaries have demonstrated the desire for alternative scales of time that explore the invisible consequences of rapid development. However, after decades of collecting oral histories in rural China and emphasizing *what* has been made to change, the filmmaker is in search of a new documentary language to express *how* ruins are gazed upon, heard, and touched. Documentary involves not only the archive of visible evidence but also the technologies with which such evidence is presented and made meaningful through repetition.

The technique of ruin-in-reverse has existed since the beginning of cinema. In one of the first actuality films that preceded the emergence of the documentary, the Lumière brothers' *Demolition of a Wall* (*Démolition d'un mur*, 1895), the demolition is visualized in a loop of two versions: one shows the wall being torn down, and the other reverses the same footage, creating the illusion of the wall's restoration. According to Thomas Elsaesser, one of the attractions of early cinema was the cinematic apparatus itself.[62] The technique of ruin-in-reverse was discovered when the film reel of *Demolition* was accidentally played backward in one of its early screenings and has been used ever since. During an era when new cinematic technologies were flaunted to attract spectators' attention, the Lumière brothers' ruin-in-reverse illustrates the appeal of visual spectacles and indicates a curiosity toward alternative experiences of time. In addition to transposing the audience to the demolition site, *Demolition of a Wall* opens a portal of time in one of the earliest instances of cinematic time travel. After the demolition is visually registered as the main event of the film in the first version, the reversal of the film's content creates the effect of reversing the time of the event and the duration spent watching it on screen. The ruin-in-reverse presents the curious case of turning back time—a cinematic attraction and emerging technology of time's representation that reflect social desires and anxieties. As time becomes increasingly rationalized and quantified during the process of intense industrialization and the expansion of capitalism, the backward motion of time creates an alternative temporal experience and fractures the homogeneity of the time of Capital. *Demolition* is an early instance when the gaze upon ruins is kept as a visual technique. What was recorded was not only the demolition of a wall but also, as indicated in the film's reversal, the fascination and desire for heterogeneous temporalities that extend beyond the present.

In Cong's experiments with ruin-in-reverse, a technique that has lost the excitement of discovery and is no longer an object of cinematic attraction, the reversal highlights the rhetoric of ruins and the meaning of their representations. No longer flaunted as a new technological innovation, *Stratum*'s ruin-in-reverse speaks to a different set of concerns with the temporalities of neoliberal post-socialism, where the reversal's backward glance becomes an essential and commodified style often generalized as post-socialist nostalgia in the forward-moving temporal logic of post-socialism. In a media environment saturated with footage of disappearances—a sign of the speed of change—asking how to cast the backward glance presents more political and conceptual challenges than a totalizing turn toward the past. As the media theorist Friedrich Kittler observes, digital technology has fundamentally changed the way questions of medium specificity should be raised and studied, since the flow of data, previously separated into the optical and the acoustic, is now united in the information network of the digital.[63] The question that concerns Chinese documentarians in the digital age is not the disregard of medium specificity but the possibility for transmedial thinking. Recycling the technique of ruin-in-reverse but reproducing it as a visual and acoustic spectacle, Cong's digital ruin-in-reverse performs an archaeological excavation that moves away from the literal representation of exterior reality and toward a media archaeology that focuses on the mediated composition of documentary reality. Through the juxtaposition of different pieces of mediated information that contribute to making demolition a screen event, ruin gazing is presented as a media composite that *is* the new reality the film documents. Confronted with the task of creating memories at a time when the speed of filmmaking always seems to lag behind the velocity of disappearance, *Stratum* lets go of the conventional method of preservation and searches instead for the techniques of ruin gazing, which form a stratum of their own kind.

Placed at the beginning and end of *Stratum*'s part A, Cong's ruin-in-reverse forms a media stratum of layers that recur with differences. While the import of the Lumière brothers' ruin-in-reverse recalls the early history of film as visual spectacle, Cong's digital version transforms the original visual experience into a multisensory one by including a soundtrack played in reverse. In an unusual ending sequence—beginning after the film's ending credits—the characters continue to walk the demolition grounds, a scene that is followed by the dramatic ruin-in-reverse. While introducing a circular structure of unending time on the visual track, acoustically the ending sequence begins with the repetitive sound made by demolition machinery before transitioning to piano music that dissipates the sound of destruction. Similar to the rhythm of repetition and structure in the sound of demolition, the piano strokes in the music are revealed to be the *Goldberg Variations*. As if leaving clues for an archaeological excavation, the filmmaker identifies the piece in a black-and-white intertitle inserted at the end with the following text in English: "Bach: Goldberg Variations; Played by: Glenn Gould; (Play Reversely)." As one of the few instances when nondiegetic sounds are included in the documentary—with the exception of the ticking sound of a clock and album music from the band Muqam Music based in Xinjiang—the inclusion of Bach's variations-in-reverse questions the role of nondiegetic sounds and music in post-socialist Chinese documentaries and opens up the possibility for transmedial thinking.

In a filmmaking tradition that emphasizes the synchronicity of sound and image, sound has played a subsidiary role meant to support the coherence of the visual track. Against this convention, *Stratum* has routinely separated the visual and audio registers by freely associating the men's conversations with images from the demolition site in part A. In a film about remembrance and alternative temporalities, *Stratum* invites the opportunity to rethink sound's relationship to the documentary image. The acoustic ruin-in-reverse—quite unlike the majestic and melodramatic sound of an orchestral symphony—echoes the structured variation and repetition of the demolition. Matching the tempo of sound and image, the multimedia ruin-in-reverse is an example of a visual experiment that borrows from a musical analogy, based on an eighteenth-century masterful rendition of inversion and repetition. Described by Gould as "music which observes neither end nor beginning, music with neither real climax nor real resolution, music which, like Baudelaire's lovers, 'rests lightly on the wings of the unchecked wind,'" the *Goldberg Variations* is a strategic choice as the film experiment considers the transmedial affinity of repetition, recycling, and inversion.[64] However, in a film conscious of the media strata it forms, Bach's music is also a recording that requires a medium, and thus suggests a set of musical documentary practices that parallel cinematic documentary practices.

In Gould—a pianist who desired to perform for recordings and denounced live public recitals—the Chinese documentary experiment finds an analogy for a new theory of musical recording. Born in 1932 in Toronto, Gould became a world-acclaimed pianist celebrated for his unorthodox interpretation of Bach's music and other classical works. His first, 1955 recording of the *Goldberg Variations* conveys a level of energy, intensity, and expressive lightness that remains unparalleled in the history of Bach recordings and performances. His tour of the Soviet Union in 1957 is still remembered by the Russian pianist Vladimir Ashkenazy, himself an accomplished Bach performer.[65] However, at the age of thirty-two and at the height of his career, Gould announced his retirement from public concert performances to begin what he considered a new musical path in recording studios. The reality of music, according to him, lies in the longevity of musical records. Also a prolific and accomplished writer, Gould predicted in his 1964 essay "The Prospects of Recording" that "the public concert as we know it today would no longer exist a century hence, that its function would have been entirely taken over by electronic media." In this essay, which outlines a new media theory of musical recording, Gould considers Jean-Luc Godard's *A Married Woman* (1964) and various ideas from the media theorist Marshall McLuhan before arriving at a radical theory of listening wherein every listener can "ultimately become his own composer." Using the example of his experience recording Bach's *Well-Tempered Clavier*, Gould describes the creation of a transcendent hybrid recording in which he combined carefully selected fragments from the original eight takes of the music.[66] The essay is not only a testament to the recording process but a thesis on the aesthetics of musical montage, a language of musical recording that is analogized to cinematic montage.[67] For Gould, as for Benjamin's concept of the dialectical image, music is born from the juxtaposition of fragments and contrasting interpretations—an idea that Cong explores in *Stratum*'s two-part structure. As described by the performing artist, the world of live performance has institutionalized the style of the single take. The assumption of uninterrupted play that is free of any mistakes imposes limitations on the imagination that can be liberated only by a new practice of recording and listening.

Gould was well known not only for his accomplished piano technique but also for numerous personal eccentricities, and his behavior was often deemed disruptive to the practice of naturalist music recording. Always spontaneously humming while he played, while the chair he sat on—a gift from his father that the pianist claimed he could not play without—made strange, squeaky sounds, such characteristics were often dismissed as arbitrary personal quirks. Yet these habits illuminate precisely a unique musical theory that emphasizes the web of relations among the pianist, the moving fingers, the vocal cords, the materiality of the keyboard, the chair, the microphone, the magnetic tape, and the studio—a network of relations buried in what Gould would consider the denaturalized style of realism found in conventional classical musical recordings that aim to simulate live performances in a concert hall.[68] When Godard and his contemporaries in the French New Wave were conducting experiments on cinema that led to dramatic shifts in the distribution of the sensible world, Gould's studio practice brought into conversation the deconstructive revolution of postwar avant-garde cinema and the institution of European classical music. His obsession with the studio—where he used a multitude of microphones and mixing techniques—creates an environment of acoustic orchestration that overlaps with cinematic strategies.

Creating long shots, medium shots, and close-ups in musical pieces, Gould's recording practices are the result of transmedial thinking, bringing together the previously separated realms of filmmaking and musical recording.[69] His attachment to material objects and his attention to recording techniques translate into a unique understanding of music as having tactile qualities of surface, angle, and texture that can be realized only in the recording studio. Performances in concert halls—a way for the audience to experience live music—lack the means to capture music that exceeds the limitations imposed by an institutionalized audible world. Cong's choice of Gould's recording of Bach evokes the memory of a studio pianist whose lifelong work is devoted to the relentless rethinking of what music is. Invoking metareflections on the medium, the musical piece, the environment for listening, and the means of mechanical reproduction (for Gould did not live to witness the digitization of the music industry), Gould's performance of the *Goldberg Variations* brings his questions of recording to bear on Chinese documentary practices.

Rather than presenting the naturalized progression of time through the conventional footage of demolition, which has been a common approach and subject in recent Chinese documentary films, *Stratum*'s ruin-in-reverse is more concerned with exploring a recurring emotional affect that still searches for a form of expression. Creating a memory without memory and a sense of loss without loss, the reversal is an experiment in capturing the pattern of transcended emotions in post-socialist China that go unnamed—emotions that do not depend on a performed context and experiences that are not grounded in a material basis.[70] Since the gaps between the spectrum of experiences and the depth of history can be presented only in the form of unrepresentable ellipses, the documentary's task lies not in providing the lost information but in a viewing experience that makes visible a form of ruin gazing that enacts participatory remembering. Reminiscent of Samuel Beckett's play *Waiting for Godot*, *Stratum*'s two characters orbit the demolition—*orbit* being a word that Gould used to describe the *Goldberg Variations*—walking, talking, and waiting for an epiphany that never arrives.[71] As the characters perform ruin gazing in the documentary, waves of emotions and childhood memories are summoned, none of which actually took place at the demolition site.

The participatory memories borrow the landscape of ruins to perform rituals of remembrance and to search for metaphors of expression, posing theoretical challenges to the aesthetic practice of *xianchang*, or recording in the here and now. Instead of the conventional account of oral history that is collected on site and as close in time as possible to the original event, *Stratum* dismisses the search for origin and invites the participatory reminiscences performed on screen as well as the improvised transmedial performances off screen. On the occasion of the film's screening in the closing ceremony of the tenth Beijing Independent Film Festival in 2013, the avant-garde musicians Liu Sola and Lin Yijun were invited to improvise a performance in front of a screen projection of *Stratum*'s part B. Trained at the Central Conservatory of Music in Beijing, Liu Sola is known for her compositions and musical performances that combine a wide range of musical styles and techniques, including jazz, blues, Chinese opera and folk music, and contemporary interpretations of Chinese traditional music. Li Yijun is the heavy metal guitarist from the Tang Dynasty Band (Tangchao yuedui). The two performed with circular rhythms that repeat and intensify. Without clearly demarcating the beginning or end, the improvisation was a striking echo of the structure and style of *Stratum*, prompting the filmmaker to preserve the performance in subsequent screenings of the film.[72]

As *Stratum* incorporates more works of improvisation, the film undergoes another stage of transformation by further distancing itself from the logic of the origin. Choosing the *Goldberg Variations* as one of its acoustic elements, the film echoes the variation form in a musical composition that consists of an aria at the beginning that is then used as a bass line in thirty variations that follow. *Stratum* sees itself as the bass line, creating variations in a family tree of extended histories. The institutional roles assigned to the documentary genre—filmmaker, subject, informant, and audience—are expected to be reversed.

Revealing and informing nothing—not the histories of affected communities nor the master plan of gentrification—*Stratum* presents an experiment wherein specific narrative content is stripped away, leaving bare the utopic pursuit of transcendent feelings (e.g., mourning, nostalgia, displacement) that characterize a unique type of post-socialist urban horror. To explore sentiments created during the condensed process of development, *Stratum* decidedly turns away from the narrative conventions of demolition in documentary films and focuses instead on creating experimental strata of temporalities. With demolition as the film's subject—the quintessential post-socialist event in which the past is torn down to make room for the future—*Stratum*'s two parts seek no beginning and no end. Perpetually caught in the status *in between*, the film leaves behind a phenomenological record in the cycle of reversals, repetitions, and inversions. According to Douglas Hofstadter's comparative analysis of "strange loops" in Bach's music, M. C. Escher's paintings, and Kurt Gödel's mathematical theorems, the variations of demolition that are included in the film are "information-preserving transformations," where "every type of 'copy' preserves all the information in the original theme, in the sense that the theme is fully recoverable from any of the copies."[73] The film's preservative function reforms an unconventional notion of preservation. As demolition replays in variations of itself in the post-socialist culture of ruin gazing, *Stratum* preserves the violent but invisible structure of extinguishing the past, of which demolition is a visible and humanly perceptible manifestation.

In Cong's documentary experiment, urban demolition—a process of disappearance and forward motion—is revealed to be a frame of Chinese realities but also a medium for representing post-socialist time. Responding to a conception of time that is no longer the collective rhythm of socialism, yet is not assimilable to the rationalization of capitalist time, the film's stratum is an example of a stand-in for a technologically produced intensive present that lies beyond representability. The visible and audible representations of the post-socialist world have created impasses that render the sensible world opaque—blind spots in the field of perception.[74] The demand for the visible evidence of China's post-socialist transformations, whether within or outside China, has created an expanding media environment that generates their visibility yet leaves behind a trail of concealment. Post-socialist China becomes more widely visible, but in specific ways that relay the desires of filmmakers, the market, distributors, film festivals, and academic institutions. Cong's *Stratum* is a unique example of representing post-socialist temporalities through ruin gazing, where the form and value of human memory is called into question in a media environment of expanding digital storage. Yet the representation of time in the digital era does not take only one form but reflects other social anxieties and desires in the imaginary of time when a different approach is taken into consideration.

The Experiment of the Intensive Present:
Huang Weikai's *Disorder*

In contrast to Cong's search for layered strata and temporal depth, Huang Weikai's *Disorder* (2009) takes the representation of time in another direction, showing post-socialist time as an infinitely expandable, intensive present that no longer distinguishes among past, present, and future. Noted for its sensationalized portrayal of urban dysfunctions in China, *Disorder* is also a documentary experiment on temporality itself and a record of post-socialist time that performs a different type of ruin gazing.

Expanding the use of urban ruin as a time-making device, the ruin in *Disorder* takes the form of man-made micro-disasters in the Guangzhou metropolitan region: unsanitary food, tangled traffic, police raids, flooded infrastructure. Providing an example of the rhetoric of contemporary Chinese ruin gazing, *Disorder*'s chaotic urbanscape associates the concept of ruin with disaster and catastrophe, signaling the end of human history and time. Not just the concrete image of piles of wreckage, "ruins evoke a transhistorical iconography of decay and catastrophe, a vast visual archive of ruination."[75] In the footage of urban chaos that *Disorder* collects, the future of Chinese urbanization heads toward imminent self-destruction, leaving the status of the present uncertain and unthinkable. Rather than reporting on a single urban catastrophe, the film is made from potentially hundreds of disorderly incidents, based on footage shot by different filmmakers and at different times and locations, made available in the digital media environment of limitless storage.[76] Engaging neither with the history nor the aftermath of a single event, *Disorder* probes the concept of time that arises from digital ruins—specifically, the necessity for a new logic of documentary time capable of transforming an infinitely expandable collection of present times into a legible form.

Based on over a thousand hours of amateur footage, making the fifty-eight-minute film involved not only selecting visual content but also conceiving a new kind of documentary time. The experiment creates a new representation of time as a stream of simultaneity—a product of the era of big data, continuous uploads, and limitless archives. As Derrida writes in *Archive Fever*, "One associates the archive, as naturally one is always tempted to do, with repetition, and repetition with the past. But it is the future that is at issue here, and the archive as an irreducible experience of the future."[77] Echoing Derrida, the film's Chinese title, *Reality Is the Future of the Past* (*Xianshi shi guoqu de weilai*), suggests a documentary reality contingent upon the concept of the future to determine the meaning of the past. The experiment of making a film out of an unsolicited archive, therefore, probes the archive's legibility and, more important, the role of an imagined future in shaping the required frame of legibility. Based on digital captures that have made a post-socialist present hypervisible, *Disorder*'s experiment responds to the cultural anxiety over an infinitely expandable collection of presences and records. Against the backdrop of this imagined future, the film is a record of urban disorder and of the emergent desires, anxieties, and cinematic rhetoric that make the intensified present legible.

Contrary to *Stratum*'s emphasis on the depth of time, *Disorder* is composed of a panoramic urbanscape that evokes the copresence of urban simultaneity. Using a wide collection of footage with different textures, resolutions, and colors, the film was digitally changed to black and white to create continuity. The film's texture mimics the surface in magnetic tapes with intentionally lowered resolution. The challenge the film confronts is not merely condensation but reconciling the sightless and machinic vision embedded in the collection of voyeuristic footage with the humanistic desire to represent the disorder of the posthuman digital archive in an orderly fashion. The experiment provides an antidote by selecting a few major strands of urban disorder, then fragmenting and rearranging them in a new orderly sequence. In the film's opening, Huang carefully edits and connects several episodes: a broken fire hydrant flooding a busy traffic intersection, a traffic accident dispute, a cockroach in a bowl of noodle soup, a police raid in an illegal shop for pawning bears and anteaters, and debtors clearing out the shelves of a supermarket. To make the representation of simultaneity legible, the film trains viewers to look for recurrent patterns in a digital data set. As the film rotates perspectives from separate incidents, the viewing experience replicates the apparatus of surveillance monitors, where events happening in simultaneity are looped in sequence on the same screen. Creating the aesthetic effects of simultaneity, the film provides the content for the filmmaker's conception of urban disorder and the instructions for patterns, loops, and repetitions that are set to recur in the metadocumentary. Contrary to the title's reference to irregularity and the violation of recognized order, the film is constructed as a stylistic effect that requires careful patterning and an algorithm for content selection.

A new concept of documentary time emerges: not the traditional succession of past, present, and future but an eternalized present time that depends on the exposure time allotted in the film. Since the footage is broken into fragments, presence in the film depends on a viewing apparatus that conjures presence through screen time, while leaving the rest in the abyss of oblivion. The documentary's treatment of footage—through fragmenting, merging, rearranging, synchronizing, and flattening—leaves behind traces of editing techniques that convey a logic of cinematic time dissolving all boundaries and differences for the effect of synchronized continuity. In the digital world, where physical distance has been eliminated by the instantaneous transmission of images and information and where the speeds of perception and representation can be technologically selected, the editing technique evokes consequences beyond the filmmaker's intention. As the experiment collects footage that sheds individual identity and focuses on a preconceived frame (disorder), the collection uncannily evokes the nonhuman, panoramic view of the city and replicates the mechanism of surveillance technologies that are ubiquitous in Chinese urban spaces. Transforming surveillance-style and voyeuristic footage into an aesthetic object, the film's aesthetics of urban simultaneity bear a striking resemblance to computer-aided perceptions that infinitely expand viewers' experience to unreachable corners of the city, while opening the door to industrialized manipulation of human vision, feeling, and sensation through new media technology.[78]

Aimed at stimulating the senses by taking viewers through the digital urban maze, the film's ruin gazing is performed in a few dream-walking sequences in which the cameras follow the trance-like movement of humans and animals walking and roaming perilously through the infrastructural space of southern China. Through the focus on human and animal bodies that enter into a dance with the urban environment, a new digital voyeurism is made phenomenologically intense. In addition to a few pieces of footage

FIGURE 3.9. The dream-walking sequence in Huang Weikai's *Disorder* (2009) provides a phenomenological anchor point for the disorienting sensorium of urban China.

showing jaywalking individuals, the film is particularly invested in a half-naked youth who walks on a busy highway. As cars and heavy trucks rush toward him, he raises his arms in dance-like movements, without any care about his perilous position (see figure 3.9). Walking with bare feet on the road's rough surface, a highway drifter introduces the sense of touch to an otherwise depersonalized collection of data. As the police approach him, the film cuts to another tactile scene, where a group of panicking pigs rush against the road barrier before being captured. The search for tactility continues in footage featuring bodies immersed in water, including human bodies moving in a flooded area, swimming in competitions, and scavenging in polluted water. Contrary to the depersonalized distant shots of heavy traffic shown near the beginning of the film, the dream-walking sequences provide a phenomenological anchor point from which the disorienting sensorium of urban China can be safely experienced. The seemingly chaotic disorder of the film follows an organizing (un)conscious that maintains conventional narrative continuity while transforming depersonalized data to information that stimulates bodily senses. The sensorial urban environment evoked in the film is an example of virtual reality and a case where new technologies of vision are given the potential to produce and shape new human perceptions, leading to capital investments and consumer demands in mechanized ways of seeing and experiencing the *reality*. As exemplified in *Disorder's* experiment with a new documentary aesthetics that mimics surveillance technology, a posthuman vision—a sightless, machinic vision that does not require the perception of human subjects—is made into a globally circulating commodity that feeds into the supply and demand for more posthuman machines of vision. The slowly encroaching industrial and technological production of new human senses broaches the subject of urban horror that this chapter has analyzed, through the examination of temporal experiences that are mediated and produced in the era of the post-.

IN THE TWO CHINESE documentary experiments discussed in this chapter, China's urbanization—a subject that made post-socialism in China visible and accessible—is revealed to be the stand-in for the condition of post-socialism that remains elusive and ungraspable. The intensive replay of Chinese urbanization in these documentary experiments reveals new technologized representations of time and poses questions about the role of documentary time in the technological production of a globally intensifying present. While acknowledging that post-socialist temporality is now a digital production, where time can be infinitely recorded, stored, and reedited, the replay of the urban reveals a response to the speed of change in China and a new fascination with and anxiety over one's digital disappearance. Using urban ruination as a time-making device, the rhetoric of ruin gazing in *Stratum* and *Disorder* implies the nostalgic desire for layered sheets of temporal depth in the former and the fascination with expansive simultaneity in the latter. Yet as digital technologies open up the possibility of continuous, infinite recording, both can be read as a response to the expansion of data that puts the definition of human time and the ethics of remembrance into question. As post-socialist Chinese documentary continues to globalize, this discussion offers a way to read the production of time, where techniques of ruin gazing are deployed as time-making devices that experiment with and at the same time shape the human sensorium in a digital media environment subject to neoliberal market demands. The production of new social rhythms, repetitions, and cycles that are disseminated through visual media takes Lefebvre's methodology of rhythmanalysis to the post-socialist digital age. But rather than reminiscing about a humanistic time embedded in an imagined lost nature after industrialization, the temporal analysis I have presented offers a new beginning to rhythmanalysis of the present—a multilayered and multimediated concept of time in demand of new methods of temporal-spatial critiques.

4

Post-Socialism in Hong Kong
Zone Urbanism and Marxist Phenomenology

Rehearsing the Disaster

Released a few months before the protesters in the Umbrella Movement occupied the central financial districts of Hong Kong, Fruit Chan's feature film *The Midnight After* (*Na ye lingchen, wo zuoshangle Wang Jiao kai wang Dapu de hong van*, 2014) soared at the local box office. Its portrayal of a postapocalyptic Hong Kong struck by an unknown disaster, its human population gone and potentially radioactive rain pouring from the sky, created heated discussions, not only on the film's allusion to the Chinese surveillance state but also its influence on the protest movement that was yet to come.[1] In the years following Hong Kong's handover to China in 1997, the end of European colonial rule in Asia and the arrival of Chinese post-socialism have created new imaginaries of the post- that remain unexamined. The Umbrella Movement represents the occasion when manifest demands for Hong Kong's political sovereignty and democracy were made.[2] Yet the image of unarmed citizens inadequately protecting themselves with everyday objects (e.g., umbrellas, goggles, facial masks, etc.) and taking action against an unknown crisis was already circulating in the public sphere a few months before the police attacked the demonstrators. Rather than attributing the origin of the Umbrella

Movement to the Chinese government's intervention in Hong Kong's electoral system, this chapter speculates a way of seeing post-1997 Hong Kong cinema as a more complex cultural landscape, where the accumulation of affects, sentiments, and feelings can be seen in a variety of genres and texts that experiment with the aesthetics of urban horror, where the gap between a defamiliarized urban landscape and cognition is deployed in the rehearsal of a future urban revolution. Through the evocation of urban horror, not as an established genre but as the creation of a horizon of public sentiments, the imaginaries of the post- in Hong Kong are translated into different forms of action and inaction.

The time is after midnight. A group of ordinary Hong Kong people board a van-bus from Mong Kok to Tai Po when Hong Kong and the world's human population suddenly disappear, leaving behind this group of strangers. As the survivors die one after another, their bodies lost to spontaneous combustion and unspecified illnesses, the uncertainty of the crisis—a totality that the film never makes clear—gradually brings together a divided group. They are last seen on their way to search for the truth in the red van that had been attacked by an unidentified group wearing black military gas masks, a scene that bears an uncanny resemblance to the police suppression in the pro-democracy movement. In the film, Hong Kong is conceptualized as a city without bodies, where the architecture is immaculately preserved, yet its designated functions are temporarily suspended (see figure 4.1). The film opens up the relationship between cities and bodies as a site of tension. A scene in which the disaster turns into a source of psychological energy and relief rather than stress proposes embodiment as a question in the zone of exception. In the midst of a crisis, the van driver, who has spent his life in perpetual transit on infrastructural roadways, exits the van after it runs out of gas. With a wanderer's spirit and a broad smile on his face, he begins dancing on the highway, his feet touching and playing with the road signs on the ground (see figure 4.2). In a city that has lost its human inhabitants, new relationships between bodies and cities are formed.[3] Whereas the film's portrayal of citizens in goggles and masks protecting themselves against the unknown is arguably a psychological rehearsal of an anticipated conflict, the van driver's dance on the highway—a replicable space without history and identity, a space that proliferates in the capitalist expansion—mirrors the protesters' desire to reimagine the conditions of their embodiment in the city, for example, by setting up tent cities with addresses and by growing a garden in the middle of Hong Kong's financial district.

FIGURE 4.1. Post-disaster Hong Kong, the city's human population stripped away, in *The Midnight After* (2014).

FIGURE 4.2. The van driver's dance on the highway—a space designed for the uninterrupted flow of people, objects, and capital—in *The Midnight After* (2014).

Rather than the sensationalized spectacle of urban destruction, the image of the disaster that the film supplies opens up a set of Marxist phenomenological questions that this chapter explores—namely, the relationship between bodies and space, phenomenology and Marxist urban theory, in the works of Merleau-Ponty and Lefebvre. Under the global post-socialist condition, where urban development transnationally expands and intensifies, Marxist phenomenology brings two modes of inquiry into conversation and asks critical questions about the body as a site of political domination and resistance, and also its role as the mediating surface of perception that remaps geopolitical forces and shapes our understanding of the individual psyche. In *The Midnight After*, the van driver's dance proposes a performative Marxist phenomenology, where the body is used to produce a different mode of embodiment that puts the existing concept of body and city into question and to provide the grounds for understanding how both are produced (and rendered reproducible) through repetition and repeatable procedures. As the dancing body suspends the rhythm of circulation and movement in the space of speed, it makes us aware, for the first time, of how time and movement in a zone of exception are ingrained in a logistics timetable and how neoliberal post-socialism has been shaping the definition of Hong Kong city, bodies, and psychological consciousness. The relationship between the disaster in *The Midnight After* and the Umbrella Movement suggests that film as a multisensory medium rehearses and produces feelings and sentiments that elude legible categories but persist and disseminate through the circulation of images. Rather than using horror as a genre convention, the film poses a cultural phenomenon that puts horror into question and explores its meanings in the global expansion of neoliberal post-socialism. By evoking urban horror, this chapter collects the images, people, temporalities, and spaces that are associated with the *production* of the affect of horror—through the rehearsals and representations of disasters and the not-yet-thinkable—that appears when transcontinental urban transformations are taking place under the flexible interpretation of the post- in post-socialism.

Rather than reiterating the origin story of the Umbrella Movement, my examination of post-socialism in Hong Kong situates the protest in a longer history of affective and sensory accumulations and intensities that complicate the definition of "embodied actions" of resistance. In *Notes toward a Performative Theory of Assembly*, Judith Butler writes, "Embodied actions of various kinds signify in ways that are, strictly speaking, neither discursive nor prediscursive. In other words, forms of assembly already signify prior to, and apart from, any particular demands they make."[4] In Butler's description, the place of action is neither discursive nor prediscursive, which is suggestive of another temporality and space not legible in the normative sequence of events and known causes and effects. I explore this spatial temporality in between discursivities through post-1997 Hong Kong cinema, where the forms of embodiment and disembodiment haunt the public imagination in a space that was created as a zone of exception in the nineteenth century and evolved from a free trade port city to a colonial financial center and is now a post-socialist special administrative region. It is the last form of Hong Kong's existence, as a post-socialist zone of exception, that remains underexamined and politically contested. However, considering the expansiveness of the zones and zoning technologies in the present, across formerly socialist and nonsocialist countries in China, Europe, South and Southeast Asia, Africa, and beyond, Hong Kong's post-socialist transformation poses a question that is not limited to the dispute of Hong Kong's political sovereignty but includes the emergence of new spatial technologies of economic extraction and political integration that rely on the flexibility and ambiguity of post-socialism.

Post-Socialism in Hong Kong

Does post-socialism exist in the former British colony of Hong Kong? After more than 150 years of British colonial rule, the handover of Hong Kong's sovereignty to the PRC in 1997 still functions as the primary lens for understanding Hong Kong's past and future. As the world's financial center and the last frontier separating the socialist and capitalist blocs during the Cold War, Hong Kong has historically been recognized as a capitalist city located between East and Southeast Asia that operates under a noninterventionist, laissez-faire colonial regime open to free trade. Given Hong Kong's integral role in the global economy, the idea of linking post-socialism to a city-state with no ostensive socialist history may seem, at first glance, an oxymoron. In recent decades, as the number of protests in the city dramatically increased following the handover, the association between post-socialism and Hong Kong may give the false impression that the city has been fully integrated into the political system of the PRC.[5] Although *post-socialism* has turned into an umbrella term that ostensibly accounts for reform-era China's totalizing transformations, the term also indicates a set of geographical and temporal boundaries that are deemed irrelevant in areas outside of the historically contingent geopolitical imaginary that is taken to be neutral and stable. Beyond the nation-state's geographical territory, socialism and so-called post-socialism represent evolving globalizing visions and projects that put the territoriality of both in flux. Whereas socialism envisions the world by overturning the empires of capitalist colonialism, post-socialism expands the existing imaginary of socialist empires with experiments in the free-market economy and political zones of exception. However, as formerly nonsocialist countries actively seek transnational collaborations to rearticulate cross-border relationships with (still) socialist China, Chinese post-socialism suggests fissures across the great divide, illuminating the post- as a newly emergent global construct. The question raised by post-socialism in Hong Kong is therefore not reducible to the city's political sovereignty but also encompasses the ongoing border-crossing history of radical deterritorialization and reterritorialization in the era of the post-.

No longer capable of sustaining the former dichotomy between East and West—socialism and capitalism—the era of the post- followed the disintegration of the rhetoric of offense and defense. From post-Mao to post–Cold War, from post-socialism to post-colonialism, the post- does not signify an end point to mankind's ideological evolution or the end of history as such, but rather indicates a camouflaged cultural field channeling global imaginaries, protocols, languages, and economic software that disguise the continuities and discontinuities of previously existing systems of domination and oppression. Therefore the question of whether post-socialism exists in Hong Kong follows a line of inquiry that unravels unchallenged assumptions that have never become fully articulated and yet already have real and historical consequences in post-socialist worlds, both inside and outside formerly socialist countries. The idea that post-socialism is a topic of interest relevant only to countries that have an apparent socialist history should be more vigorously evaluated. To borrow Shih Shu-mei's words: "Post-socialism ought to be considered as a condition affecting the entire world. The collapse of the Soviet Empire and the end of the Cold War reconfigured the world in specific ways. For instance, the Cold War divided the world around a particular kind of dichotomy of East and West—socialism and capitalism—not the East and West of Orientalism and Occidentalism. The collapse of this dichotomy has given rise to a new dichotomy with a different geographical pivot—the North and the South—as a way to understand the economic inequality of the world."[6] Shih's passage makes lucid the appearance of new geopolitical and geographical configurations of the world that are replacing Cold War divisions. But rather than new sets of dichotomies, the global condition of the post- has not been fully explicated, which is the point of origin of the present inquiry. On one hand, *post-socialism* refers to a set of concrete strategies of managing and deploying the human, political, economic, and environmental resources in the era of the post-—in this case, between Hong Kong and the special economic zones in the Pearl River Delta. On the other, it is also the virtual condition that expands the logic of "neoliberalism as exception" as, for example, in Hong Kong's integration in South China's economic archipelagoes of exception zones under the principle "one country, two systems."[7]

Whereas post-socialism has often been used to describe China's social transformations since the economic reforms of the late 1970s, it should be emphasized that post-socialism was always already a global phenomenon not exclusive to the territorial space of the PRC. Under the scheme "socialism with Chinese characteristics," China still exists as a socialist political entity, where the post- functions as a transnationally maintained virtual space whose governing strategy is the international deployment of exception. Therefore the examination of post-socialism in Hong Kong broaches a subject more complex than the applicability of the term in the former colonial city. Occupying an in-between space—between capitalism and socialism—post-socialist Hong Kong is one of many zones of exception set up for economic and political experiments that are designed to allow for maximum profitability and political integration without disruption to the political imaginary of the nation-state.

Not a uniform experience throughout the world, post-socialism in Hong Kong refers to Hong Kong's transterritorial urban transformation, which extends beyond its urban center. Linking Shenzhen, Dongguan, and Zhuhai—rapidly urbanizing Chinese cities close to the border—post-socialist Hong Kong is part of a network of interconnected urban archipelagoes made up of special economic zones. Comparing zones to repeatable and programmable templates for making economic urban enclaves that do not benefit the majority of the population in their host countries, Keller Easterling characterizes the ramifications of zoning as a new global epidemic in the postwar era. Evolving from free ports in the mid-1500s to the 1930s, to export-processing zones in the late 1950s to 1970s, and now taking the form of special economic zones, economic and technological development zones, and science industrial parks, zoning urbanism has been a transformative state instrument in forging international trade relations through the technology of exception.[8] Expanding with unprecedented speed and scale, China's special economic zones are in a class of their own. In a real place that nevertheless exists nowhere, the zone is the physical and psychical manifestation of the market-driven logic of exception at the core of Chinese post-socialism as a global phenomenon.

Under the socialist regime and a globally imagined post-socialist condition, the *nowhere* is now everywhere. Not only are the exception zones, which are fueled by direct foreign investment, rapidly proliferating as a new species of nonplaces; the expanding network of urban enclaves also alludes to an extraterritorial urban future that is yet to come. In an urban society that is both and neither socialist nor capitalist, the future of urban China will likely refer to the intricate network of economic archipelagoes that exist primarily for the maximization of monetary profit for a new global elite class. Writing before zoning technologies transformed the East and Southeast Asian landscape in the aftermath of the urban-centered May 1968 protest in France, Lefebvre suggests in *The Urban Revolution* a hypothesis that comes closer to present-day reality but that is still suspended in a futurity yet to arrive. He writes, "An *urban society* is a society that results from a process of complete urbanization. This urbanization is virtual today, but will become real in the future." For this Marxist theorist who devoted a lifetime to the study of the urban problematic, the urban phenomenon is paradoxically a virtual object—a nonexistent existence. Tracing the city's evolution—from the original political city to the mercantile city, from the industrial city to the globalization of the urban—Lefebvre notes the obsolescence of an empiricist methodology that treats the city as a set of tangible facts and an object fixed in time and space. He also emphasizes the transition from the city to an urban society, where the urban is distinguished from the city as an "illuminating virtuality," a "paradox," a "negation of vision," "concrete contradiction," and a "presence-absence." As societies become more urbanized, the urban totality recedes further into an abyss of reflections and refractions in tension with direct knowledge. "The urban is veiled; it flees thought, which blinds itself, and becomes fixated only on a clarity that is in retreat from the actual," Lefebvre writes.[9] Almost fifty years after Lefebvre's initial prediction, the question contemporary society confronts is not whether urbanization has advanced to the stage of completion but how to deal with the continuity of a totalizing process for which we have only fragmentary analytical tools.

The *urban* is an emergent object of the future, an impossible-possible that nonetheless requires a solution in the present. The logic of exception made room for the post- in Chinese socialism. The ideological space of exception also directly translates into the proliferation of zone urbanism, where competitiveness is sustained by the colonization of land and labor resources through the expansion of the urban fabric. Controlling wages and limiting affordable housing, the zone of exception is replacing historical cities as the new site of capital accumulation. Clustered around airports, container ports, and inland expressways, exception zones are organized and designed according to the logistical need for uninterrupted movement of global shipments, bypassing the interests of the residential population. The post-socialist global geography is witnessing a radical and violent reterritorialization, with the possibility of a future geography reduced to replicable zones that feed into a logistical empire aimed at eliminating distance and time.

The rise of zone urbanism adds a sobering layer of present reality to the virtuality looming on the future horizon. However incomplete and ungraspable, the not-yet-arrived future already has a material weight on the present that remains elusive and at times incomprehensible. The future is already confronted in the present, leaving behind traces of anxieties, dissatisfactions, and desires of resistance that are communicated through some of the least expected means. As one of the first treaty ports opened to the West in the aftermath of the First Opium War in 1842, Hong Kong epitomizes the colonial, post-colonial, and post-socialist state technologies of exception. Since the early 1980s, various transitional tools have been used in both the state and the private sector to ensure Hong Kong's integration into the special economic zones in Guangdong, Guangxi, and Fujian provinces. These include the controversial construction of the new Hong Kong International Airport at Chek Lap Kok, the expansion of the city's container port, and the numerous bridges and expressways connecting Hong Kong to Chinese cities on the mainland.[10] The imaginary of the post- in Chinese post-socialism is materialized through an infrastructural revolution—both physical and financial—that spectacularizes the condition of exception.

Hong Kong's infrastructural boom began in the early 1980s and arguably transformed the city into a megacenter of transit—a transport super city that bypasses the local while servicing the elitist circulation of financiers, shoppers, and the international business class.[11] After Hong Kong's real estate market climbed to an all-time high shortly before plummeting to dismal lows in the Asian financial crisis in 1997, land and housing speculation witnessed dramatic fluctuations before prices soared to record highs in recent years.[12] For mainland investors and corporations, the city's land and properties have become a financial hedge against the depreciation of the renminbi and the Chinese government's antispeculation measures. While an international and local class of elite developers and speculators strategically benefit from the zone of exception, Hong Kong's indeterminable in-between status creates an indefinite condition of accumulation by dispossession.[13] Exceeding the framework that reduces the "Hong Kong question" to a crisis of postcolonial identity, the city's post-socialist condition generates a rapidly evolving network of systematic inclusion and exclusion through state-sponsored technologies of deterritorialization. Hong Kong is at the center of an expansive site of experiment. Mutative and replicable, Hong Kong goes beyond the physical existence of the city, becoming a code name for a set of protocols, programs, procedures, and spatial software of urbanization—with Chinese characteristics.

Space is not only produced but rendered reproducible.[14] Under the post-socialist condition, the developmentalist logics of capitalism and socialism are fused in the limitless conquest of space, both abstract and concrete. Space has always been the basis of Capital's *concrete abstraction*, produced to be reproduced and conceived for its exchangeability. Written as a continuation of the way Marx's *Capital* deals with space, Lefebvre's spatial analysis unfolds through developmental stages before arriving at the conscious awareness of the violence of space in an industrial-capitalist modernity. Building upon and also challenging Marx's original focus on production, *The Production of Space* introduces the concepts of reproduction, repetition, and reproducibility in an understanding of space that renders obsolete the idea of space as a fixed and readily legible entity. Focusing on patterns, rhythms, and the repetitiveness of everyday life—with the body as a mediating point of contact between the social and the individual—spatial analysis in Lefebvre's formulation is not confined to the physical location of factories, dormitories, shopping centers, and roadways that represent the post-socialist zone architecture. "The concept of the city no longer corresponds to a social object," Lefebvre writes.[15] The urban problematic refers to the elusive presence-absence of an urban fabric that becomes concrete through reproduction and repetition. The production of space refers to the loss of the physical dimensions of space as they are replaced by the technologies that synchronized global time, by which every movement in the capitalist chain is calculated to optimal efficiency. Occupying a significant role in the carefully choreographed post-socialist production and distribution chain in the Pearl River Delta, the case of Hong Kong and zone urbanism in South China alludes to a larger problem at hand. The familiar routines of transportation, land speculation, and zoning are interlinked practices motivated by the logic of abstraction. Under the post-socialist governance of exception, space becomes an easily manipulated concept, an idea dispossessed of its material basis and in radical contradiction with the possibilities of *lived* space.

Post-socialist Hong Kong is a schizophrenic space. It is, on one hand, a finance capital of supreme abstraction that reduces the city to a calculable set of data, and on the other, a space under intense pressure to physically accommodate its human population. Indeed Hong Kong has devised new means of acquiring land with the creation of artificial islands and land reclamation.[16] Since the 1990s this process has accelerated as part of Hong Kong and China's zone urbanism. From the artificial islands that became Hong Kong International Airport and the Disneyland Resort to the expansion of Victoria Harbor, the post- in post-socialist Hong Kong is tied to the emergence of nonplaces—spaces of transit without history or identity—that circulate goods and people in East and Southeast Asia.[17] Following the Closer Economic Partnership Arrangement between Hong Kong and the PRC that opened the door for mainland tourists, Hong Kong has been designated a city of consumption and leisure that is easily accessible to Chinese consumers.[18] During Hong Kong's transition from a colonial port city to the PRC's special administrative region, the city was increasingly imagined and managed as an abstract space with a rationalized function: to homogenize, unite, and subsume scattered fragments by a violent force that combines state technology and neoliberal desires. As the city center expands vertically upward for more commercial space and as the auction of land creates scandalous bidding wars that overinflate prices, Hong Kong is increasingly transformed into a city without bodies, its population and human inhabitants stripped away.[19] This idea of the city without bodies exerts a haunting presence in post-handover Hong Kong cinema, bringing into focus the emergent tension between the politics of dispossession and strategies of repossession.[20]

Elusive and flexible, post-socialism in Hong Kong is both concrete and virtual. Its ambiguity probes the limits of the established regimes of legibility that are coded in capitalist and socialist systems. The future is uncertain, which is a unique feature in the imagination of the post-. Yet it is on the basis of future uncertainty that Hong Kong's presents and pasts are reimagined, reorganized, and rematerialized. The not-yet-arrived future is already ingrained in the city's present-pasts, leaving behind powerful *affective residues* and *emergent feelings* that seek the language of expression.

History requires lenses of legibility. While the realities of historical events recede into the open-ended indefiniteness of textuality, the lenses remain and leave behind traces that continue to exert powerful influences over human perception. In the recent history of Hong Kong, one of these lenses is the handover in 1997. Signifying the end of European colonialism in Asia, the event also gestures toward the popularized narrative of the rise of China and the resurgence of the Chinese Empire. In the aftermath of the Cold War, the world was in need of a new geopolitical framework for mapping new synergies and divisions. The year 1997 emerged, not necessarily as a pivotal moment in Hong Kong history considering the continuity of colonialism, but as a convenient cultural space for the world to conceptualize powerful illusions of discontinuity, separating Hong Kong history into before and after, colonial and post-colonial, and British and Chinese.[21] As a symbolic dividing point in global discourses that focus on measures of democracy, freedom, and civil liberty, the year 1997 had a heightened visibility during the symbolic transition of global powers, from the West to the East. Lacking a viable and nuanced alternative, post-1997 Hong Kong is increasingly perceived as a city of the unfree, obscuring a longer history of deterritorialized post-socialism that began before the handover. My reading of post-1997 Hong Kong cinema is therefore evocative of historical continuities not reducible to the handover as a singular event.

Extending beyond the year 1997, and encompassing an urban network that crosses national boundaries, the post-socialist condition in Hong Kong in its most visible form can be understood as an economic phenomenon and a regional strategy of political integration. However, post-socialism in Hong Kong is also a part of the globalizing condition of exception and has engendered a wide range of semisocial experiences, vague dissatisfactions, and speculative feelings; each is an articulation of presence that is not yet legible in the existing structures of feeling. Neither discursive nor prediscursive, the range of speculative feelings from post-socialist Hong Kong lacks the legible sociality of the Umbrella Movement that took place in 2014. Present and yet lacking a legible framework of correspondence, the affective landscape of post-socialist Hong Kong is representative of emergent feelings shared across national borders, connecting ramifying spaces of exception in the geopolitical shift to a post-socialist future. While public protest provides visible evidence of dissent, this form of protest already articulates a particular kind of relationship between protesters and the protested. By seeking recognition and acceptance, the expression of specific demands often precludes the necessary task of understanding emergent feelings as a continuously forming and formative process.

These emergent feelings are communicated and embedded in specific urban representations and imaginaries. Tracing the aesthetics of urban horror in Hong Kong cinema opens up connections between the violence of the post-socialist condition and the space of resistance. Rampant in the post-1997 (i.e., post-handover and post–Asian financial crisis) cinematic representations of Hong Kong, the emergent feelings associated with Hong Kong as a zone of exception may disappoint those looking for the articulation of an authentic Hong Kong identity that is represented in the realm of culture. The assumption that the city has lost its culture furthermore obscures the productiveness of Hong Kong as one of Asia's dominant cultural producers in broaching the contested and elusive imaginaries of repossession. In the era of the post-, the year 1997 is the dividing line between different modes of aesthetic production. Whereas pre-1997 Hong Kong cinema is read through the lens of a New Wave cinema that parallels the desire to see and retain a fleeting Hong Kong–ness before it actually disappears, the post- in post-1997 cinema is much more difficult to define and is often subsumed in the alternating and contradictory rhetoric of resurgence and decline as filmmakers emigrate northward to the mainland Chinese film industry.[22] Hong Kong cinema as a subject has always exceeded a narrow focus on individual filmmakers' aesthetic practices and alludes to the intricate entanglement of aesthetics and Hong Kong's geopolitical position in the post-socialist world.

Under this premise, post-1997 Hong Kong cinema represents an emerging and neglected cultural field of intangible feelings and experiences. Rather than resorting to an interpretation that emphasizes the unique singularity of Hong Kong as a hybrid culture, post-socialism in Hong Kong should be probed as a globalizing condition that operates under the veil of isolation. Dispelling the rhetoric of neither-nor—neither capitalist nor socialist, neither Chinese nor British—the void that has been structurally ingrained in Hong Kong's political, economic, and cultural imagination evokes productive negativities that defy the meaning of nothingness. Saturated with feelings, reactions, and responses, the state of exception is in the process of being reclaimed. For the many people who live, pass through, and work in the post-socialist condition of exception, the global circulation of cinematic images mobilizes emergent transnational networks of communication that are in the process of formation. The future has already been confronted, yet the traces left behind remain indeterminate and unassimilable. Thus the examination of post-socialism in Hong Kong warrants new approaches to aesthetics and politics as well as their connections under the post-socialist condition, where exception gives rise to new aesthetic forms.

The correspondence between Fruit Chan's disaster film and the Umbrella Movement poses a new question on the future of the image. From not yet legible perceptions to vague dissatisfaction, feelings evoked in post-socialist Hong Kong cinema *precede*, in many ways, the events to come. Instead of being the mimesis of social reality, cinema "negates the categorical determinations stamped on the empirical world and yet harbors what is empirically existing in its own substance," Adorno says in his definition of aesthetics in the devastating aftermath of World War II.[23] Yet juxtaposed in the same sentence, a gap is noticeable between what Adorno calls the empirical world and the empirically existing *other* in art that is the intangible but present essence of the truth. Unreachable and unsettling, the public sentiment of horror that Hong Kong cinema rehearses lies not in the reality that disaster happened but that it has always escaped recognition.[24] The empirically existing reality, as Adorno shows, does not correspond to the empirical world but exists as a negative presence that can be given no use-value in the instrumentalizing logic of capitalist developmentalism. Therefore the Hong Kong films collected in this chapter were not chosen for their commercial value or popularity but because their production spans 1997 to the mid-2010s. Through the films of Fruit Chan, the question of the future of the image spectrally returns as the films are viewed from the lens of post-socialism in Hong Kong, wherein exists an archive of public sentiments that accumulate and intensify in the filmmaker's persistent portrayal of an abject Hong Kong that intentionally defiles the image of a prosperous city.

Feeling is a form of thought that resides in the ephemeral shadows cast in the changing shades of light. There is always a gap between a film's explicit intention and an undercurrent desire that it is powerless to resist or realize. The question of feelings and affects in post-socialist Hong Kong cinema is thus not reducible to the biographical sketch of individual filmmakers or the speculations on their intentions. Created by a combination of social forces, Chan's films contain an embedded powerlessness that is the opposite of paralysis. Instead this powerlessness is the formative anticipation of a future sociality that is reshaping the cinematic present. Unlocking the present of the post-—a neoliberal ideological space that relies on the dissemination of suspension, exception, void, and vacuum—requires an examination of the post- and the bodies-spaces it engenders in contemporary Hong Kong cinema.

Fruit Chan, Marxist Phenomenology, and Post-1997 Hong Kong Cinema

Based on a serialized internet novel, Fruit Chan's *The Midnight After*, or *That Morning, I Got on the Red Van from Mong Kok to Tai Po* (the Cantonese title), crystallizes the post- in the imagination of an unthinkable disaster. After midnight, a disaster with an inexplicable connection to Japan's 2011 Fuku-shima nuclear meltdown is about to strike, wiping out the entire popula-tion of Hong Kong and possibly the world beyond. Hong Kong is reduced to a ghost city where all human bodies are mysteriously lost to spontane-ous combustion. Speculating that there has been a nuclear disaster or an outbreak of an infectious disease previously unknown to the world, the survivors—sixteen passengers and one driver in a red van—are seen wear-ing surgical masks and safety goggles salvaged from a local supermarket. The slow-motion panoramic shot of the group, a film technique commonly used for the introduction of action heroes, creates a sharp contrast between a group of ordinary Hong Kongers' will to fight and the protective gear that apparently falls short. Neither tragic nor comic, or perhaps both at the same time, the image invites contemplation as it resists decipherability. The bodies in assemblages and bodies as assemblages evoke a collective presence that challenges previously existing relations among Hong Kong's social groups, city center and suburban satellite towns, and competing definitions of Hong Kong. Through the process of becoming—a symbiotic emergent unit that Deleuze and Guattari describe as the bringing about of a new way of being through the transformation of originally existing relations—Hong Kong as a future sociality is seen as an emergent possibility.[25] The same image of ordinary citizens using assemblages of everyday items—umbrellas, plastic wrap, goggles, glasses, towels, and masks—to defend against abrasive chemi-cal weapons would be repeated on the streets of Hong Kong in the Umbrella Movement only a few months after the film's theatrical release.

The conventional allegorical reading of a cultural text as the reflection or representation of empirical social reality is confronted with an imminent fail-ure to produce meaning. Not only is the separation between fiction and reality difficult to maintain, but the question of *what* the film is about reveals a his-torical and theoretical aporia that remains buried in the great divide between aesthetics and politics. Between the film and the protest movement, a new image of historical consciousness is born. Belonging to neither the past nor the future, the assemblages of bodies in goggles and masks emerge from the visual fragments of both and constitute the materiality of the present. They are the epitome of Benjamin's dialectical image—an unfinished image that exists in the constellation of fragments and reveals the regime of visibility that pre-determines our senses.[26] The uncanny similarity renders both incomplete but opens up a rhizomic channel of communication that extends feelings, com-pletes thoughts, and delivers action. *The Midnight After* did not predict what took place in the Umbrella Movement. But it is a spark that suddenly flashed up against a darkened network of thoughts as the neoliberal imaginary of the post- obscures the legibility of the present and forecloses meta-analytical thinking. With the number of protest movements rising steadily in post-1997 Hong Kong, the myth of the post- as uninterrupted economic prosperity and security is rapidly deteriorating. The visual and sensory infrastructure of vague dissatisfaction is expanding and harbors a future sociality that leads to a revolution of the senses. Aesthetics is not determined by politics. It is through sensory channels that the political is given new meanings.

Reflecting on the "imagination of disaster" and the technologized visuality of cinema, Susan Sontag considers "the most profound dilemma" created from cinema's capacity to visualize the wildest, unthinkable possibility.[27] What is the value of thinking about, and now seeing, the unthinkable? Is the visualization of the impossible-possible a means to prevent the abhorrent or an instrument to normalize it? These questions, raised by Sontag at a time when science fiction was becoming a popular genre in the aftermath of the Second World War, have become even more relevant today, when the imagination of disaster is now fully integrated into the global military-industrial complex of mediatized warfare and terrorism. In a detailed account of the growing symbiosis between cinematic technologies and military warfare, Paul Virilio makes the dystopic observation that the "actual can no longer be distinguished from the potential."[28] What for Sontag has the unexplored and ambiguous potential for resistance, for Virilio signifies the more pessimistic total annihilation and displacement of the human senses. The eye's function is transformed into a weapon of destruction, and technologically enhanced vision in the era of modern warfare means the realization of and the participation in unthinkable disasters. The implication of the imagination of disaster is therefore twofold. It is, on one hand, a sobering rehearsal of the crises of humanity, and on the other hand, a spectacle of destruction that integrates disasters in everyday life and a new psychic infrastructure of fear that fuels the industries of war.

However, the intentional obliteration of disaster as visual spectacle in *The Midnight After* raises a different issue. In response to the exploding number of available images of disasters from around the globe, there is fatigue and exhaustion. The more often such horrors are seen, the less they are capable of engendering meaning. For example, the obsession with ruin and ruination has developed into specific genres of ruin porn popular in postindustrial societies. Usually devoid of human figures, ruin porn refers to the aesthetic practices that transform catastrophic landscapes into sites of sensory pleasure.[29] Without asking what disaster means and which representation the concept engenders, the critique of the "imagination of disaster" may easily lose focus while the critical capacity of the term becomes obscured. Contrary to being a universal and ahistorical concept, Chan's depiction of a Hong Kong disaster prompts an examination of the imaginative faculty as the embodiment of a shadow record on the limits of visibility, perception, and cognition. When disaster is given a material form, the normative distribution of the sensible and the possible world is challenged and redistributed. Not only do sight and hearing lose their given social functions, but the system that provides them with value and meaning is also put into crisis. Disaster has a form and tradition that complicates the pleasure of the spectacle. The imagination of disaster comes with a history of discontents, anxieties, actions, and solutions.

Whereas post-1997 in Hong Kong is characterized as the era of protests and political action, these are not separable from a broader-scale movement of consciousness between actions that are taken on the street and the formation of a new structure of feeling. The overlapping image of Hong Kongers responding to disasters in Fruit Chan's film and the subsequent Umbrella Movement confirms a channel of communication and a sensory network that extends from one to another. The juxtaposition of the film and the political movement opens up the possibility of reading into a collection of images whose mutual reverberation brings the past and the future into a present that had never been lived or recognized before.[30] In response to rampant state and financial technologies of abstraction in the era of the post-, the connection shared between *The Midnight After* and the Umbrella Movement represents a violent moment of rupture in the dominant regime of visibility that regulates discontent by separating cinematic fantasy from the empirical world of reality. As the boundary between the possible and the impossible blurs, the details of Chan's cinematic disaster bring about a shadow archive of a future that has already arrived. Examining a disaster that exceeds the visible spectrum, the following analysis delineates the unfolding of the future in the past and explores the historical content of post-1997 Hong Kong's imagination of disaster.

A Disaster That Exceeds the Visible Spectrum: *The Midnight After* (2014)

At two o'clock in the morning, the camera's casual glance at the time accentuates the boisterous interior of a gambling house before the camera exits onto the lively and crowded streets of Mong Kok, one of the busiest commercial shopping districts in Hong Kong. As if mimicking the social rhythm of a city that never sleeps, the opening sequence of the film alternates between the dizzying and blurred movement of people and traffic and the nondescript flow of information displayed throughout the city's extended network of digital billboards and LED screens. In its initial appearance, Hong Kong is represented as a phantasmatic network of virtual movements where the intrinsic logic of post-socialist neoliberalism is on full display. Moving too fast for the human eye to discern, post-socialist Hong Kong is the epitome of the visible-incomprehensible—a Hong Kong conceptualized from the perspectives of financiers, planners, politicians, and speculators. The city appears by disappearing into a space of abstraction—indistinguishable, illegible, and noncorporeal.

The initial image of Hong Kong as a city of hypermediation and abstraction is contrasted with a postdisaster Hong Kong where the physical infrastructure remains but the human population has been stripped away. When survivors on a van, their bodies fragile in an abandoned city, are confronted with a troop of black-attired men in military gas masks and a possibly infectious virus that causes the body to combust, the film highlights the tension between bodies and cities, abstraction and corporeality, and dispossession and strategies of repossession.[31] Over the course of one night, during a routine trip from Mong Kok to Tai Po, the reality known as Hong Kong ends, leaving behind a group in a crisis that is never given clarity. In distinct before and after shots, the film depicts predisaster Hong Kong as an excess of bodies and movements that literally overwhelm the frame but offers a contrasting image of the post- that evokes the concept of nothingness. From the panoramic shots of expressways devoid of traffic to a downtown missing its population and a communication network that goes silent, the cinematic disaster is depicted as the contrast between movement and stasis, abundance and lack. The disaster coincides with the imminent disappearance of Hong Kong's human inhabitants, making literal the posthuman amid Hong Kong's postdisaster.

In a city locked in the aggravating condition where land is speculated as capital, Hong Kong's dwindling supply of affordable housing has worsened in recent years as the city has been redesigned to fulfill its function as a major transit center connecting East and Southeast Asia. Linking the special economic zones and manufacturing centers along the PRC border in the Pearl River Delta to the rest of the world, the special administrative region of Hong Kong is increasingly integrated in the infrastructural hardware and software of transportation that have created an urban enclave among the economic archipelagoes of exception zones. In contrast to the notion of the post- as an ideological vacuum, the post- of post-socialism in Hong Kong is the principal economic logic governing an accelerated infrastructural integration by air, land, and sea. The post- indicates the transformation of Hong Kong into an integrated modern logistics hub and a global center of transportation, especially for multinational developers.[32] Post-socialism in Hong Kong has a physical and material form. From the Guangzhou-Shenzhen Expressway to the Hong Kong–Zhuhai-Macau Bridge, infrastructural roadways—many of which were modeled after US highways and tunnels—helped stimulate industrial, commercial, and residential development in towns and cities along the newly developed routes. While the double zoning strategy affords Hong Kong cheap supplies of labor and land from its sister city, Shenzhen, the intensive and successful development of Shenzhen has also been a source of anxiety, raising concerns over the eventual demise and replacement of Hong Kong. In short, the further Hong Kong's urban fabric extends, the more it finds itself embedded and locked in the unknown. The infrastructural extensions broadened Hong Kong's economic influence, but the imageries of tunnels and expressways are treated with more pronounced ambiguity and uncertainty in the cultural realm.

Considering the apparently prosperous infrastructural boom in the post-socialist era, the appearance of tunnels, bridges, and expressways in the depiction of a disaster in Hong Kong invites a second look at the relationship between bodies and the city they inhabit. The postdisaster is the posthuman in Hong Kong, as suggested in *The Midnight After*, in which an intact city, a functioning van, and emptied-out transportation infrastructure are left behind. As if foreseeing a future that already exists, the posthuman landscape of Hong Kong embodies the cultural logic of neoliberal post-socialism, where the principle of abstraction dissolves away every corporeal being. In the latest development of zone urbanism, systematic management of structural unemployment and housing shortages means permanent bodies are no longer required. The city of the future will be dependent on transient populations of laborers and the global elite class. The disappearance of Hong Kong's human population illustrates a disturbance across the field of vision. Under neoliberal post-socialism, the old dichotomy between visibility and invisibility as indicators of presence and absence falters. Humans do not simply disappear but are rendered invisible, the cumulative result of repetitive transient movements too rapid and systematized for the human eye to discern.

On an ordinary night, the Tai Po–bound van-bus passes through the Lion Rock Tunnel that connects Hong Kong's downtown districts to the peripheral towns. In this space of transit, Chan's camera focuses on a transient moment: the blink of an eye. In the split second when all passengers and the driver close their eyes—the literal representation of closing the old regime of visibility—they are transposed to a new reality that exceeds the previous visible spectrum. During the moment of temporary blindness, the unthinkable has taken place: the unstoppable flow of capital has come to a standstill. The ephemeral blackout is the condensed image of a (self-)destructiveness, a witness to the end of the existing social hierarchy, law, and order—an image of death and potential rebirth that remains unseen but whose effects are explored as an emergent visuality and sociality.

Disinterested in the spectacle of destruction that is conventionally focused on densely populated downtowns, *The Midnight After*—whose Cantonese title emphasizes the movement of transit—relocates the scene of the disaster to Hong Kong's infrastructural transportation network. Characterizing expressways, tunnels, airports, train stations, and bridges as the quintessential *nonplaces* of supermodernity—places that are real but lack histories or identities—the anthropologist Marc Augé explores new species of spaces, especially spaces of transit that are creating new patterns of consumption and production and are redefining the sociological understanding of place. In his initial definition of the term, Augé writes, "If a place can be defined as relational, historical, and concerned with identity, then a space which cannot be defined as relational, or historical, or concerned with identity will be a non-place."[33] As the gateway that connects South China's special economic zones to the world, post-handover Hong Kong is not only a special administrative region but also the integration of a political and economic zone of exception. This integration is most clearly manifest in the city's historical and emerging role as East and Southeast Asia's "transport super city."[34] With an integrated infrastructure that specializes in movement, Hong Kong has a history of transportation—embedded in its container ports, expressways, and the new international airport—that embodies its success as a capitalist city. However, as *The Midnight After* draws attention to the unfolding crisis on the van, which is passing through the nondescript space-time of a tunnel, the tension between the city as a space of residence and a space of transit is brought into the open. The non- in Augé's formulation of "non-place" is not antithetical to the traditional definition of place. He writes, "Place and non-place are rather like opposed polarities: the first is never completely erased, the second never totally completed; they are like palimpsests."[35] From the scene of the tunnel and the mobile site of the moving van, the film probes the impossible possibility of a transient sociality and solidarity while opening up the potential meaning engendered in the space of negativity.

An active filmmaker since the 1990s, Fruit Chan is known for his film trilogies on the subject of Hong Kong after 1997—*Made in Hong Kong* (1997), *The Longest Summer* (1998), and *Little Cheung* (1999)—and the allegorical presentation of post-handover relations between Hong Kong and China through female prostitutes' bodies and mobilities in *Durian Durian* (2000), *Hollywood Hong Kong* (2001), and *Public Toilet* (2002). Known as the "handover" and "prostitute" trilogies, these films unfold the ever-shifting power relations between Hong Kong and mainland China.[36] Always avoiding the clichéd image of Hong Kong as a city of finance, Chan focuses on sites, people, and objects of negative vision. Capturing the elusive metropolis through exotic fruit, animals, children, and women, Chan constitutes Hong Kong through the practice of looking away, turning the gaze away from the very thing that blinds sight and from the urban-as-concept that the mind's eye is conditioned to see, creating a delirious blindness and an urban mirage that his films consistently subvert. Since *Made in Hong Kong*, a film that depicts a group of alienated young Hong Kongers with a crisp lyricism of pessimistic nihilism, Chan has launched a career as a collector of abject bodies living on the margins of Hong Kong's social strata. Seeing Hong Kong through wet dreams, semen, shit, shed skin, and severed limbs, Chan's cinema is full of abject bodies and body parts that linger against the shadowy and dark urban landscape of Hong Kong in cemeteries, slaughterhouses, brothels, slums, public toilets, and numerous public housing estates that mirror the history of unaffordable urban living. In the transport super city, Chan's human subjects live under the condition of perpetual displacement, where the ideas of home and homeland fracture and recede infinitely. The non- in Augé's nonplace is filled with the reality of living in the invisible margins of the transport city, outside the seamless infrastructure of airport lounges, high-speed trains, amusement parks, and air-conditioned shopping centers. The new species of nonplaces creates in reality an unequal spectrum of accessibility hidden in the shadow and under the visible façade of post-socialist Hong Kong's infrastructural boom. In a space increasingly designed for transit, neoliberal post-socialism discriminates and creates new inequalities by granting or denying access to the infrastructure of global mobility. Turning the camera toward Hong Kong's recent spatial and societal transformation, Chan's Hong Kong landscapes that are mediated by abject bodies are imbued with feelings and sentiments that open up a new Marxist phenomenological structure of perception and probe the silhouette of a global system that lies beyond representability.

In works that accentuate self-exile and displacement, Chan portrays the city as landscape-in-abjection and suggests cinematic Hong Kong as the architectural unfolding of the phenomenological experiences of urbanization in neoliberal post-socialism. From the low-flying airplanes that lurk behind the scenes of suicide and murder in *Made in Hong Kong* to the all-encompassing, scam-filled cyber network on social media in *Hollywood Hong Kong*, the city's infrastructural development is captured at the liminal margins of visibility and animated as connected points of intensity that probe the relationship between the city's human population and its infrastructural networks. Capturing articulations of feelings that are not yet namable, the relations between bodies and the infrastructure of speed calls for a new object of phenomenological study—the phenomenology of infrastructural space—mediated through the body as the interface of sensory knowledge and potential action. In architectural and software designs that are intended to create unobstructed flow and movement, the place and meaning of the body in a transport super city undergoes a crisis. Though the body's movement is vulnerable to calculated manipulation and assignment in the master plans of Hong Kong's infrastructural design, Fruit Chan's collection of abject bodies recenters the body as a site of knowledge formation. Rather than resorting to the traditional anthropocentric divide between human and nonhuman, body and environment, Chan's Marxist phenomenology of infrastructural space probes the entanglement of the body as a site of knowledge and its intensified subjection to logistical procedures, protocols, and itineraries. Since Hong Kong is deeply embedded in a global financial and transportation infrastructure, as well as the demand and supply chains of nuclear energy in South China's special economic zones, the eruption of environmental hazards and disasters poses a literal and philosophical existential crisis to human bodies in residence in the region.[37] Chan's focus on bodily mutilation, inexplicable combustion, and other symptoms of the body can be viewed as an emerging urban phenomenology that contests the definition of the body as a passive object that merely responds to external stimuli, while rendering it possible to rethink the body as an interactive medium that disrupts and revises what we presume to know as feeling, seeing, and hearing.[38]

For Lefebvre, the response to spatial abstraction that proceeds in developmental stages under capitalist industrialization is lodged in the body as a central figure of resistance. Presented as a roadmap to the right to "difference," or what Lefebvre calls "differential space," *The Production of Space* focuses on the deconstruction of several spatial categories—absolute space, abstract space, contradictory space, and differential space—the last being the final stage in the teleological movement toward the development of consciousness. Constantly emphasizing the significance of lived space and space as lived experience, the Marxist urban theorist mentions the body throughout the text but provides only a general blueprint for engaging the body as a figure of resistance. Conceptualized as the central figure through which difference may be envisioned, the body in Lefebvre's description is a space of the transcendent and beyond. He writes, "Today the body is establishing itself firmly, as base and foundation, *beyond philosophy*, beyond discourse, and beyond the theory of discourse." Its disruptiveness originates from sensory functions that Lefebvre emphasizes throughout the text:

> Thanks to its sensory organs, from the sense of smell and from sexuality to sight (without any special emphasis being placed on the visual sphere), the body tends to behave as a *differential field*. It behaves, in other words, as a *total* body, breaking out of the temporal and spatial shell developed in response to labor, to the division of labor, to the localizing of work and the specialization of places. In its tendency, the body asserts itself more (and better) as "subject" and as "object" than as "subjectivity" (in the classical philosophical sense) and as "objectivity" (fragmented in every way, distorted by the visual, by images, etc.).

For Lefebvre, the body's sensory organs, especially the nonvisual senses, need restoration in the urban grid of abstraction.[39] However, the gesture toward redefining and relocating the body through its sensory organs should not be confused with the romanticization of human senses as a part of innate biological nature. According to Merleau-Ponty, the phenomenological study of human perceptions and senses is meant to radically challenge, rather than affirm, the scientific understanding of sensation, which insists on the separation between nature and culture, defining senses and sensations as pure biological responses to the external environment.[40] When Lefebvre conceptualizes the body as the space of transcendence capable of creating ruptures and discontinuities, the emphasis on the body should be distinguished from a simple biologism where the body is the site of inherent knowledge. Drawing from a phenomenological understanding of the body, Lefebvre's Marxian figure of resistance brings back the body as a site of consciousness in Marxist urban theory. As a medium and a form of mediation, the body creates distinctions—between inside and outside, legible and illegible. Restoring the body and its senses means challenging the existing relations between the perceptible and the meaningless, thus conjuring a new field of perception and conscious possibilities.

Throughout Chan's trilogies, the prominence of the body, especially the filmmaker's idiosyncratic obsession with the physical materiality of the body—including its decay, fluids, smell, and mutilation—illuminates a way of seeing and recording Hong Kong's post-socialist urbanscape through the conjuring of certain bodies and body parts. To illustrate the Marxist phenomenological approach to Hong Kong's urban space through which new knowledge and consciousness about Hong Kong is produced, a body-centered analysis reveals a corporeal landscape that performs the body and its presence in opposition to the forces of abstraction.

Hong Kong as Corporeal Landscape: Early Fruit Chan Films

In *Hollywood Hong Kong*, a magical realist black comedy that depicts shanty-town residents' sexual liaisons with a mainland Chinese prostitute, the Hong Kong body is visualized as male, excessively obese, and always drenched in grease and sweat. In contrast, the film's mainland body is gendered female, and its femininity is transformed into the cultural site where Hong Kong's relations with the *other* are established and negotiated. The Chinese actress Zhou Xun portrays a seductive woman with an impenetrable psyche, the mainland prostitute Dong Dong, who, by various means of seduction and manipulation, preys on a butcher's family. Dong Dong sleeps with the father and his young adult son, and her feminized mainland body depicts Hong Kong's post-handover cultural ambivalence toward the mainland *other*, whose cultural reputation oscillates between the dangerous femme fatale and the precarious sex worker. Adopting multiple pseudonyms and virtual online identities, Dong Dong appears as different embodiments of mainland femininities, slipping in and out of the Hong Kong imaginary of the seductive Shanghai girl and the innocuous and caring neighborhood sister.[41] Free-spirited and unpredictable, Dong Dong has a post-handover *otherness* that has evolved from the stereotypical masculinized femininity typically associated with femininity in socialist cultures. Her "mainlandness" is no longer marked by legible traits of otherness, such as accent, clothing, or other markers of social status. The body's surface as the signifier of difference ceases to be tangible and conjures instead the film's magical realist fantasies of sexual contamination, physical contact, and masturbatory touch that dramatize the *no longer* in the newly entangled self and other.

In the film's treatment of Dong Dong's feminine body—an elusive and spectral body—the mainlander is seen through her body's movement, swinging up and down and back and forth on a swing set, summoning while at the same time hiding the traces of her presence. Juxtaposing and blurring footage set in the shantytown and in the characters' dreams, the film is haunted by the presence that is everywhere and nowhere: a body that swings freely in and out of the (un)consciousness of the shantytown's residents, a visual spectacle that is the source of both desire and fear. As Shih Shu-mei argues in "The Geopolitics of Desire," the intensified integration among China, Hong Kong, and Taiwan has created specific kinds of cultural symptoms where the negotiation of new identities and relations often manifest through the negotiation of gendered bodies and sexualities.[42] To imagine the sexualized *other* and to construct his or her place in a rapidly changing geopolitical environment is a way of negotiating and oftentimes mending previously existing borders, boundaries, and thresholds. Drawn to the swing as a visual device and a game of appearance and disappearance, Chan's *Hollywood Hong Kong* conjoins, through Dong Dong's body, two adjacent worlds where the existence of one threatens to eliminate the other's. Set in Tai Hom Village, Hong Kong's biggest squatter village before its demolition in 2001, the film focuses on the narrow corridors and makeshift rooftops. Seen, smelled, and touched from the perspective of a pig butcher's family that resides in the village, the urban slum is architecturally dilapidated and also rendered as animalistic, full of grease, excessive fat, and grotesque bodies. In a city of animals, the landscape of male bodies becomes contiguous with the pigs they rear and roast for human consumption. Used by the film as the visual frame that surrounds the prominent towers of Hollywood Plaza—one of the biggest shopping centers and residential towers in Kowloon East—Tai Hom Village lurches at the foot of "Hollywood," forcefully remapping the two onto the same spectrum of visibility.[43] Swinging her body high and above the claustrophobic rooftops of the urban slum, Dong Dong flies in the air, the distance between Hollywood Plaza and Tai Hom Village turned into a simulated reality dependent on the height of her swing. Belonging neither here nor there, yet capable of infiltrating both, Dong Dong's body-on-swing rehearses the appearance and disappearance of her presence. Similar to the *fort/da* (gone/there) game Freud observes in a child's play and describes in *Beyond the Pleasure Principle*, Dong Dong's spectral *dis*appearance illustrates the compulsion to repeat in the game.[44] In the child's game of throwing away (gone) and relocating a beloved object (there)—the rehearsal of separation and reunion—the threshold between

FIGURE 4.3. In Fruit Chan's *Hollywood Hong Kong* (2001), the body of a mainland woman is conjured and eliminated and suspended in a state of perpetual vanishing.

the self and the other becomes distinguished and fortified and the object objectified. The absence of the other is tolerated, while her disappearance becomes pleasurable and gratifying. Through the body-in-motion—a body in cyclical movements—the body of a mainland woman is conjured and eliminated and suspended in a state of perpetual vanishing (see figure 4.3). Neither present nor absent and neither living nor dead, Dong Dong's body is the new undead where Hong Kong's anxiety and ambivalence toward the mainland is reflected in the reproduction of women's spectral vanishings and returns.

The film *Durian Durian* centers on the life of a mainland woman named Yan who journeys from the Heilongjiang province in northeast China to work as a prostitute in Hong Kong. Chan's portrayal of mainland migrants defies the group's traditional association with political and economic refugees and asylum seekers and explores the intensifying entanglement between self-imposed displacement and a new chimera of post-socialist cosmopolitanism, creating the illusion of cosmopolitan travel and social mobility for solitary Chinese female migrants in the integrated network of post-socialist economies of exception. Disregarding the typical concern for human rights and economic inequality, Chan portrays mainland sex workers leading a contradictory double life as cosmopolitan travelers whose motivations to work and travel reveal the desire for, rather than the necessity of, movement.

Reversing the journey from Hong Kong to Heilongjiang, *Durian Durian* returns Hong Kong's *other* to a place where she rightfully belongs but that in the end turns into a phantasmatic place of origin. Hong Kong's anxiety toward the return is mapped onto the film's female subject, whose desire to be elsewhere remains a blind spot and a sign of affinity.

In female-centered dramas that skillfully utilize the female body to mediate Hong Kong's post-1997 anxieties, Chan's collection of post-socialist mainlanders in Hong Kong has raised issues concerning the city's future under "one country, two systems," which is set to expire in 2047. The inclusion of foreign female bodies opens up the space of gendered bodies as a cultural site where the renegotiations of borders and boundaries are performed. However, the same question of bodies as a site of emergent consciousness can be posed for the films' cinematic bodies that are not in tension but in contiguity with Yan's and Dong Dong's bodies of otherness. As a historical port city and a recent zone of exception, Hong Kong is a place that can only be constructed out of its shifting relationships with the *elsewhere*.[45] Describing Hong Kong culture without origins or ends, Ackbar Abbas theorizes the city's existence through the prism of perpetual displacement. Hong Kong is always already an impossible possibility—a location in the mise-en-abîme, a virtual location in the abyss of simultaneous traces. Chan's cinematic rendering of mainland women has provided a space for discussing Hong Kong's changing relations with China since 1997. But given the films' departures from the earlier narrative of assimilation—constructed upon Hong Kong's fantasy of cultural and economic superiority in the cultural scene of the 1990s—the films' ambivalence toward the *other* signals the collapse of the distinction between self and other.[46] While the otherness of the other looms in excess without a corresponding framework for comprehension, the otherness of the self—a self also constructed upon shifting concepts of borders—remains the blind spot in the (re)location of Hong Kong.

The fetish of women's bodies in Hong Kong's urban milieu is dependent upon an urban environment that accommodates and fetishizes foreign bodies. In *Hollywood Hong Kong*, a film that plays on the juxtaposition of doubles, Dong Dong's exotic *otherness* is matched with the performative self-exoticization of Tai Hom Village as animalistic and carnal, the kernel of primitive desires. The Chu family, whose surname has the same pronunciation as *pig* in Cantonese, problematizes perceptions of the local in the traditional dichotomy that separates the local from the *other*. Tinting the shantytown in bold variations of the color red, Chan makes Hong Kong oscillate between two seemingly incommensurable sites of consumption, one referring to the clean and air-conditioned Hollywood shopping plaza, and another the nearby Tai Hom Village, where the Chu family earns their living servicing the city's conspicuous rituals of meat consumption. In an unconventional opening, the film begins with a shot of the Chu family—father and two sons—sitting half-naked in their delivery truck as they return from an off-site slaughterhouse to their barbeque shop in the village. Intentionally fragmenting the human subjects through close-ups of their round bellies and other indistinguishable body parts, the opening credits are "stamped" on meat surfaces, mimicking the routine procedure designating the meat's origin and itineracy in Hong Kong's meat market. The skins of men and animals are no longer distinguishable, and the opening credits foreshadow the fate of both. In sequences that follow, the Chu family repetitively performs the labor of cutting, dissecting, treating, moving, and roasting whole pigs in the hot and humid summer, making the provocative allusion to the precarious position of Hong Kong that resembles the meat on the plate. Portrayed through the desiring bodies of men, including the Chu family and the shantytown resident Keung, the meat-consumers become easy prey for online schemers who lure with another kind of meat: the young and exotic flesh of mainland women.

If Dong Dong's elusive body illustrates the profound ambivalence toward the mainland *other* after 1997, the portrayal of Hong Kong has shifted from the possessor of cultural superiority to primitive, exotic, and animalistic meat-eaters whose instinctive desires for food and sex entrap them in the bottomless pit of desire and deceit. Between the film's two female mainlanders, Dong Dong, who seduces Keung in a scheme that extracts money from men who sleep with her, receives the most attention. However, the film is haunted by another presence—the doctor, scientist, and businesswoman Dr. Liu—whose flowery rhetoric and venture capitalist idea for a medical experiment makes her an acoustic siren that turns her listeners into stones. Liu's experiment would use animal uteri to produce human babies, mocking the fantasized alignment of capitalism and socialism, where fetishized surplus value masks the complicity between power systems. From the mismatch of Keung's severed hand to the experiment on post-socialist and posthuman babies, *Hollywood Hong Kong* exploits the logic of exception in "one country, two systems" in an array of cinematic puns. Working like the butcher's incisive knife, Chan's camera fragments the male body and cuts it apart. Disassembling and reassembling body parts, the film turns the violence of deterritorialization into a comic tragedy, painstakingly enumerating the sequence of events that contributes to the acceptance and normalization, rather than the rejection, of the new body-assemblage. After his hand is chopped off by scheming gangsters midway through the film, Keung help-lessly lies on the operating table, under the care and knife of Dr. Liu. As the camera zooms in to show in full detail the severed hand and its replacement part, the close-up reveals the tattoos on both body fragments: a newborn animal with a dragon head and snake tail. A visual pun alluding to the Can-tonese and Chinese phrase *tiger head snake tail* (*futau-semei/hutou-shewei*), the hand-as-assemblage is a coded message that mocks the inconsistency of grand openings and meek endings.[47] The men who consume meat like they consume women's fetishized bodies in the virtual world of pornography find themselves trapped in the same network of commodified fetishism. The eater of meat in turn becomes meat on the plate for cash-hungry predators. The Hong Kong they inhabit transforms into an animal kingdom, a City of Animals.

Depicting human and pig/animal bodies in similitude, Chan explores the physicality of his Hong Kong characters by evoking the suppressed animal traces in humans. In a reading of the animal and its philosophical conceptu-alizations from Aristotle and Derrida, Akira Lippit observes that the animal exists in the state of "perpetual vanishing," a spectral existence that lingers in the world *undead*.[48] Incapable of using language, animals are distinguished from humans by their lack of ability to engage in the activities of writing and discourse. Forever outcasts in the realm of communication, animals are linked to the liminal space of dreams, crypts, and the unconscious, their lack of human functions turned into a fertile ground for imagining different kinds of limits—in language, visibility, and presence. To imagine animality is to animate silenced muteness and untold secrets, bringing humanity to its liminal threshold. In the soon-to-be-demolished shantytown Tai Hom Village, the villagers are seen constantly engaged in activities that blur the boundary between the village's human and animal inhabitants, their lives *alternating* between repetitive cycles of eating, sleeping, and roasting pigs in the butcher shop. Rarely leaving the village and reticent about Hong Kong's contemporary affairs, the father and elder son in the Chu family appear, like a coded message, through a screen presence that cuts apart and frag-ments their bare bodies like chunks of meat. Almost touching the meat, in camerawork that exposes the pores and fissures of the skin, *Hollywood Hong Kong* presents a carnal and tactile landscape that is too close to be seen. The visible-but-illegible resonates with the film's two iconic sequences, in which the youngest son, Tiny, tries to send signals to Dong Dong in Hollywood Plaza's resident towers, which overlook the shantytown. Signaling across the prominent sign of Hollywood Plaza, Tiny shouts and waves his hands, although his signal is not recognized until his father joins in with a giant red flag. Mocking the failure to see something right in front of these characters' eyes, the film transforms Hong Kong into the City of Animals, where the characters' consumption and becoming-animal illuminate the symptom of illegibility. As the urban environment chases away animals and animal traces in a utopic vision of global cities, the film races against time to capture the imminent disappearance of humans, animals, and the space they cohabit. Hong Kong appears through the cinematic capture of disappearing animal species, whose perpetual death and reincarnation illuminate a cinematic fantasy that moves freely between life and afterlife.

In films that intently focus on Hong Kong's foreign others—illegal immigrants, Southeast Asian domestic workers, and mainland prostitutes—Chan's affective and often sympathetic depiction of *others* works like a mirror in which Hong Kong appears in layered reflections as an alienating and alienated city. Before Hong Kong was Chan's City of Animals, it was first the City of Ghosts in *Made in Hong Kong* (1997), the City of Oblivion in *The Longest Summer* (1998), and the City of Money in *Little Cheung* (1999). Shown as menacing, hollow, and materialistic, but also the subject of melancholy, nostalgia, and tenderness, the Hong Kong in Chan's films is the invisible *other* that escapes the field of vision, documenting Hong Kong's ambivalent self-relations beneath the realm of visibility. As Chan's camera captures the way Hong Kong sees *others*, it also records how the city sees itself, intertwining city and bodies and accumulating feelings and sensations. While the city has been preoccupied since the 1980s with forging new relations with China, its relationship with the self has transformed into an illegible site of anxiety and trauma.

In *The Longest Summer* (*Huinin yinfa dakbit doh/Qunian yanhuo tebie duo*), Hong Kong appears as the City of Oblivion that has lost its ability to remember. Following a group of ethnically Chinese Hong Kong soldiers discharged from the British Army, the film painstakingly constructs their psychological transformation as the city is demilitarized in preparation for the handover. In a film that mourns the loss of Hong Kong through nostalgia for military male comradeship, the waning of British–Hong Kong masculinity becomes an affective medium for new channels of collective feelings that encourage the formation of new communities. As the soldiers take off their British military uniforms and change into civilian clothing, the former code of racializing their Hong Kong bodies disappears, leaving the bodies bare and vulnerable. No longer engaged in the strenuous duties of the army, the soldiers struggle to make their transition to postmilitary life, working odd jobs as a security guard, a subway assistant, and a local gangster. Short on money, the group decides to embark on one last mission together and rob a local bank, bringing about disastrous consequences.

As the quality of these soldiers' lives rapidly deteriorates in the months leading up to the handover ceremony on July 1, their anguished feelings of loneliness and betrayal are buried beneath the spectacular summer fireworks frequently displayed in the celebratory events of 1997. Each event is paired with a violent atrocity conducted or experienced by the former military members. Alluding to the contentious Airport Core Program, which was used as a political strategy to ensure Hong Kong's financial stability, one of the ex-soldiers, Ga Suen, assassinates his target during the fireworks celebration when the British prime minister Margaret Thatcher inaugurated the operation of the massive Tsing Ma (Qing Ma) Bridge in April 1997. Part of the US$20 billion infrastructure development that included the new airport and expressways and rail lines to better integrate Hong Kong and its peripheries, Tsing Ma Bridge is one of the world's longest suspension bridges, linking the airport on Lantau Island to the New Territories.[49] Appearing numerous times in the film and punctuating different moments of an escalating crisis, the bridge evokes the unrepresentable but lived condition of being in between, in permanent suspension. Documentary footage of the rituals of celebration—fireworks, speeches, crowds—are inserted elliptically, tearing open the deep rift between the spectacular celebration and the void of its meaning. "In That Year, Fireworks Were Especially Plentiful," the film's Cantonese title plainly states, leaving to interpretation the "fireworks" that are ambiguously defined and multifariously rich. When the main protagonist, Ga Yin, embarks on a shooting rampage, the unbearable loss of his former comrades to invisible consequences following their discharge materializes in an outburst incomprehensible to society at large. Leaving behind no record of his suffering, Ga Yin is shot in the head. A year after the handover, there are fewer cars on the street and traffic has improved. Ga Yin runs into an old acquaintance but is unable to recognize her. As the camera zooms in, a tiny hole is revealed in the lower back of his head. The vessel of his memory is removed, containing feelings, resentments, and regrets that no one else knew. Hong Kong is the quintessential City of Oblivion. Stories arrive and depart, imprinting traces that are neither possible to remember nor possible to forget. The city that the ex-soldiers vowed to protect stands in silent witness, without any sign of acknowledgment, like an object of desire that never returns one's gaze.

Unable to establish a mutual relationship, Chan's characters become indistinguishable from the supposed *others* in Hong Kong society, adrift in the city they claim as home. In *Little Cheung* (1999), a film that explores the psychological landscape of Hong Kong during the handover through the perspective of a nine-year-old boy, Hong Kong is perceived as the City of Money. Working in his father's restaurant as a delivery boy, Little Cheung makes his entrance in voice-over narration. As he bikes through the familiar streets of his neighborhood, his voice calmly declares his assessment of the adults in his life: "Everything is for making money!," a rule that applies to his father and mother, the Filipino domestic worker, and the rest of the world. The handover for Little Cheung means the disappearance of three women in his life: his doting grandmother; the domestic worker who substitutes for his mother; and his childhood companion, whose illegal status leads to her deportation. Departing one after another in the summer of 1997, these women represent irretrievable losses, sentiments, and attachments that overwhelm the nine-year-old, whose emotion exceeds the language available in the City of Money. "Cash only," as the boy's father always reminds him before he goes out on his delivery errands. The alienation between Little Cheung and his parents is fully captured in the daily rituals of incommunicability, where conversations begin and end with questions about money, frustrating both the coming-of-age boy and the adults earning a living in the city of commodification.

Whether through the ghosts of young adults in *Made in Hong Kong*, the ex-soldiers in *The Longest Summer*, or the lonely son in *Little Cheung*, Chan's early films bring into view a range of bodies that transform Hong Kong into an animated environment and a site of consciousness. As Merleau-Ponty says in *The Primacy of Perception*, "The perceiving mind is an incarnated mind."[50] The anthropological shift of focus across gender, class, and age groups illuminates corporeal landscapes *imagined* by corporeal minds. Imagination, which is also the appearance of something, is already a signifier of presence, contrary to its common dismissal as pure absence. Although Chan's films consistently symptomize through the conjured bodies of ghosts, vanishing women, and animals, their presence does not guarantee legibility. The films are records of blind spots, nonperceptions, and the incommensurable gap between embodiment and disembodiment, capturing and evoking the affect of urban horror, where bodies are visualized in a state of permanent suspension—fascinating and unsettling and a threshold to post-socialist Hong Kong as an un/known territory. Accumulating bodies-in-transition, bodies-in-movement, bodies-in-exile, and bodies-in-displacement, Fruit

Chan's Hong Kong is a crowded city where the speed of the bodies-in-motion blurs their visibility. As Hong Kong continues to expand the physical and virtual infrastructure connecting itself to special economic zones in China, the heightened speed of connection obscures individual bodies into streams of movement, creating underexposed presences that leave behind indiscernible traces.

However, in a set of films that explores the intricacies of Hong Kong–China relations produced when the connections and traffic between Hong Kong and the Chinese special economic zones intensify, Chan proposes the allegory of Hong Kong's geopolitical position in the post-socialist world and the emergent landscape of affective intensities concerning borders in the global proliferation of zones—specifically the ways in which borders are reconceptualized in a presumably borderless world. From the spectral appearance of a mainland woman whose elusive sexuality bewitches the entire village of men in *Hollywood Hong Kong*, to the imagination of an invisible and border-trespassing disaster in *The Midnight After*, Chan's Hong Kong is haunted by bodies, viruses, radiation, and other elements at the limits of visibility that paralyze the concept of traditional borders. For the survivors in the posthuman Hong Kong, their final ride in the red van, as they head toward Hong Kong's highest peak in search for truth, is interrupted by unexplained violent attacks from an unidentified troop of men. The scene highlights the neoliberal imaginary of a borderless world as illusory. One's mobility in the zones and the freedom to move are paradoxically the result of intensified regulation in a carefully engineered borderless environment. The zone of exception is made of new borders that change Hong Kong's urban architecture—influencing the designs of cross-border bridges, expressways, and rail links—and the invisible infrastructure regulating bodies, movements and intimate relationships.

Urban Horror at the Border:
Erratic Violence in a Borderless World

Drawing attention to the question of borders in the proliferation of zones, the filmmaker Ann Hui turns to the bodies-spaces in borderlands and border landscapes. In their study on the significance of borders in global capitalism, Sandro Mezzadra and Brett Neilson write against the notion that borders are disappearing. In what they call "postdevelopmental geographies," the appearance of zones and economic corridors in developing countries and in unpredictable forms is at the core of a new market rationality that is shaped by flexibility. They write, "We are confronted not only with a multiplication of different types of borders but also with the reemergence of the deep heterogeneity of the semantic field of the border. Symbolic, linguistic, cultural, and urban boundaries are no longer articulated in fixed ways by the geopolitical border."[51] The violence of economic and political integration in the zones stems from the unpredictability of border-making in the era of the post-. The disappearance of the physical border and the mutability of new borders between Hong Kong and the Chinese special economic zones reshape the human relations in a border town. Through the atrocities of Tin Shui Wai, a border town of new immigrants from China known for numerous cases of family tragedy and domestic violence, Hui's films that are based on real events open up a conceptual horizon for thinking and feeling about the incomprehensible that continues to multiply and leave behind affective excesses and residues that have no name.

Pointing the camera at the borderland that conjoins the two zone cities of Hong Kong and Shenzhen, Hui's two-part film, *The Way We Are* (*Tinshuiwai dik yat yu ye/Tianshuiwei de ri yu ye*, 2008) and *Night and Fog* (*Tinshuiwai di ye yu mo/Tianshuiwei de ye yu wu*, 2009), lays out the structure of feelings in the zone and in newly developed lands where every resident is a new immigrant, subject to varying degrees of movement and displacement depending on age, gender, job opportunity, and rent for housing. Both films are set in the border town Tin Shui Wai, in the northwest periphery of Hong Kong, where Shenzhen's developing skyline can be seen in close proximity to the natural ecology of Mai Po Nature Reserve, part of the Frontier Closed Area created during the Cold War by the British government to secure Hong Kong's separation from the mainland.[52] Established in 1951 after the United Nations embargo against China following the Korean War, the buffer zone extends twenty-six kilometers along the Hong Kong–China border. Closed off to developers and residents, the frontier of Hong Kong has gradually transformed into a natural habitat for migratory birds, wetland insects and animals, and various plant species.[53] Opening *The Way We Are* with black-and-white photographs of butterflies, crabs, and wetlands that have claimed the buffer zone as their natural habitat, Hui's camera transitions to the towering public housing complexes that crowd the town of Tin Shui Wai, where many new immigrants from the mainland and locals from Hong Kong reside. While the Cold War decree unexpectedly created a biosphere of wildlife in a buffer zone frozen in time, the camera's deliberate pause on the dense forest of concrete buildings adds to the visual residue of the border ecology and probes the web of relations and dependencies embedded in the new town of Tin Shui Wai (see figures 4.4 and 4.5).[54] Constructed in the early 1980s on reclaimed land

FIGURE 4.4. Black-and-white photographs of butterflies, crabs, and wetlands in a nature preserve at the border between Hong Kong and Shenzhen in *The Way We Are* (2008).

FIGURE 4.5. The camera transitions from black-and-white shots of the wetland to colored shots of residential towers in the border town Tin Shui Wai, probing the web of relations among zones, nations, nature, and people in *The Way We Are* (2008).

from the area's abundant fishponds, the town is in an enclosed and remote location, making it a peripheral space. Originally established as a bedroom community for an emergent class of workers, Tin Shui Wai was turned into a low-income residential area by the British colonial government in 1992. However, the town was unable to compete with the new pool of labor from China's special economic zones, so the plan of creating labor-intensive industries nearby fell to dust, leaving behind a ghostly residential infrastructure that now accommodates a different group of human inhabitants.

Hui's cinematography often juxtaposes two urbanscapes, in Hong Kong and Shenzhen, separated and connected by an uncanny sea of greenery that is now designated the Hong Kong Wetland Park, an ecological mitigation area intended to compensate for the wetland lost to the Tin Shui Wai New Town development in 1998.[55] Gazing ambivalently at the scenic walkways and tranquil wetland, the mise-en-scène of *Night and Fog* re-creates a phenomenological spatial setting for the human tragedy that took place in 2004, when a Hong Kong man brutally murdered his mainland wife and their two young daughters in the border town. Instead of focusing on an individual case of psychosis, *Night and Fog* reenacts the murder by returning to the original site of trauma. Replaying, remembering, and reconstructing an intimate relationship that ends in violent destruction, the film proceeds by regressing into a lost time and space filled with memory gaps and ellipses, where the scenic surroundings of Tin Shui Wai enter into ambiguous relations with the human subjects living there. Physically located at the border, the town transforms into a symbolic gateway that mediates relations between Hong Kong and its others. A zone belonging neither to the inside nor the outside, the tranquil wetland that connects the two zones also marks the extreme danger and violent aggression that are manifested in the ordinary setting of everyday life, in conflicts over everything from the taste of food to the value of money. Uncovering layered bureaucracy in Hong Kong's legal system, which maintains the Chinese woman's "foreign" status in her marriage to a Hong Kong man and thus denies her social welfare and protection in an abusive relationship, *Night and Fog* explores a post-socialist border system — in the form of erratic violence — that seeps into the texture and intimacy of everyday life. Through the daily cycles of eating and cooking, sleeping and waking, and entering and exiting women's shelters, the relationship between an older Hong Kong man and his young mainland spouse has a cumulative intensity that in the end escalates out of control. After a brutal rape scene that leaves the female protagonist, Wong Hiu-ling, bloodied and sitting on the pavement, the camera quickly glances toward Shenzhen's gloriously lit skyline. Across the darkened wetland, Shenzhen emerges like the city of light that outshines Hong Kong. Under this gaze, the preserved land is hardly a symbol for the romantic notion of untouched nature, but rather shows a post-socialist nature born of the displacement and development of zone urbanism—a geopolitical ecology.

Hong Kong and Shenzhen are two zones becoming one, touching each other in a porous wetland. Yet their conjoined fabric—driven by the logic of seamless integration in frictionless post-socialism—gives rise to mutative and nomadic boundaries that erupt in a new history of erratic violence and accidents. The adoption of a new technology means the adoption of a new accident.[56] The invention of the ship means the invention of the shipwreck. The creation of nuclear reactors means the repetition of nuclear disasters— from Chernobyl to Three Mile Island, from Fukushima to present and future post-socialist exception zones. However, the case study of Tin Shui Wai, a zone of exclusion created by the spatial technology of exception, reveals the mutative and unpredictable nature of accidents, which make the relation between origin and materialization indirect and intangible. The deterritori-alization of zones leads to the violent reterritorialization of intimacies that dramatically redefines the normative scale of disasters and creates an un-equal spectrum of impact where certain bodies bear the brunt of an invisible and cumulative violence. In the juxtaposition of Tin Shui Wai and the pre-served wildlife surrounding it, the polar extremes of neoliberal post-socialist accidents are brought to the forefront—melancholic, paradoxical, and vis-ibly incomprehensible. The disappearance of the border—a border retired to nature—means the enactment of new borders that are constructed upon the contingent articulation of violent expulsion. The death of the Sichuan-Shenzhen woman highlights not an individual case of domestic violence but an ecology of violence constituted by law, politics, economy, and culture that elucidates the atrocity at the border as a socially produced human tragedy. The affect of horror here takes a new urban form, whereas Hui's camera lingers on the thriving wildlife and nature in the preserved land, their fate subject to the past and future demands of zoning.

THIS CHAPTER BEGAN with a set of speculative questions on post-socialism in Hong Kong. Through Hong Kong cinema and the bodies-spaces that are introduced in the network of image circulation, the emphasis on "*in* Hong Kong" revises and challenges the spatial and temporal assumptions of Chinese post-socialism and opens up a new terrain for understanding both the spatial and cultural transformations that are created in the deterritorialized form of neoliberal post-socialism. In a time in Hong Kong film history that is dominated by the narrative of decline, as Hong Kong filmmakers emigrate to China to make blockbuster coproductions tailored to the Chinese audience, the sentiment that Hong Kong culture is disappearing is intensified. However, precisely at the moment when the sentiments of decline and disappearance disseminate and accumulate—and constituting a horizon of sentiments and feelings that lack legible categories—a new landscape of bodies-spaces emerges, where specific images, people, temporalities, and spaces are associated with an affective mode of excess. Produced under the condition of a deterritorialized post-socialism—an emergent economic and political rationality that is mutative and unpredictable—the forms of embodiment and disembodiment that we see in Hong Kong cinema are already rehearsing feelings and actions toward the anticipated unknown. Emerging across multiple genres, the cinematic evocations of urban horror suggest a range of bodily performativities that foreground the crisis of embodiment in expanding zones of exception. Exceeding horror as a commodified genre, the Marxist phenomenology of recent Hong Kong cinema probes what horror means in the dream of a borderless world, producing and reopening senses that reenvision the place of the body and the potential space of resistance.

5

The Ethics of Representing Precarity
Film in the Era of Global Complicity

Urban Horror at the Museum

The room was covered in tree branches and leaves. Spectators—families, lovers, and children—made themselves comfortable lying down on hand-painted, cabbage-shaped pillows and wrapped themselves in blankets. The Malaysian Taiwanese filmmaker Tsai Ming-liang's film *Stray Dogs* (*Jiaoyou/Excursions*, 2013) screened in the background, its images and sounds accompanying the museum attendees as they entered the world of sleep. For people who stayed awake in the special screenings, spending the night at the Museum of National Taipei University of Education meant not only an opportunity to watch the film but also a simulated experience of excursion. The film's portrayal of a father and his two children living in a ruin overtaken by nature in the heart of bustling Taipei cues a few themes at the installation site: mattresses that are laid on crumbled tree leaves and debris, pillows that are specially made to provide the audience interaction with an object the father fondles with feelings of loneliness, and concerts and talks that are held amid fallen tree branches to simulate the aftermath of a powerful typhoon that further drives the film's characters to the depth of desperation. Inside the museum—a space for the exhibition of art—the bleak experience of living an invisible and precaritized life is transformed into an experience of spending the night away from home before going back to the ordinary world. But before one takes a moralistic stance and judges the installation as the aestheticization of a scripted urban horror that transforms life in precarity into a commodifiable spectacle, it is important to consider the new questions that are proposed by the night at the museum and film's transformation into an experiential and phenomenological art—on the meaning of aesthetics that renders precaritized and marginalized life experiences in simulated representations.

In a characteristic production by Tsai, which features no plotline, narrative, or storytelling, *Stray Dogs* can be described as a multisensory, cinematic collage of phenomenological interfaces that induce visual, acoustic, and haptic sensations in viewers. In Tsai's sensory cinema, extreme long takes are used to accentuate the prolonged scenes of characters eating bento, sleeping and snoring on a bed, and standing for hours at work in the howling wind and rain. Leaving details of the characters' personal histories and their futures unknown, Tsai's camera is interested only in filming the fundamental care that the human body requires—an aesthetic practice the filmmaker uses to connect characters' bodies on screen and the audience's sensory organs off screen. As characters in the film consume food, drink water, get washed and cleaned, desire and become the objects of desire, the images that are projected in the installation become indistinguishable from the spectators' bodies in the museum that require the same kind of attention and care. The camera's prolonged gaze at the characters' bodies—observing minute details, from the movement of the nostrils to the rhythm of breathing and the process of consuming every piece of food in an ordinary bento box—is aimed at creating and discovering sensations and activating new organs of perception. The minutes-long take on a character sleeping and snoring, for example, evokes a new temporal experience and perception of time mediated by the sleeping body, alluding to another realm of existence that parallels the existing world but escapes legibility. In short, the bodies asleep in the museum next to the images of sleeping characters projected on exhibition screens mediate new feelings and affective modes of existence. However, Tsai's urban horror at the museum also highlights the entrance of film into the institutional space of museum art and probes a new web of relations between collaborating neoliberal institutions that are interested in producing feelings as commodifiable experiences and image-making as a practice of resistance.

FIGURE 5.1. The father holds an advertisement placard of Farglory-developed urban apartments in *Stray Dogs* (2013).

Funded by the Farglory Group, a transnational construction enterprise and real estate developer established in Taiwan in 1969, *Stray Dogs* bleakly depicts a financially challenged father working long hours to earn a living by standing at a busy intersection and holding an advertisement placard of Farglory-developed urban apartments. Surrounded by cars and people streaming past, the father is a lonesome figure, isolated and confined to his work station (see figure 5.1). Rather than explicitly raising class consciousness or creating a social movement, the film (which won awards for best director and best leading actor at Taiwan's Golden Horse Awards) ironically turned into a tool of publicity that boosted sales for Farglory and helped create a positive corporate image.[1] The contrast between the film's affective and aesthetic investments in depicting contemporary displacement and its complicity in the financial institutions it critiques represents the new scene of neoliberal art production, where strict boundaries can no longer be drawn. As the artist and filmmaker Hito Steyerl asks, "How can one think of art institutions in an age that is defined by planetary civil war, growing inequality, and proprietary digital technology? The boundaries of the institution have become fuzzy."[2] Yet for Tsai, the significance of the market and the source of funding have always been present. In the *Stray Dogs* exhibition, the idea of a family-friendly night at the museum is undoubtedly tied to sales strategies to help attract audiences and to sell film tickets. "The attendance was getting better. However, it wasn't enough. My pernicious habit of personally selling tickets started to wriggle again," says Tsai in the notes to the solo exhibition.[3] In addition to the night screenings, the filmmaker also improvised talks and discussions where the audience was invited to participate in activities associated with the film, such as eating drumsticks (referencing a long take in which the father devours every part of a drumstick in his bento) or hugging pillows as though they were objects of desire (referencing a scene in which the father draws a face on a raw cabbage, and then kisses and munches on the cabbage-face).

With full acknowledgment of the market forces that shape the definition of art in the contemporary world, Tsai's night at the museum is one of many improvised activities and diligent campus tours that sometimes involve selling tickets in crowded landmarks or outside cafeterias in order to attract an audience that Tsai and his longtime crew strove to create. Therefore the question posed by Tsai's version of urban horror at the museum is more complex than the mere acknowledgment of complicity and probes another urgent issue. Especially at a time when the sights and sounds that are meant to represent the violence of a mutative neoliberalism are funded and produced by institutions of financial capital, how to rethink the future of the image and the future of art becomes the challenge that contemporary artists and filmmakers need to face. Tracing a Malaysian Taiwanese filmmaker's aesthetics of slow, phenomenological, and invisible horror that challenges the existing definitions of being and nonbeing—referring to modes of existence that are managed and assigned according to the values of neoliberalism—this chapter examines the ethics of representing precarity in the era of global complicity.

As Butler theorizes in essays written after September 11, 2001, the notion of precarious life describes what she observed in the wake of new wars and the threats of violence: "Some lives are grievable, and others are not; the differential allocation of grievability that decides what kind of subject is and must be grieved, and which kind of subject must not, operates to produce and maintain certain exclusionary conceptions of who is normatively human: what counts as a livable life and a grievable death?"[4] Drawing from the writings of Emmanuel Levinas on the human face as a site that mediates the relations between the self and the other, Butler's theorization of precarious life is a call to confront a new value-assignment system that is mobilized by the war on terror and by an expansive economic-geopolitical governmentality that is systematically reproducing the condition of precarity for the extraction of profit and the avoidance of shared social responsibility. The concept of precarity is further developed in subsequent texts that expand the question from the legibility of life to forms of contemporary political and economic systems that distribute life's meanings and strategically assign vulnerability.[5] As previous chapters of this book illustrate, life's exposure to contingency, accident, and death has intensified in recent decades. The notion of precarity speaks to new forms of creating and managing the status of nonbeing that were previously unimaginable. Yet limited existing tools are available for understanding the frames of reality that are deployed in state or self-imposed censorship, in social media, and in other mechanisms of mediation that structure our senses and perceptions.

Therefore the question posed by the work of a Malaysian Taiwanese filmmaker and artist—whose multilayered identity already evokes a contingent structure of meaning-making that manages legibility—lies in the aesthetic practice about precarious life that is produced under the neoliberal condition of intensifying precarity. Rather than providing ethnographic portrayals of precaritized people, communities, nations, animals, or the environment, and accumulating histories of precarity in each film, Tsai's filmmaking practice centers on an inherent logic of subversion by reinventing sensory experiences that lead to a fundamental shift in the perception of the *givenness* of the world. The phenomenological experiences of slowness, noises, and the sight of nothingness that are distributed across different films contribute to building up a communication channel, where slowness becomes the new social rhythm, noise the new sound, nothingness the new sight, and nonbeing the new state of being. The value and meaning of the new sensory world remain ambiguous and are subject to change as Tsai's work moves fluidly across neoliberal art's multimedia platforms. However, such contingency and mutability characterize the condition of contemporary art-making. A filmmaker-artist's obsession with selling tickets personally to his audience implies an affective drive invested in the future of the image. What this speculative future means and what images, sounds, landscapes, and people the drive conjures and materializes are explored in this chapter. Tsai's aesthetics of the phenomenological image, the way of seeing life in precarity is linked to the geopolitical space of Taiwan—a precarious island, an island of precariousness that is caught among competing global empires and belongs neither here nor there—whose urban landscape provides the fundamental spatial language for imagining a precaritized and precaritizing world.

A Malaysian Taiwanese Filmmaker Sees Taiwan:
Urban Horror and the Landscape of Precarity

As a colony of Spanish, Dutch, Chinese, and Japanese empires that later served as the front line between the capitalist and socialist blocs during the Cold War, Taiwan occupies a quintessential in-between space. Strategic negotiations between competing global empires have a long history in the island. Geographically separated from mainland China by the Taiwan Strait, and culturally steeped in the legacy of Japanese colonial rule (1895–1945), Taiwan presents a distinct case from Hong Kong, which was part of a European colonial empire and is now a politically integrated special administrative region of the PRC. However, though China, Hong Kong, and Taiwan share linguistic and cultural common ground, new synergies and divergences have emerged since the late 1970s, as the condition of the post-provides a new global imaginary for transnational economic cooperation. Surrounded by contested waters, where territorial disputes among China, Japan, and the Philippines continue to the present day, Taiwan nonetheless remains geographically isolated from the landmass of Asia that frames Hong Kong's post-socialist visibility. The island nation's continuous struggle to balance an internationally recognized political sovereignty and the revitalization of a stagnating economy—the result of fierce competition with and dependence on China's labor resources and materials—provides a specific context that frames Taiwan's visibility in the cultural and political realms.

Like a code name for the unspeakable, Taiwan embodies a recurrent structure of negative presence. Rather than referring to a physically tangible space, *Taiwan* refers to the historical condition of subjection to multiple systems of inclusive exclusions. To confront the question of Taiwan's visibility therefore involves the task of first recognizing that the object in question is never a fixed entity waiting to be discovered but a systematically reproduced condition of nonbeing that challenges existing modes of representation. In other words, the task of seeing Taiwan requires a critical reflection on the limits of collecting loosely identifiable locations and people that are labeled as Taiwan. The island's overt and covert colonial histories leave behind traces of strategic nonrecognition, creating a cryptic landscape that keeps in memory a recurrent state of nonbeing that in turn seeks a language of expression.

From the perspective of Tsai Ming-liang, for whom filmmaking involves the meticulous deconstruction of naturalized perception and the reorientation of the senses—a process that continuously redefines the threshold between being and nonbeing—seeing Taiwan is both a problem and a challenge. Existing neither here nor there but kept as an economic organ in the competing cartographies of global empires, Taiwan presents the condition of structural marginality, a state of nonbeing that the filmmaker projects onto human subjects and objects on the verge of disappearance. Taiwan's appearance in Tsai's films from the 1990s to the 2010s suggests more than a background setting. Amid decades of intensifying economic integration with China and political and military pressure to relinquish political sovereignty, the island is presented as a landscape of precarity produced and managed by those interested in its economic and political value.

Born in Malaysia and of Chinese descent, Tsai Ming-liang, who later immigrated to Taiwan, has become known internationally as a Taiwanese filmmaker influenced by postwar French New Wave cinema, especially the urban films of François Truffaut. Haunted by the animosity of the city that Truffaut explores through the perspectives of Antoine Doinel as a child, a teenager, and a young adult—played by the actor Jean-Pierre Léaud, who appears in multiple Truffaut films—Tsai's metacinema follows the actor Lee Kang-sheng. Together, filmmaker and actor embark on a lifelong partnership creating cinematic visions of Taiwanese and Southeast Asian cities in crisis. Sitting uncomfortably within the traditional framework of national cinema, yet celebrated for the international fame they attract to Taiwan, Tsai's films are rarely discussed for their Taiwaneseness. In contrast to the prolific discussion of Tsai as a queer filmmaker, the relative silence concerning the significance of Taiwan in his filmmaking, which explores intersecting positions of marginality, indicates a problem that exceeds the framework of singular identity politics.[6]

For the international audience attracted to Tsai's films through global art house venues, Taiwan is a vague description of the films' minimalist and otherwise defamiliarized urban settings, which could represent any number of urbanizing societies in the world. For audiences and scholars interested in understanding Taiwanese histories, the films' treatment of Taiwan—through the filmmaker's idiosyncratic collection of bathrooms, construction sites, abandoned apartments, and disappearing urban spaces facing demolition—presents a landscape that is illegible as Taiwanese. In both cases, Taiwan's appearance in Tsai's films is dismissed either as an aesthetic background or as an imaginary setting that lacks historical and political significance. The *real* Taiwan is considered a lack, and one that transcends the visible frames of the films. The real island is presumed to be absent in Tsai's films. Yet its absence suggests opaque layers of unreadability and is evocative of the visible-incomprehensible discussed throughout this book. Despite Tsai's being hailed as a Taiwanese filmmaker, Taiwan is paradoxically missing in his films, which suggests an illegibility that highlights the inadequacy of the existing frame of interpretation.

The minimal engagement with a conventionally defined Taiwan in Tsai's work contradicts Taiwan's supposed transparency as a neutral background space. Instead Taiwan presents a recurrent space of opacity created by the island's encounters with capitalist colonialisms, where conflicting genealogies of colonial, postcolonial, and neocolonial histories coexist and continue to be strategically suppressed and deployed under competing regimes of veridiction. Considering the island's successive colonizers and colonial histories that parallel the expansion of global capitalist imperialism, its contemporary condition of negative presence is constructed upon a cumulative history of illegitimation. Taiwan in Tsai's films appears as an empty and abstract urban landscape that seems devoid of any historical reference. This empty landscape refers to neither the specific histories of Taiwan's former colonizers nor the uncovering of lost memories, records, or archives. Portraying economically developed Taiwanese cities as ghost cities haunted and tormented by constant rain, drought, flood, decay, and other forces of nature, these films probe the constructed limit of the grid of legibility. From Tsai's ruinous urbanscape, Taiwan is made to appear as a manipulated state of nonbeing, a condition in the transnational global network that abstracts bodies, cities, and nations for their economic and political value, leaving behind ghostly presences that require a new language and system of articulation.

For a transnational subject making films about precarious lives set in an island of nonbeing, Tsai presents the Taiwanese urbanscape as a language of precarity that draws from the island's past and future, at a moment when Hong Kong—a zone of exception that is deployed for the purpose of integration—is viewed as a potential model for the future of Taiwan. Constructing an urban landscape haunted by illegible presences, Tsai's metacinema—whose films complement, remember, and repeat each other in a metafilm that intensifies the films' intertextuality—speaks to a global epidemic capable of subjecting entire nations, zones of exception, and human and nonhuman beings to a state of sanctioned nonbeing. Taiwan thus lies at the core of an emergent crisis landscape. The global translatability of Tsai's Asian urban apocalypse cannot be dismissed simply as apolitical aestheticization. Rather, its global translatability provides an opportunity to ask questions about an expanding global system of precaritization that assigns vulnerability transnationally.[7]

Taiwan as an apocalyptic landscape is composed of prolonged and intensive looks at objects, scenery, and human bodies and faces that, through the camera's mediation, lose their prefigured signification and transform into a sight that is not yet thinkable. Distinct from the clichéd depiction of human suffering that satisfies the humanitarian impulse—a recurrent structure of representation that depends on the separation between a universalized construction of human and nonhuman others—Tsai's static and eventless urbanscape accentuates limitations in the existing spectrum of representation.[8] For example, Tsai expresses his fascination with a mundane but indescribable urban landscape that becomes the spatial protagonist in *Stray Dogs*. The filmmaker writes:

> A lake appeared in the script.
> The father takes his son and daughter boating at the lake.
> He is completely drunk
> and wants to kill himself with his children.
> The children hide in the tall grasses by the lake
> and wait for their father to sober up.

"I can't remember how many times I have revised this opening scene and how many times I have changed it to something else again. Yet the lake always remained," recalls Tsai. The lake that haunts him is a mundane urban space and part of an everyday landscape in Asian cities that is hypervisible but illegible as an affective space in any traditional category (see figure 5.2). From the perspective of the film's protagonists—a homeless father and his two children who live in an abandoned urban ruin surrounded by giant trees and greenery—the lake is evocative of a paradox. It is on one hand a lifeline, a daily crossing and a pathway to the city center for work and other excursions that sustain their meager life, but on the other hand, it is an entrapment that locks them in the socioeconomic hierarchies of the neoliberal urban fabric. As the Malaysian Taiwanese filmmaker recalls, "I searched everywhere for a place like that [in Taiwan]. . . . In front of the Japanese colonial office building, there was a very large pond. There had been plans to construct new buildings. But when they dug out the foundations, water flowed out and construction was halted. It was abandoned and soon overgrown with grass and trees. It turned into a lake."[9] Out of time and out of place, this lake turns into a conceptual abyss, a visible-incomprehensible, a site that illuminates the gap between vision and cognition, an aesthetic form that evokes urban horror.

Within the film, the lake is at once an urban oasis and a natural playground for the children and a psychological abyss where the father contemplates suicide and the murder of his children. Beyond the film, as the

FIGURE 5.2. The lake in *Stray Dogs* (2013), an artificial oasis formed in the symbiosis of man-made gentrification and the reclaiming force of nature.

filmmaker describes it, the lake is everywhere in developing Asian cities, where the ebb and flow of construction leave behind numerous *in-between* sites.[10] They are caught in between construction and destruction, the no-longer and the not-yet, and the legible and illegible. Their status depends on a contingent value-assignment system that creates different modalities of value and valuelessness and exposes groups of people and their ecological environment to injury, violence, and death.

Evoked by the phenomenological experience produced by a film that accompanies Tsai's discovery of a new crisis landscape, a new type of intensely felt presence—through immersive episodes of watching human characters sleep, cry, and breathe, and nonhuman agents (mostly urban ruins) as they disappear and fall out of sight—emerges along with a new structure of feeling. Not the scripted horror aimed at inducing a physical response from the body, the horror in this case refers to the knowledge of not knowing and the feeling of not knowing how to feel, for the characters living in precarity and for the viewers who watch the condition of precarity in a work of art. The indeterminacy persists as an open-ended question, returning at unexpected moments when the audience exits the screening and engages in the same everyday rituals of feeding, working, and resting. The films create a new sensory organ through a phenomenological link established by the performance of the body, shaping the affective intensities that define the present time.

Contrary to the assumption that the cinematic visibility of capital's abjects—referring to precarious lives that are neither subject nor object—creates an ethical relationship between the onlooker and the marginalized subjects on screen, Tsai's characteristic long takes of human bodies breathing, sleeping, eating, urinating, longing, singing, and crying pose an unresolved question of the future of cinema: What ethical relations should one have with the bodies in media circulation that are now visible everywhere?[11] Suspending the conventional narrative structure, the films resist *telling* the story of marginalized lives, an act that relies on preconceived notions of horror, abuse, and exploitation. Letting go of the scripted narrative of horror that has become the conventional way of establishing a relationship between onlookers and marginalized others, the films' depictions of daily trivialities and basic human functions criticize the cinematic desire to give a voice to less privileged subjects.[12] Instead of transforming the nonhuman to the human, the deliberate evacuation of narrative storytelling and the acoustic tracks filled with silence and noise exist as reminders of the unassimilability of precarious lives in a conventional humanizing framework that replicates the structure subjecting these lives to the state of nonbeing. Therefore Tsai's metacinema relies on a method of recycling that simulates the rhizomic development of multiplicitous narratives, where the same actors, objects, behaviors, and spaces reappear in repetitions and differences. The intertextual and metaphoric montage of faces, bodies, characters, and encounters blurs the boundaries among individual films, encouraging interpollination in the production of meaning and resulting in intimate yet distant sensations of déjà vu and familiarity. Depicting no past or future, these films replace conventional storytelling with a phenomenological state of existence in which legibility is subject to the forces of contingency.

Portraying precarious lives on a precarious island, Tsai's films explore an emergent crisis landscape that replaces scripted horror with a visual and acoustic landscape of emptiness, where the concepts of "nothing" and "nothingness" are represented as a new modality of knowledge not assimilable to the prior modes of being and nonbeing. According to Leszek Kolakowski, the history of Western philosophy can be summarized in the phrase *metaphysical horror*, referring to his observation that philosophy's quest for meaning always ends in nothingness. However, this nothingness is not a literal nothing but a history of ideas—such as God, the absolute, cogito, ego, and I—that attempt to understand what exists beyond the immediately perceptible world. Even if the quest always ends in nothingness, the desire is real, and the drive to ask is a tendency of being human. The nothing in question is never no-thing, but a concept that is placed beyond the established order of the world, that exists like a "specter of never-ending uncertainty" bound to reappear.[13] Whereas Kolakowski explores nothing as Western philosophy's confrontation with its own limits of knowing, nothing as a central concept in Asian Buddhism has reemerged in recent comparative studies of Buddhism and Western critical theory, especially Marxism, psychoanalysis, and poststructuralist theory.[14] Taking up the intersection between Marxism and contemporary Buddhism that share the same historical situation of global capitalism and the same utopian possibilities in the critique of the present, the analysis of Tsai's cinema of precarity focuses on highlighting the filmmaker's exploration of a Marxist-Buddhist aesthetics of nothingness.

In Tsai's short film series *The Walker* (2012)—*Walker* (*Xingzhe*), *Sleepwalk* (*Mengyou*), and *Diamond Sutra* (*Jingang jing*)—Lee Kang-sheng plays the Chinese Buddhist monk Xuanzang from Wu Cheng'en's celebrated sixteenth-century novel *Journey to the West*. Xuanzang traveled from China to regions that are now Pakistan, India, Nepal, and Bangladesh during the Tang dynasty (seventh century), bringing back Buddhist scriptures and teachings that shaped Buddhism in China and opened the imagination of China's frontiers. Performing a walk with deliberate, intense slowness in bustling cities like Hong Kong, Lee's character is dressed in a red robe. The movement of his body is out of sync with the rhythm and speed of neoliberal urban space. In an interview, Tsai explains his fascination with the Buddhist monk:

> I wanted to make a film about walking, and Xuanzang came naturally to mind. . . . Walking was difficult, especially during Xuanzang's time. Where was India and what did India mean would only remain an ambiguous idea. . . . Therefore I admire him. There was an idea motivating him. This idea could be very simple. It was about bringing enlightenment to the world. Why does the world need enlightenment? He must have sympathized with the people. But don't you think the way people live now also deserves sympathy? This is a much busier and faster world, with more needs to satisfy. But in the end, these pursuits may only lead to an empty void.[15]

Freely interpreting Xuanzang's walk and his Buddhist teaching—a mode of association that should be distinguished from the cinematic adaptation of Xuanzang's ideas—Tsai is not proposing an erudite study of Chinese Buddhism but an experiment with concepts that challenge the given values of

FIGURE 5.3. Tsai Ming-liang's *Journey to the West* (2014) features Lee Kang-sheng as a Buddhist monk who walks with deliberate, intense slowness in the streets of Marseille, France.

capitalist societies. Lee's slow walk covers select Asian cities, then is subsequently continued in *Journey to the West* (*Xi you*, 2014), the last installment of the *Walker* series that references the sixteenth-century novel, reaching as far as the streets of Marseille, France (see figure 5.3). Presented as a work of cinematic art and a live performance in *Xuanzang* (2014), where Lee slowly walks across a theater stage, the series turns the human body into a medium of time and space, producing new conceptions of temporalities, spatialities, and sensations that are not commensurable with the modes of perception conditioned by the capitalist demand of speed, utility, and quantifiable results. The walk that consists of nothing—no event, no beginning or end, and minimal movement—is driven by a desire that remains ungraspable. From Tsai's perspective, the *Walker* series shares an affinity with Xuanzang's walk fourteen hundred years ago. The walk fascinates because it is motivated by the desire for enlightenment—a threshold and limit separated by many hundreds of years of geographical, economic, and political differences yet remains a structure in search of a better world that keeps returning.

Performing slowness as an aesthetics of nothingness, the temporal phenomenology of Tsai's recent work has translated into a unique way of seeing and sensing Asian urban space, which is a deliberate choice of setting for Tsai's portrayal of life in precarity. From the usage of silence and noise that challenges the boundary between culture and nature, to the focus on trivial daily acts that one does alone, such as taking a bath or boiling water, Tsai presents a collection of nothingness from which he develops a Marxist-Buddhist aesthetics of emptiness. Contradicting the logic of utility, meaning, and being, the sights and sounds of nothingness are surprisingly everywhere and embedded in the most intimate textures of everyday life in Taiwanese and Southeast Asian cities. Existing as the illegible *othered* city, as if in another spatial-temporal dimension, the shadow presence of the other city and its inhabitants becomes a cruel reminder of the existence of multiplicitous modes of being and the givenness of the system of legibility that controls the assignment of value and valuelessness according to the capitalist definitions of utility and waste. Rather than reciting stories of abuse that further subject precarious lives to the state of nonbeing, Tsai's empty crisis landscape exposes the senses to the realm of nothing. Portraying alternative rhythms of time and the various social vantage points of the films' recurrent characters, the collection of nothing challenges the preconceived notion associated with the concept of nothing as lack or void. The cinematic experience of nothing results in the senses' reorientation, hinting at alternative social orders and channels of communication.

Circumventing the representation of densely populated Asian cities through images that evoke speed and movement, Tsai's empty crisis landscape suggests a different kind of political unconscious: not the desire to remap Taiwan and its geopolitical position in the global world system, nor the strategy of exoticizing and commodifying Taiwan as a developing country in the market of global visual culture, but the recognition of bodies, cities, and nations in a state of precarity, existing neither here nor there, but always strategically conjured for economic and political profitability. As the filmmaker says, "I am talking about people in limbo. We don't always fit nicely into our environment, and sometimes we are neither here nor there."[16] Providing the context, material condition, temporality, and space for thinking about a position of perpetual marginality—required to maintain a preexisting system of legibility that underlies global empires, economic social class, heteronormativity, and more—Taiwan as a precarious island motivates the collection of illegible presences through which a transnational landscape of precarity highlights not marginality per se but the conditions that intensify under neoliberal post-socialist economic processes of re- or deterritorialization, in which precarity is sanctioned. Under this premise, Tsai's crisis landscape of nothing provides a new aesthetics to address the condition of living with insecurity and contingency, a language that evokes the horror of not knowing, not recognizing what is already happening and within one's intimate proximity.

The Anatomy of an Apartment as Crisis Landscape

The world is counting down to the end of the millennium, the year 2000 only seven days away. Yet an apocalypse has already taken hold of Taiwan. Tsai's *The Hole* (*Dong*, 1998) begins with a black screen. The news of the apocalypse arrives without visual representation; instead fragmented pieces of information about a spreading epidemic and an involuntary quarantine arrive through the film's audio track, which simulates broadcast news. The lack of visual input creates a sense of chaos enhanced by conflicting viewpoints, both from the protesting residents who are forced to abandon their homes and from patronizing government officials promising a quick solution. "I think they should just light a fire and burn us all, together with the garbage!" says a resident living in abandoned apartments in the quarantine zone that has been denied garbage collection services, where human lives are left like overflowing trash. As the voice of an official from the water company offers more bad news—water service will be discontinued in the quarantine zone starting at midnight, January 1, 2000, and all residents are under mandatory evacuation—the emotional tone used to convey this decision further highlights the themes of isolation and marginalization, as well as the strategic creation and management of nonbeings made in the name of public interest.

Foucault observes that governmental reason in its modern form no longer deals directly with people and things but with the "interests" they represent:

> On the basis of the new governmental reason—and this is the point of separation between the old and the new, between *raison d'État* and reason of the least state—government must no longer intervene, and it no longer has a direct hold on things and people; it can only exert a hold, it is only legitimate, founded in law and reason, to intervene, insofar as interest, or interests, the interplay of interest, make a particular individual, thing, good, wealth, or process of interest for individuals, or for the set of individuals, or for the interest of a given individual faced with the interest of all, etcetera. Government is only interested in interests.

Not concerned with individual bodies or communities, the new governmental reason no longer exercises the power of government over specific subjects and things, but over what Foucault calls the "phenomenal republic of interests," where the calculations and exchanges of interests replace the true value of things.[17] The protesting, angry voices of residents whose bodies and faces never appear in *The Hole* become acoustic reminders of bodies in disappearance, not because they do not exist but because their presence depends on the value assigned to them. Set in a public housing apartment complex awaiting demolition in Taipei, *The Hole*—which literally refers to a hole between upstairs and downstairs apartment units, made by a plumber who goes missing—is representative of Tsai's collection of abandoned and ruinous apartments located in the heart of densely developed urban centers in Taiwan and Southeast Asia. Tsai's portrayals of Asian cities in competition with one another in the global neoliberal economy center on a crisis landscape haunted by the scarcity of human bodies. Yet the absent presences of these bodies seep through the materiality and texture of the built environment that, like the Mystic Writing Pad discussed by Freud, retains memory traces even after the surface memory is erased.[18]

Often stripped to the walls, with minimal furnishing or other household items, the apartments and other residences are old, empty, moldy, flooded, leaking, or without running water, and infested with pests or cockroaches. As Tsai transitioned from 35mm film to digital filmmaking, a change he made between *Visage* (*Lian*, 2009) and *Stray Dogs*, the dilapidation of apartment buildings, construction sites, and more acquired new, vivid details through digitally enhanced sharpness.[19] In *Stray Dogs*, the first feature-length film Tsai made with a digital camera, the interior scenery is composed of vivid and extreme close-ups of cracks, peeled paint, and moldy, blackened walls in a rundown building. Positioning the camera in intimate proximity to the wrinkled and curled up surfaces of the wall, where the material histories of paint, plaster, water stains, and other elements accumulate over time, the slow-moving camera functions like an invisible hand, touching and remembering histories that can only be allegorized in a child's story (see figure 5.4). Told by a little girl who is scared of the cracks devouring the house, the story that fills the audio track concerns a community of frogs living in a pond. Tired of being weak and mistreated, the frogs pray to the fairy for a king for protection but end up being eaten by the crane their supposed savior sends. "Are there cracks in the wall because of ghosts?" the girl asks. "The wall is sick," answers one of the women in the film, Chen Shiang-chyi. As the camera continues to follow dark, indecipherable marks that spread throughout the building, the origin of the cancerous growth is never revealed. The personal histories among the film's three women (Yang Kuei-mei, Chen Shiang-chyi,

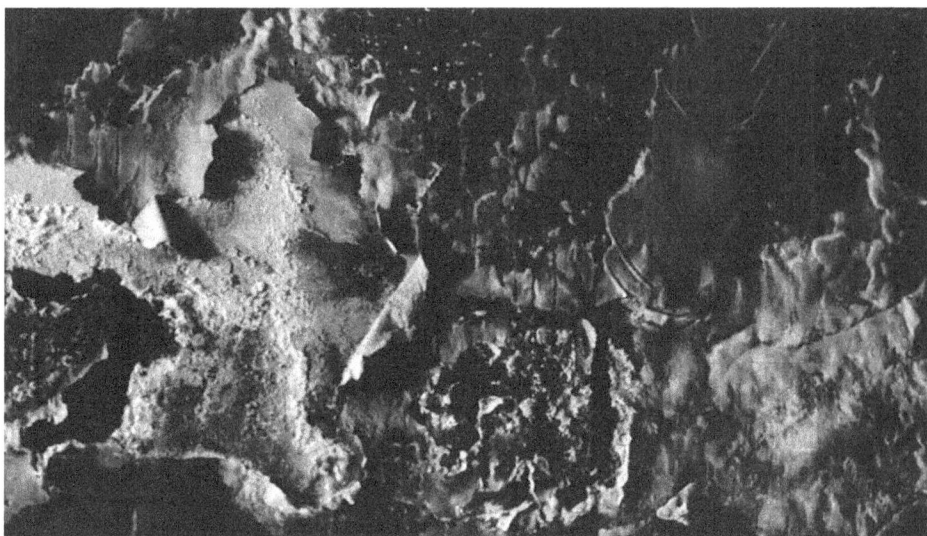

FIGURE 5.4. Positioning the camera in intimate proximity to the wrinkled and curled up surfaces of the wall, Tsai's slow-moving camera functions like an invisible hand, touching and remembering histories that can only be allegorized in a child's story in *Stray Dogs* (2013).

and Lu Yi-ching) and Lee Kang-sheng, whose relationships develop in different forms across different films, are like the buried histories in the wall. They unfold in the canvas created by the close-up but are coded in the secret ink of history that leaves behind only strange lines and shapes. Although a recent digital production, *Stray Dogs* continues Tsai's experiments with the landscape of precarity, from which he develops a language to see, sense, and hear the negative presences of lives lived in precarity. Rather than proving their existence, the films' focus on secrets and histories that cannot be told directs attention to the structures that make disappearance possible and that disguise the traces of violent subjection.

Relying on the spectral returns of actors, spaces, objects (like the rice cooker), pet fish, and other cinematic body-spaces, Tsai's filmmaking fundamentally defies the capitalist economic principle embedded in the definition of a film that is bound by the concept of an event and the desire to avoid wasted time.[20] As characters (played by the same actors) develop their relationships across films and encounter their recorded selves from the past, the infinitely multiplying possibilities drastically expand the boundaries of perception, presenting a challenge to the existing limitations of the sensible world. According to Rancière, who revises the conventional Marxist approach to aesthetics as the effects of politics, aesthetics should be reconsidered as the dominant social force reshaping the distribution of the sensible world, responsible for delimiting the distinctions between space and time, the visible and the invisible, and sound and noise. Rethinking aesthetics as the "configurations of experience that create new modes of sense perception and induce novel forms of political subjectivity," Rancière's utopian approach to aesthetics essentially highlights an imaginative space of transcendence that nonetheless provides a way of thinking about aesthetics as a dominant historical regime that conditions perceptible channels of communication.[21] The film, or what can be conceptualized as a metafilm that Tsai is making across time, fundamentally challenges the social function and meaning of film as a set of reproducible practices that reflect the rationalizing capitalist logic of efficiency (i.e., the convention of screening time, the concept of the cinematic event, etc.). To understand Tsai's cinematic investment in precarious lives it is first necessary to consider the filmmaking practice that sets his work apart from that of his contemporaries in the Sinophone world.

Working with the same crew, the same faces, and the same characters, Tsai challenges the capitalist logic of waste and disposability. Approaching film as a medium whose images of the past and future are allowed to coexist, Tsai emphasizes the afterlife of images and fundamentally resists a film consumption culture built upon amnesia. Victor Burgin, in proposing the concept of a "remembered film," suggests that *film* should be understood as the virtual extension of a film's interior content and its afterlife to shape new rhizomic meanings in one's encounters with sounds and images over a lifetime.[22] A similar point is made by the filmmaker and writer Raoul Ruiz, who describes the experience of film as a "fragmentary *rebus*" that resembles the process of making dreams through "random juxtapositions of diverse elements across unrelated spatial and temporal locations."[23] Tsai makes films that are uncontainable in themselves. They seep out of the screen and the temporal duration of the film, suggesting the existence of a deterritorialized affect that is neither here nor there. One of Tsai's techniques involves the exploration of the face as a time machine, a platform for the coexistence of temporalities. Inviting some of the most iconic faces in cinematic history to be part of his films—including Jean-Pierre Léaud, the French New Wave actress Jeanne Moreau, and Chinese *wuxia* genre hero Miao Tian—Tsai uses the face as a multisensory screen that triggers sudden flashes of meaning.[24] The aged and sullen face of Miao, for example, becomes the embodiment of the taciturn and distant father in Tsai's films but never ceases to play a double role, continuing its part in King Hu's *wuxia* masterpiece, *Dragon Inn* (*Longmen kezhan*, 1967), which made Miao an international star during the Cold War. Similarly the recurrence of Lee Kang-sheng and Tsai's regular female cast undoes the singularity of meaning attached to their physical bodies.

Depicting the body not as a superficial surface that has ephemeral cultural values but as a corporeal being with insatiable physical and emotional desires, Tsai's cinema of precarity explores the fundamental definition of *life* as the universalizable cruelty of existence. The body that requires constant food, fluids, and emotional care is made into one of the films' crisis landscapes, where the fragile corporeality of the body is performed in resistance to the neoliberal production and management of life for its economic value. Cruelty has been historically associated with violent behavior, atrocity, and acts that inflict pain and human suffering. As a technique of governmentality, cruelty lies at the heart of criminal prosecution, penal punishment, and other technologies of biopolitics that compete to produce the definition of life. When the playwright and theater director Antonin Artaud wrote about his vision for a "theater of cruelty" during the interwar era in early twentieth-century France, he put forth cruelty as a principle of artistic production, defining the social function of art as action against the dominant regime of perception. In *The Theater and Its Double*, Artaud begins with a call to make a "culture-in-action." He writes, "We must insist upon the idea of culture-in-action, of culture growing within us like a new organ, a sort of second breath." The culture-in-action is the making of the theater of cruelty. Referring to a practice of art that shows the audience the overbearing truth rather than a conventionally defined definition of cruelty as sadism or physical bloodshed, Artaud writes, "One can very well imagine a pure cruelty, without bodily laceration. And philosophically speaking what indeed is cruelty? From the point of view of the mind, cruelty signifies rigor, implacable intention and decision, irreversible and absolute determination."[25] The making of a theater of cruelty, based on Artaud's description, requires persistence and discipline. In describing cinema's relationship to thought, Deleuze's *Cinema* books crystallize in a discussion of cinema's capacity to induce the powerlessness of thought. While moving images may easily take control of one's thoughts, Deleuze argues that these moments of powerlessness are precisely the locus of philosophy. Citing Artaud, Deleuze summarizes the theoretical affinities they share: "In short, it is the totality of cinema-thought relations that Artaud overturns. . . . If it is true that thought depends on a shock which gives birth to it (the nerve, the brain matter), it can only think one thing, *the fact that we are not yet thinking*."[26] Such is the birth of thought and what Artaud calls culture-in-action. In the case of Tsai's emphasis on a bodily nothing—bodies that are in their natural states of breathing, sleeping, eating, and other functions—the body landscape is a mode of the theater of cruelty. The body is re-presented as a cultural space that is not yet thinkable and that, through the recurrence of characters, transforms into a site of compulsive returns, where irresolvable dilemmas, both personal and societal, stubbornly replay.

The Plumber Is Missing: *The Hole* (1998) and
the Collection of Dysfunctional Bathrooms

Having established a filmmaking practice that puts the disposability of the body in question, I return in this section to the scarcity of human bodies in densely populated Taiwanese and Southeast Asian cities. If these bodies are made to disappear under the global neoliberal conditions that subject them to nonbeing, the exploration of life in precarity depicts a correspondent urbanscape in crisis. An idiosyncratic collection of spaces in abjection in Tsai's work—including dysfunctional bathrooms, flooded apartments, and broken elevators—suggests a burgeoning philosophy of the powers of horror. Julia Kristeva defines the abject as neither subject nor object. The abject is a state of non/being that puts one on the edge of nonexistence and hallucination that, if acknowledged, threatens one's sense of self and life. Yet the abject's indeterminate state and its disrespect of borders, positions, and rules draw attention to the fragility of the law, questioning established identities, systems, and orders.[27] Translating the abject into a cinematic urban form, Tsai's collection of dysfunctional bathrooms, for example, is not meant to represent the clean or the unclean but to show the insufficiency of the divide, which conceals a space where the fundamental state of being human, a state the filmmaker explores as universal, is put on display. The bathroom provides a view of developing Asian cities from a unique perspective usually kept invisible. In a place where the most basic human needs are tended to, the body is also given a new set of meanings. In the filmmaker's utopian egalitarianism, all bodies are fundamental units of desires. Desiring food, water, air, intimacy, and care, the body channels, performs, and remembers these needs. The cycle of needs repeats itself. Life consists of alternating fulfillment and disappointment. The bodies that occupy the space of the abject are made to exist through their human needs, while at the same time exposing the cruelty of existence as the repetition of desires that overflow and return cyclically.

Often nonfunctioning, flooded, or lacking water, bathrooms and toilets in Tsai's films suspend modern conveniences. The plumbing system's paralysis releases bodies from their ingrained daily routines and from the value systems that distinguish among sexes, sexualities, ethnicities, and social classes. As abjected social spaces that are often considered private, the bathrooms induce behaviors that highlight the fragility and artificiality of meaning-making systems. Introduced to Asia as part of colonial modernity during the late nineteenth and early twentieth century, the infrastructure of plumbing technology refers to the systematized protocol of waste management but also the social construction of public health as a concept and a set of governmental technologies of biopolitical control.[28] Tsai's bathrooms raise questions about uncovering a public history of violence where value systems separating the self and otherness are reproduced in the urban technology designed to handle and dispose of waste—a concept that is created in the systems that assign value, function, and utility to specific social groups, nature, and the environment. By temporarily suspending the grid of legibility, Tsai's dysfunctional bathrooms generate no feelings of disgust or repulsion but rather provide a space of conflict where bodies as matters of public interest and bodies made of fundamental human needs create new tensions against the value systems of neoliberalizing Asian cities.

Tsai conveys the bathroom—whether private or public, male or female, modern or traditional—as an emergent cultural site for staging, shaping, and structuring the question of subjectivity in the neoliberal era of radical dispossession. Observing the emergence of the "apartment plot" in postwar American film and popular culture, Pamela Wojcik suggests that the apartment is the mise-en-scène and highlights the ways in which the apartment plot provides a lens to historicize the conceptions of family, work, sexuality, and urban space.[29] Illuminating the cultural significance of the apartment in conditioning the visibility of nonheteronormative, nonwhite, and other nonconformative lives, Wojcik proposes a method of reading the fluidity between an architectural space and its afterlife in the cultural realm. Tsai's "bathroom plot," in the same vein, presents a set of cultural artifacts imbued with historical significance. When Tanizaki Junichiro wrote in the early 1930s about Japanese-style bathrooms in *In Praise of Shadows*, the contrast he observed between Japanese- and Western-style toilets turns into a philosophical treatise on shadows and light. Whereas the former leads to an aesthetic realm of shadow play, indiscernible shapes, and infinite possibilities of ambiguity, the latter is characterized as the light of exposure that distinguishes between the clean and the unclean, the visible and the invisible, and the modern and the rest. He writes, "The cleanliness of what can be seen only calls up the more clearly thoughts of what cannot be seen. In such places the distinction between the clean and the unclean is best left obscure, shrouded in a dusky haze."[30] Commenting on the materiality of "modern sanitary facilities"—pure white porcelain, metal fixtures, and electric lights and heating—Tanizaki transforms every detail of the modern bathroom into a piece of evidence for the encroachment of a new regime of visibility dependent on the logic of excessive illumination and exposure. The Japanese-style toilet provides a counterpoint for thinking the (il)legibility of the body that has become overexposed in the regime of light and sanitation, transforming the site of self-care into an intimate panopticon that manages biopolitical definitions of meaning and nonmeaning.

In the context of post–Cold War Taiwan, where closer economic integration between the PRC and the rest of the Sinophone world provides the historical setting for the emergence of the bathroom plot, Tsai's focus on toilets, bathtubs, and a plumbing crisis probes the body as a site of political subjectivity. As the end of the Cold War initiates new migration trends in the reterritorialization of economic networks, the relations among Taiwan, China, and Southeast Asian countries are increasingly conditioned by shifting labor demands, creating a new class of transnational migrants whose mobility and displacement are determined by the economic values assigned to their bodies. Tsai's collection of bodies-bathrooms is characterized by bodies-in-precarity who occupy the space and by the focus on bodily temporalities in the state of needing care. The camera's long takes patiently wait for the acts of relieving, cleaning, renewing, and caring for oneself and others, suggesting the bathroom as a space for bodily performativity and new types of community and (homo)sociality.

While dysfunctional (and functional) bathrooms exist throughout Tsai's metacinema, *The Hole* is a particularly salient example. The film shows a city in paralysis, a rain-drenched and virus-infested Taiwan where a plumber goes missing in a quarantine zone overfilling with garbage. The film begins with a crisis of waste management. Like the garbage that continues to pile up, residents in a public housing community have been abandoned by the government. Isolated and cut off from the infrastructure of sanitation, the residents' crisis turns into a series of frustrating, comical, and fantastical encounters with others and the self, beginning with the hole the plumber makes between two apartments before going missing himself. Commissioned by French Television La Sept Arte as part of a world cinema project titled "2000 Seen By: An International Collection," *The Hole* represents Tsai's vision of a near future to come, seen by many as the end of the world and the end of human civilization.[31] Popularly believed to be the beginning of a new millennium, the year 2000 was also culturally significant because of the theological interpretation of the Christian apocalypse in the Book of Revelations, when the Second Coming, the return of Christ, would lead the world to salvation. As Christianity plays a sizable role in universalizing the imaginary of global doom, the connection between religion and the end of human civilization quickly transformed into a media franchise that at the same time desires and fears what Susan Sontag calls the "imagination of disaster" and the "aesthetics of destruction." Commenting specifically on postwar science fiction genres, Sontag writes, "In place of an intellectual workout, they can supply something the novels can never provide—sensuous elaborations. In the films it is by means of images and sounds, not words that have to be translated by imagination, that one can participate in the fantasy of living through one's own death and more, the death of cities, the destruction of humanity itself."[32] During the transition between two millennia, the dystopic setting of *The Hole* may lead to speculation that the film was created to participate in the global franchise of the disaster genre. However, as the film's opening suggests, Tsai's approach begins with a void, a crisis landscape that sets itself apart from the conventional postwar disaster genre, whose cinematic technologies create what Sontag calls "sensuous elaborations," highlighting the indiscernibility between fetishization and critical reflexivity embedded in the genre itself.

Devoid of visual spectacles, the disaster in *The Hole* centers on life in an abandoned public housing community, where apartments are examined not simply as architectural spaces but as forms of urban living, that is, patterns of behavior and psychological states. In contrast to the mansions and penthouses that lie at the heart of the urban imaginaries of neoliberalizing Asian cities, the apartments in Tsai's work always evoke an urban limbo. In Bih Herng-dar and Chen Yi-ling's study of gender's relation to Taiwan's housing problems, they observe a recurrent patriarchal logic in the Taiwanese government's neoliberal approach to the issue of housing. As a developing country under the leadership of an authoritarian government since 1949, Taiwan's public policies are primarily focused on state-led stimulants for economic development. With housing defined as a mercantile consumer good, the lack of affordable housing is masked by a government-endorsed neoliberal discourse that delegates the issue of homeownership to the private sector.[33] This framework directly affects specific social groups: women, singles, queers, and foreign migrant workers. This social-gender-economic class of people who do not conform to reproductive heteronormativity bear the invisible burden of rising housing costs and social scrutiny.

Drifting and lingering in apartments, abandoned buildings, construction sites, parks, and bathrooms, precarious lives appear and disappear in Tsai's depiction of urban wastelands. The bathroom in particular is a site of haunting that returns and presses for more questions. Like the apartment plot that provides a cultural space for imagining nonheteronormative and nonconforming lives, the collection of bathrooms is motivated by specific kinds of social unconscious. Starting with the clogged drain that stays mysteriously flooded and unclogs of its own will in Tsai's first feature film, *Rebels of the Neon God* (*Qingshaonian Nezha*, 1992), Tsai's crisis urbanscape continues through *The River* (*Heliu*, 1997), where the father struggles with a leaking roof throughout the film, which depicts the incestuous sexual encounter between father and son in a public bathhouse. In *The Hole*, a plumber visits Lee Kang-sheng's apartment and disappears after drilling a hole between his apartment and the one downstairs. As the film progresses, the woman living downstairs (played by one of Tsai's recurrent cast members, Yang Kuei-mei) grows increasingly frustrated as the hole turns into a peephole where sounds, voyeuristic gazes, and bodily fluids from Lee pass through. Agitated, the woman employs a wide range of antisurveillance techniques—filling the hole with a mop, taping up the hole, and spraying pesticide against spying eyes—but to no avail. After the news broadcast announces that a French virologist, Dr. Carpentier, has helped identify the contagious epidemic known as "Taiwan fever," caused by the "Taiwan virus," the woman downstairs begins to display symptoms, first a flu-like fever, followed by bug-like behaviors such as crawling, photophobia, and the tendency to hide in dark and humid corners. The hole in the film is not only the architectural hole between two apartments but also a symbolic fracturing of a claustrophobic architectural segmentation designed to economize space. With no spoken dialogue, the film accentuates the distance and isolation among urban residents while uncovering new sensory channels where, for example, a character's involuntary sneeze in the bathtub opens up a new cinematic dimension of exuberant sexual and flirtatious fantasies in a lip-synced musical dance performance.[14] The silence of the film creates new modes of listening and visual spectatorship, challenging the existing regime of perception and values.

As the woman becomes infected with the virus, her exaggerated crawling around the apartment is paired with a flirtatious phone call she makes to the plumber, whose identity remains unknown. In Franz Kafka's *The Metamorphosis*, the hardworking salesman Gregor Samsa turns into a bug one morning after waking up from a dream. While dramatizing the unimaginable physical transformation, the novella centers on the psychological mentality of the insect Gregor eventually becomes. One of his favorite pastimes, for instance, is hanging from the ceiling. While he enjoys the sensation of aloofness, viewing the world upside down also provides an expanded perspective that is no longer confined to the vertical social hierarchy that defined his former human life. Utilizing every part of Gregor's apartment to stage his physical and psychological metamorphoses, Kafka describes the family's clearing of furniture and objects to make way for the bug's gigantic body. Without worldly possessions, feelings of euphoria and freedom emerge. Changing bodies and perspectives provides a new form of extrication. The rationalizing logic of the capitalist accumulation of wealth, social status, and upward mobility undergoes a crisis, exposed as a former distribution of the sensible world that is no longer applicable. Similar to Gregor, the woman in *The Hole* is released from her former routine of labor after the infection. When the connected apartments become flooded—the man's toilet flush upstairs causes an inexplicable leak in the apartment downstairs—the woman mops the floor, transports huge bundles of tissues away from the water, and sits on the toilet with a bucket on her head to stay dry. The labor of maintaining cleanliness is parodied in the scene where the woman is seen hoarding a room full of tissues in a flooded apartment during Taiwan's rainy season. However, as she succumbs to the disease, the end of her misery arrives when her cruel and childish neighbor sends down a helping hand. The hole is a meeting point for uncontainable desires of intimacy and acknowledgment in search of a channel of communication.

The bathroom plot—full of allusions to the possibilities of touching, contact, proximity, and exposure—is motivated by secret presences. Nicolas Abraham and Maria Torok call these secret presences a crypt, based on Freud's case study of Sergei Pankejeff, the "wolf man" whose childhood trauma stays encrypted in the prelinguistic stage. His multilingual background encases his memory in complex wordplay, ciphers, and rebuses.[35] In Derrida's reading, the crypt refers to a paradoxical exteriority that exists inside the interstices of the psychological interior.[36] More complex than the unconscious itself, the crypt is part of an inexpressible self within the conscious mind that lacks the means of communication. Collecting not only bathrooms but also behaviors, the space of the bathroom does not reveal presences, conscious desires, or existing histories; rather, it focuses on existences that compulsively return but are hidden in negative forms. From Lee Kang-sheng and his father's sexual intimacy in the dark public bathhouse in *The River* to Chen Shiang-chyi's monotonous cleaning of the public toilet that functions as a gesture of care and tribute to the disappearing old theater house on its last day of business in *Goodbye, Dragon Inn*, the collection of bathrooms alludes to a pattern of returning. The socially marked space and time that are conditioned by the logic of disposability paradoxically become the site where feelings surface, linger, and emerge. The bathroom plot is essentially a way of reexamining the cultural logic of disposability while opening up new ethical questions about the condition of precarity.

The visibility of the characters, objects, and spaces that appear in Tsai's films poses a problematic of presence. Conforming to neither the stereotype of the victim or the oppressed, nor the demand to hear their humanized voice, Tsai's approach to precarious life relies upon the deconstruction of the established regimes of the visible and audible world. Only when the givenness of the established order of the senses is challenged can the history of violent erasure and the strategic management of nonbeing resurface. The existence of the crypt—a kernel of knowledge that remains incommunicable through language—challenges the role and function of language as a means of communication. What is said conveys as it simultaneously conceals. As Tsai's films operate without the conventional means of communication—such as spoken dialogue, camera movement, and plot—they probe the existence of undeliverable experiences that can find no linguistic means of expression. Yet the films are hardly mute and in fact are saturated with an unconventional soundtrack of noises that are not audible as narrative sounds. The attentive mode of listening to the sounds of storms, raindrops, breathing, eating, kissing, and urination constructs an acoustic space conventionally suppressed in narrative cinema. Employing sounds associated with emptiness, unintelligible noise, or simply *lack*, Tsai's circumvention of spoken language and narrative dialogue suggests the development of an *acoustic visuality* that counters the commodified demand for the voice of those living in limbo, belonging neither here nor there.

Acoustic Visuality: *I Don't Want to Sleep Alone* (2006), Kuala Lumpur, and the Politics of Noise

Throughout Tsai's career as a filmmaker, he made only one film with a conventional nondiegetic musical soundtrack. Composer Huang Shu-run's work for *Rebels of the Neon God* won the award for best original score at the Golden Horse Film Festival in Taiwan for an acoustic track that seems to perfectly simulate the blinking neon lights and the night world of Taipei through a rhythmic repetitive tempo and low-bass beats.[37] Despite its success, Tsai considers the postproduction soundtrack, which essentially changed the meaning of the film, an utter failure. Searching for a philosophy of sound that will reorient the senses, the filmmaker's subsequent films deploy a silent soundscape that complicates the notion of having or assigning a voice to specific social groups—a practice that potentially replicates the management of being and nonbeing in the neoliberal value system.

Difficulties of communication have always preoccupied theorists and artists who portray urban mental life. While Tsai gave full attention to this theme in his earlier films, failures of verbal communication seem to reach an extreme in his first feature made in Malaysia. Released shortly after the SARS pandemic that transformed all of South China, including Hong Kong and Taiwan, into isolated quarantine zones, *I Don't Want to Sleep Alone* (*Hei yanquan*, 2006) dramatizes the impossibility of verbal communication amid a pandemic that requires every citizen to wear a face mask. As families and friends are forced to surveil themselves to contain the disease, interpersonal relationships go into crisis, creating invisible wounds that remain unaddressed.[38] In a condition in which verbal communication is made literally impossible, language is put to the test. Introducing a new character to the cast, representing the foreign migrant workers from India and Indonesia working in Malaysia, the film addresses the community of workers living across multiple linguistic and cultural borders, where languages contribute minimally to meaningful communication. Creating a soundtrack without words, *I Don't Want to Sleep Alone* presents an acoustic space of nonvoices with the multifarious collage of Malay folksongs, Bollywood music, the sound of clacking mahjong tiles, and the repetitive and deafening noise of construction machines. When given these audio cues, viewers enter a zone of indiscernibility where the distinction between sound and noise, culture and nature, signifying and signified is exposed as a social construction. The sound/noise landscape of Kuala Lumpur opens a new sensory channel, where listening as a mode of knowledge undergoes a dramatic shift. Alluding to the migrant population whose spectral presences are everywhere in the urban fabric of rapidly developing Asian cities, working in construction sites, doing domestic work, and providing care for seniors, the film's collection of indecipherable noises simulates their experience of multilayered displacement. Introducing conflicting notions of realities, the environment becomes surreal for the precarious lives forced into movement, exiled in the perpetual search for economic opportunities.

I Don't Want to Sleep Alone stars Tsai's usual characters Lee Kang-sheng and Chen Shiang-chyi, whose relationship and history remain a mystery since *What Time Is It There?* (*Ni nabian jidian*, 2001). The film follows two disabled young men—the homeless guy and the paralyzed guy, according to the ending credits—both played by Lee. The relationship between the two, whose states of existence put the definition of life into question, is never clarified. They may be strangers, look-alikes, or twins, or they may be in one another's dreams as they lie in bed, waiting for recovery and nursed by the coffeehouse waitress played by Chen or the Malaysian migrant worker Rawang. The two characters are introduced in the opening sequence, first in a static long take that shows the paralyzed Lee lying motionless in bed with his mouth slightly open. The motion of the wind blowing through the window curtains creates a sharp contrast between the world outside and the character's vegetative state. The radio plays Mozart's opera *The Magic Flute*, but we are never sure if he is able to hear it. The scene suddenly transitions to Lee's cinematic double, who has long hair and a beard, walking around Kuala Lumpur, momentarily sharing the same frame with Chen as they stand staring at food in front of a local food stall. Lee and Chen's relationship receives more narrative development as they wander around the city for a place to cuddle. However, Lee's flirtation with multiple characters, including Chen, her boss at the coffee shop, and Rawang, who takes meticulous care of him, allegorizes an ephemerality that does not last. Like the neon flower torch that glows with changing colors in the dark street of Kuala Lumpur (an object that appears throughout the film), the experience of the homeless Lee may be a dream of the paralyzed Lee, who stays in a state of perpetual sleep. The indiscernibility between two distributions of the sensible world sets the tone for *I Don't Want to Sleep Alone*. But the connection between two worlds takes a dramatic turn when a life-threatening haze engulfs the city of Kuala Lumpur. The audience learns from the radio that a wildfire, possibly started by illegal migrant workers, has broken out in nearby Indonesia, producing a dense haze over the Malaysian peninsula.

Malaysia, a former Portuguese, Dutch, and then British colony in Southeast Asia, gained independence in 1957. Among countries worldwide, it has the largest ethnic Chinese minority population (about one-third) by percentage of total population. When the Treaty of Nanjing signed over Hong Kong as a British colony in 1842, the treaty also opened five ports to foreign trade: Canton (Guangzhou), Amoy (Xiamen), Fuzhou, Ningbo, and Shanghai. The opening of Chinese ports intensified trade-related migration and travel, and the number of Chinese settlers in Malaysia reached its high point in the late 1920s, before the colonial government tightened immigration control out of concern over the number of foreign Chinese residents.[39] Tensions escalated between the ethnic Malaysian population and the Malaysian Chinese who were considered squatters in an increasingly competitive labor market under British colonial rule. In the tumultuous moment following the end of World War II, the British administration declared the Malayan Emergency (1948–60), sanctioning military persecution and attacks on the Malayan Communist Party and its guerrilla wars, which were led by overseas Chinese who fought in the anticolonial war against Japan. The violence extended to any ethnic Chinese civilians accused of aiding the insurgencies. The mechanisms of state-led suppression and persecution resulted in involuntary repatriations and deportations of Malaysian Chinese to their "home" countries, leaving behind memories of trauma that persist in contemporary Malayan-Chinese ethnic relations.[40] After the war against ethnicized communism, the Malaysian government implemented the New Economic Policy in 1971 with the explicit goal of enhancing the economic prominence of its Malay population. As Carolyn Cartier observes, the Malaysian government's pro-Malay policy and unpredictable attitudes toward the Chinese community prompted a prominent second wave of immigration, when the skilled Chinese diasporic population relocated to new host countries such as Australia, New Zealand, Canada, and the United States. Working-class Chinese laborers who sought higher compensation in countries such as Taiwan and Japan left behind wives and children in Malaysia, creating what is characterized as "the globalization of husbands" and the "localization of wives."[41]

In Tsai's films, audiences generally receive minimal information about characters' background and history, and *I Don't Want to Sleep Alone* is not an exception. But this tension becomes allegorized in the middle-aged coffee shop owner who flirts with the homeless Chen when her husband disappears on business trips. Present only as an economic agent during business transactions, such as selling the house, the husband leaves behind a void that the wife desperately tries to fill. The exodus of Chinese men also means the influx of underpaid temporary foreign workers from other parts of Asia, especially Indonesia and Bangladesh.[42] Before the economic recession of the Asian financial crisis in 1997, Malaysia's rapid postwar economic development attracted an influx of foreign workers, both illegal and legal. With 1.2 million documented and an estimated eight hundred thousand undocumented workers, the most serious social and economic problem faced by both workers and the Malaysian state is a shortage of housing.[43] Since most migrant workers work in major metropolitan centers such as Selangor and

FIGURE 5.5. Adding to the dream-like quality, a butterfly lands on Lee Kang-sheng's shoulder just moments before dropping to its death in the impenetrable and bottomless pool in *I Don't Want to Sleep Alone* (2006).

Kuala Lumpur, the economically underprivileged workers have to compete directly with local citizens for limited available housing. Therefore it is not a coincidence that one of the double Lees in the film has the role of a homeless Chinese man who has been bullied and saved from the street by the construction worker Rawang, whose tender nursing eventually turns into helpless love. Although the film later reveals that Rawang lives in the same building as the café waitress Chen and her boss, numerous shots of Rawang as he squats in the bathroom scrubbing either the mattress or the homeless Lee's underwear make implicit reference to squatting—temporarily staying in abandoned or unused parts of a building—as part of life in precarity.[44] The surrealist scene where Lee squats in front of what appears to be a pool, fishing inside the abandoned construction site where Rawang has been seen working, portrays the experience of displacement as the most realistic unreal. Adding to the dream-like quality, a butterfly lands on Lee's shoulder just moments before dropping to its death in the impenetrable and bottomless pool (see figure 5.5). With long and meandering staircases that seem to lead to multiple dimensions, the construction site also functions as an enchanting maze where lovers hide, find, and lose one another in its engulfing darkness.[45]

Tsai's portrait of Kuala Lumpur, like many of the Taiwanese cities he portrays, bypasses its flashy and urbanized downtown and focuses on abandoned urban sites on the verge of disappearance. As a Chinese Malaysian who has relocated to Taiwan, Tsai chooses to identify with women and Malaysia's migrant workers, whose presence in the city becomes a visible dilemma as the state's wavering economic policies re-create a patriarchal economic caste system. The film's focus on life in precarity speaks to the buried histories of violence in being Chinese in Malaysia and a new crisis of displacement that the filmmaker sees in globalizing Asian cities. Utilizing the motif of the double—double lives, double characters, and the city covered in haze and the darkness of the night—the film creates shifting perceptions of the reality that, through its multiplicities and infinite extensions, allows for the coexistence of distinct lives and perspectives. However, questioning reductive coevalness and commensurability, the film ends with an image of three characters in a love triangle—Lee, Chen, and Rawang—sleeping peacefully on a mattress that slowly floats across a dark pool of water at a construction site (see figure 5.6). Perhaps dreaming the same dream, or perhaps not, the coexistence of these characters mirrors the film's structure of multiplicity, leaving their relationship to the dreamers.

As the film's titles suggest—*I Don't Want to Sleep Alone* in English and *Dark Undereye Circles* (*Hei yanquan*) in Chinese—it is a work obsessed with sleep, sleeplessness, dreams, and the shadows of the night. Considering Tsai's focus on precarious lives, the obsession with sleep and dreams refers to the condition wherein visibility is minimized and visuality comes alive. The smog that engulfs the city persistently veils what the eyes can see but leads to the opening of an acoustic visuality that is not simply the equivalent of an audio soundtrack. In his discussion of the voice as a subject of philosophical inquiry, Mladen Dolar observes that there are two conventional ways of understanding the voice: as a vehicle of meaning and as a source of aesthetic admiration, as in the example of singing. Using hiccups as another example, Dolar suggests a third definition of the voice, as an excessive remainder that may disrupt spoken language's meaning. In reality a blind spot that disturbs the easy solicitation of meaning or aesthetic admiration, the voice opens up a zone of indeterminacy and undecidability.[46] This particular ambiguity becomes a new way of rendering reality in cinema, as suggested in Žižek's study of a Lacanian *real* that is always elusive.

Compared to Tsai's previous films set in Taiwanese cities, *I Don't Want to Sleep Alone* has additional layers of linguistic complexity. Whereas characters in his films usually highlight urban alienation by staying silent, this

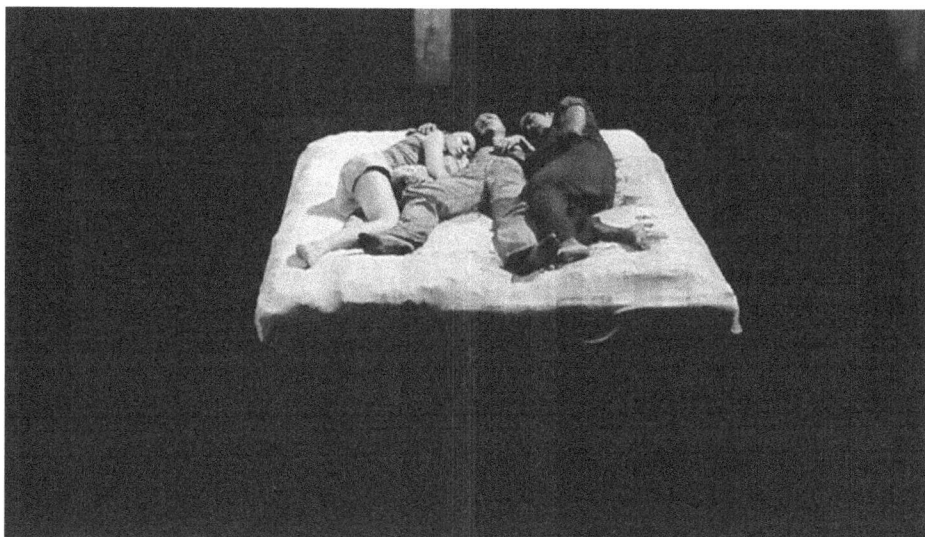

FIGURE 5.6. *I Don't Want to Sleep Alone* (2006) ends with the three characters in a love triangle sleeping peacefully on a mattress that slowly floats across a dark pool of water at a construction site, evoking the coexistence of multiplicities.

film literally makes verbal communication impossible. To maximize incommunicability, the haze that compels everyone to wear homemade face masks (made of plastic bags or disposable bowls) seems an additional obstacle to prevent the use of language. Although Tsai has revised his earlier style of adding musical inserts where songs' flirtatious lyrics exteriorize characters' interior desires, diegetic music from televisions and radios in the film's mise-en-scène plays a similar function. Characters' desires seep into the environment, when Rawang enjoys the Tamil love song "Gundu Malli" after he gently washes and caresses the homeless Lee's clothes in the bathroom and when Chen joins pedestrians in front of a record store and listens to a romantic duet before eloping with Lee to the abandoned construction site. These moments easily elude attention but punctuate the film as affective openings that secretly leak the characters' desires, leaving the gap between their taciturn faces and the flamboyant music open to speculation. Evoking a space of indeterminable ambiguity, Tsai's soundscape conjures desires and traumas that elude material representations. Whether diegetic or not, the musical inserts, the honk of a horn, and the film's prevailing silence open up pathways to different temporalities and affective spaces. Without verbal communication, the voices of these characters exist among a broad spectrum of sounds that transgress the arbitrary boundaries between language and noise, presence and silence, and culture and nature. Creating an acoustic visuality that expands existing modes of listening and seeing, the film fundamentally challenges the concept of sound as a mechanism of reproduced inclusion and exclusion. The state of precarity seeps through the ephemeral fragility of sounds, and the rest falls into irrecoverable oblivion.

For a filmmaker often identified as Taiwanese, the label opens up a realm of excessiveness—from Taiwan's political sovereignty to its ethnicities, languages, and histories—that continues to be subjected to the competing imaginaries of global empires, including China, the United States, and Japan. However, from the perspective of the filmmaker, the multiple systems of inclusive exclusion at the intersection of post-socialist neoliberalism, global empires, and heterosexual patriarchy transform Taiwan into a crypt where shadows of lives without legible bodies present an ethical crisis that, like the devastating effects of the wildfire and the catastrophe of Taiwan fever, speaks to a universalizing condition. The filmmaker's return home to Kuala Lumpur results not in the sentimental nostalgia for a place of origin but in the expansion of the landscape of precarity by recalling the violent history of state-sanctioned persecution of Malaysian Chinese during the Cold War, when the definition of life was subjected to the assignment of economic and political values. Defying the capitalist definition of nothingnesss—a strict division of presence and absence based on assigned values—Tsai's empty cities, empty soundtrack, and empty bodies connect Malaysia to Taiwan, and Hong Kong to France. The nothingness overflows the narrow definition of lack and begins to accumulate as kernels of desires, traumas, protests, and resistances. The mold, leakages, and cracks that permeate Tsai's urbanscape suggest the diagnosis of a global pandemic, wherein the symptoms take the form of excessive growth that is beyond control and always already there. Prone to imminent returns, these leakages test the logic of disposability, while gesturing toward future hauntings in the violent grid of legibility that is contingent upon the forces of dominant global powers. The films of Tsai Ming-liang provide the possibility of seeing contemporary Asian urban space as the locus for theorizing the state of precarity, casting a wide network of ethical questions whereby life's being and nonbeing are subjected to evolving value systems that begin with the body and extend to the city, the nation, and other creative forms of destruction. Produced in the era that is characterized by global complicity, Tsai's cinematic practices suggest a number of strategies of resistance as the filmmaker continues to transform the meaning of film. As his image migrates from theaters to internationally circulating DVDs and performance and installation experiential art at the museum, a multimedia sensory platform is set in motion, producing and disseminating cinematic sensory organs that paralyze the givenness of the world. The aesthetics of resistance lies in the contingency of perception and the limits of visibility, wherein exist the new ethics of representing precarity.

Epilogue

Urban horror cinema sets realities in motion, raising questions about the affective forces of the image in the era of hypermediality. To close this book, I return to where the book began—on the speculative futures of Chinese cinemas—to propose a final speculation on the future of the image and its potentialities as a force of resistance.

In a book about film written at a time when film is considered old media in the emergent field of new media studies, the emphasis, as each chapter illustrates, is no longer the medium specificity of film that theorizes a technology-led sensory revolution. Rather, the emphasis is on film as image-making practices across multiple platforms and media technologies in the image-saturated present that choreograph the meaning and nonmeaning of the image in a set of operations that create and frustrate expectations. Commenting on the transition from paintings to synthetic images, Rancière takes up the question of the future of the image in a conscious reflection that tries to avoid "a certain idea of fate and a certain idea of the image [that] are tied up in the apocalyptic discourses of today's cultural climate." At the beginning of *The Future of the Image*, written in response to the unspoken assumptions about the power of the image in the age of synthetic digital media, Rancière asks, "What is being spoken about, and what precisely are we being told, when it is said that there is no longer any reality, but only images? Or, conversely, that there are no more images but only a reality incessantly representing itself to itself?"[1] Rancière's discourse reveals that the relationship between image and reality has still not been solved, regardless of the image's transition of medium specificity from literature to painting, photography, film, and computer software.

Reading the opening scene of Robert Bresson's *Au hasard Balthazar* (1966) and the camera's operations, Rancière gives a new definition of the image: "The image is never a simple reality. Cinematic images are primarily operations, relations between the sayable and the visible, ways of playing with the before and the after, cause and effect." For Rancière, the image does not refer to the donkey, two children, and one adult in the opening scene, but the "operations" that produce "a discrepancy, a dissemblance." The image arises from the orchestrations of what one expects to see and the dissemblance of what is shown.[2] The gap between what the mind is socially conditioned to see and the camera's operations that frustrate the expected rendition of reality is the definition of the image that opens to a futurity rather than foreclosing an end. The question of the future of the image is thus central to understanding the role of cinema in producing the public sentiment of urban horror. Literally refusing the conventional representation of cities and monsters—or what the mind is socially conditioned to see—the evocation of urban horror relies on the operations of dissemblance and alternates between the creation of expectations and frustrations. The realities of globally expanding neoliberal post-socialism are set in motion, revising and challenging the existing images of the urban and horror and revealing both to be emergent concepts whose meanings are shaped by the lived histories of the present.

For readers who are searching for the familiar tropes of ghosts, monsters, and specters that are representative of the return of the repressed—the resurgence of past traumas and violence that continue to haunt the present—the urban horrors presented in this book frustrate expectations, yet for a specific reason. Different from the Freudian theorization of repressions and returns that provides an account of the psychological mechanisms of memories and symptoms, urban horror is derived from Engels's industrial horror, where the sentiment of horror is evoked in correspondence to an anticipated future and the possibility of an aggravated calamity.[3] The emphasis is on the speculation of the future that is reshaping the legibility of the present, rather than repressed desires and anxieties of the past. Urban horror arises not because of the confrontation with cultural taboos or encounters with the abject but the paralysis of existing tools of comprehension and response. Thus the book has offered a new approach to horror that shifts the focus from reading the visible forms of monstrosity to the diffusion of horror and the speculation of the future of the image. Through the cinematic operations of dissemblance that disjoins and conjoins disparate realities—such as *Yellowing*'s juxtaposition of the realities of festivity and urban revolution—new realities are set in motion, creating actions that ramify.

However, the potentiality of film as the public channel of dissent does not simply refer to the utopic realization of possibilities for action. According to Giorgio Agamben, the notion of potentiality depends on impotentiality—the potential *not to act*. In his reading of Aristotle's *De Anima*, Agamben unravels a way of thinking about potentiality as "not a logical hypostasis but the mode of existence of this privation." Potentiality does not literally refer to the presence of actuality or mere existence as such, but actuality's privation (i.e., a *present absence* as the mode of existence). Therefore he writes, "The greatness—and also the abyss—of human potentiality is that it is first of all potential not to act, *potential for darkness*." Rather than reading a set of films and labeling them as political based on overt signs and actions of resistance, the notion of potentiality allows us to uncover a space of indeterminacy. Whereas the transnational circulation of film opens up a channel for challenging the existing hierarchical order of the sensible world, it elucidates not only the possibility for action but also the impotentiality of nonaction. Only until all impotentiality is exhausted can true potentiality emerge.[4] Films produced in the intensifying Chinese neoliberal post-socialist era collectively demonstrate not the clear presence or absence of the forces of resistance but the indeterminacy of cumulative affects that suggest a future potentiality inclusive of the possibility of nonaction. Both possibilities of action and nonaction exist in the social relations film mediates, until a spark reconstellates the chain of events that will (or will not) lead to legible forms of public protest. Urban horror is an excavation of the affective space of indeterminacy, where the threshold for embodied actions of protest is rehearsed, imagined, and negotiated.

In the era characterized by the end of the revolutions, where the conception of the post- presents a temporal imaginary of an anticipated future that reverts back to socialism and capitalism, the crisis the present era confronts is the lack of a framework to describe the present as well as a future that is devoid of the forces of resistance. This crisis has been aggravated in recent years, as Chinese post-socialist technologies of state surveillance permeate every fabric of the PRC and expand to nearby Sinophone countries, where public channels of protest—such as the physical gathering of a protesting crowd—are increasingly narrowed. Yet rather than mourning the loss of the forces of resistance—a sentiment that can be characterized as a symptom born after the atrocity of the Tiananmen Square protest—the thesis that this book proposes, written after the supposed end of revolutionary times, is the fundamental redefinition of revolutions in the contemporary era. Shaped by global complicity, the arts of protest are sponsored and created by the same institutions of power that ramify existing crises. Yet complicity describes only the problem, not the nuanced responses, negotiations, and reactions recorded in post-revolutionary Chinese cinemas that illustrate a history of the affective rehearsals of revolutions that cannot otherwise be told.

Produced in the changing geopolitical climate of the aftermath of socialism, when the imaginary of the post- gives rise to the new post-socialist mythology of unlimited economic and political expansionism and integration, urban horror speaks to the massive infrastructural and urban transformations that advance new technologies of producing space and rendering space reproducible. The elimination of the Cold War divide between capitalist and socialist blocs is rapidly restructuring the divisions of East and Southeast Asia, Europe and Africa, and East and West, probing post-socialist histories beyond the borders of formerly socialist countries. As new zones, airports, megaports, and factory cities emerge in a global urban transformation that is remaking the world into an integrated logistics route for the traffic of capital, the articulation of borders, boundaries, and hierarchies does not disappear. Instead borders become increasingly unpredictable, exposing the bodies and lives that inhabit these spaces to more contingent forms of violence.

This book is an opening to a way of seeing, sensing, and experiencing what I theorize as Sinocentric neoliberal post-socialism that is meant to describe the proliferation of elsewhere, nowhere, and nonplaces as the strategy of governance in the contemporary world. Transcending the traditional concept of a city or a place with a history and an identity, the nowhere (i.e., island pockets of exception) relies on the logic of isolated exception and poses new challenges to forming a transnational and comparative network of resistance. *Urban Horror* is an attempt to open up the space of comparison and to rethink the speculative forces of resistance that are happening across regions not limited to the Sinophone world, where the urban form (un)expectedly becomes the medium producing affect. Their powerful presence probes the existence of new technologies of producing *space* that challenge the existing tools of mapping, referring not to the visible evidence of spatial expansion but to the map of injury, vulnerability, dispossession, precarity, and death that is reconstellating the networks and channels of dissent and awaiting future practices of affective mapping.

Notes

Introduction. Urban Horror

1. See Chow, "China as Documentary." Chow describes the era of hypermediality as the age of digital hypermediality, where digital technology has been fundamentally transforming the meaning of the image, the logic of capture, and the process of image dissemination and transmission.

2. Moretti, "Dialectic of Fear," 83, 87, 91.

3. Halberstam, *Skin Shows*.

4. Zhang, "Song at Midnight."

5. See a detailed analysis on the sensationalization of *Song at Midnight*'s horror leftism in Braester, "Revolution and Revulsion."

6. Shih, *The Lure of the Modern*.

7. Terada, *Feeling in Theory*.

8. Rancière, *The Politics of Aesthetics*.

9. Lefebvre, *Marxist Thought and the City*, 6.

10. Engels, *The Condition of the Working Class in England*, ix, 65.

11. Miller, *History and Human Existence*.

12. See a discussion of Sartre's visit to China in Shih, "Is the Post- in Postsocialism the Post- in Posthumanism?," 28.

13. Rockmore, "Merleau-Ponty, Marx, and Marxism."

14. Merleau-Ponty, "Marxism and Philosophy," 129.

15. See "The Theory of the Body Is Already a Theory of Perception," in Merleau-Ponty, *Phenomenology of Perception*, 235–403.

16. Karl Marx writes, "A mule is a machine for spinning cotton. Only in certain relations does it become capital. Outside these circumstances, it is no more capital than gold is intrinsically money, or sugar is the price of sugar. . . . Capital is a social relation of production. It is a historical relation of production" (Marx and Engels, *Selected Works in Two Volumes*, 159–60).

17. Lefebvre's book is loosely organized by the spatial categories that he develops as tools to read the different types of production of space, with "differential space" as

a method of producing "difference" in an otherwise homogenizing system of space production. For example, he writes toward the end of the book, "The formal theory of difference opens itself onto the unknown and the ill-understood: onto rhythms, onto circulations of energy, onto the life of the body (where repetitions and differences give rise to one another, harmonizing and disharmonizing in turn)" (*The Production of Space*, 373). This is a passage that draws attention to methods of producing difference (producing differential space) that still requires inventive experimentation.

18. Lefebvre, *The Production of Space*, 170.

19. Lefebvre, *The Production of Space*, 395.

20. For example, see Campanella, *The Concrete Dragon*, and Chung and Chang, *Great Leap Forward*.

21. For a collection of essays on comparative politics that focuses on different post-socialist pathways in East Central Europe, including Poland, Czechoslovakia, the German Democratic Republic, Hungary, Bulgaria, and Romania, see Stark and Bruszt, *Postsocialist Pathways*.

22. Drucker, *Post-Capitalist Society*.

23. For a detailed discussion of anticipation and post-socialist time, see chapter 3. For the temporal politics of anticipation, see Derrida and Stiegler, *Echographies of Television*.

24. Dirlik, "Postsocialism?," 43.

25. Zhang, *Postsocialism and Cultural Politics*, 12.

26. McGrath, *Postsocialist Modernity*, 1–2.

27. Shih, "Is the Post- in Postsocialism the Post- in Posthumanism?," 28.

28. For a provocative study that counters the Eurocentric origin of neoliberalism, see Bockman, *Markets in the Name of Socialism*.

29. For example, Wendy Brown begins her book *Undoing the Demos* by highlighting the irony in the discourse of democracy after the Cold War. She writes, "In a century heavy with political ironies, there may have been none greater than this: at the end of the Cold War, as mainstream pundits hailed democracy's global triumph, a new form of governmental reason was being unleashed in the Euro-Atlantic world that would inaugurate democracy's conceptual unmooring and substantive disembowelment. Within thirty years, Western democracy would grow gaunt, ghostly, its future increasingly hedged and improbable" (9).

30. In *The Birth of Biopolitics,* his well-known text about neoliberalism, Foucault argues that power no longer operates through the traditional form of state sovereignty in neoliberalism, which is a new system that redefines state power. He writes, "The state does not have an essence. The state is not a universal nor in itself an autonomous source of power. The state is nothing else but the effect, the profile, the mobile shape of a perpetual statification [*étatisation*] or statifications, in the sense of incessant transactions which modify, or move, or drastically change, or insidiously shift sources of finance, modes of investment, decision-making centers, forms and types of control, relationships between local powers, the central authority, and so on. In short, the state has no heart, as we well know, but not just in the sense that it has no feelings, either good or bad, but it has no heart in the sense that it has

no interior. The state is nothing else but the mobile effect of a regime of multiple governmentalities" (77).

31. Foucault, *The Birth of Biopolitics*, 77.

32. Foucault, *The Birth of Biopolitics*, 121.

33. The phrase *neoliberalism "with Chinese characteristics"* comes from Harvey, *A Brief History of Neoliberalism*, 120–51.

34. Shih, *The Lure of the Modern*, 349–50.

35. For a detailed study of China's infrastructural expansionism (imperialism), see Miller, *China's Asian Dream*. The book provides a detailed account of China's empire-building visions in Xinjiang, Central Asia, Russia, Laos, Cambodia, India, Pakistan, Sri Lanka, Myanmar, and Vietnam.

36. Harvey, *A Brief History of Neoliberalism*, 120–51.

37. Dirlik, *Complicities*. While observing different cases of authoritarian capitalism in Asia, Dirlik discusses what it means to talk about a "China model" that may be used to describe China's neo-authoritarian economic reform. He concludes that if there is a China model, it is defined by the willingness to experiment with different models rather than a set of definitive procedures.

38. Chakrabarty, *Provincializing Europe*.

39. For a political theory on dispossession and precarity, see Butler and Athanasiou, *Dispossession*.

40. See Miller, *China's Asian Dream*.

41. Lefebvre defines the urban fabric in this way: "The *urban fabric* grows, extends its borders, corrodes the residue of agrarian life. This expression, 'urban fabric,' does not narrowly define the built world of cities but all manifestations of the dominance of the city over the country. In this sense, a vacation home, a highway, a supermarket in the countryside are all part of the urban fabric" (*The Urban Revolution*, 3–4).

42. Lefebvre, *The Production of Space*, 99–100, 54.

43. For a general introduction to changes in the Sinophone and East Asian cultural industries in recent decades, see Davis and Yeh, *East Asian Screen Industries*.

44. Chow, "China as Documentary."

45. Chow, *Entanglements*, 4.

46. Chow, *Entanglements*, 5.

47. See Benjamin, "The Work of Art in the Age of Mechanical Reproduction." See also Baudrillard, *Simulacra and Simulation*.

48. Rancière, *The Politics of Aesthetics*, 13.

49. Foucault and Miskowiec, "Of Other Spaces."

50. The idea of socialist cognitive mapping is borrowed from Toscano and Kinkle's chapter "Seeing Socialism" in *Cartographies of the Absolute*, 78–100.

51. For a Marxist critique of post-socialist nostalgia, see Dai, "Imagined Nostalgia."

52. For a detailed discussion of the phantasmagorias of the interior, see "Paris, the Capital of the Nineteenth Century," in Benjamin, *The Arcade Project*, 14–26.

53. Barlow, *The Question of Women in Chinese Feminism*.

54. For a detailed but concise history of the shifting definitions of femininity in twentieth-century China, see Barlow, "Femininity."

55. See Davis and Yeh, *East Asian Screen Industries.*

56. Beatriz Colomina introduces a detailed analysis of the house in Euro-American modernist architecture (Le Corbusier and Adolf Loos) that she deconstructs as the assemblage of framing devices, including thresholds, windows, stairways, walls, mirrors, and furniture. These visual and sensory devices in architecture and interior design create dichotomies between interior and exterior, feminine and masculine, and public and domestic, as well as viewing positions that produce and frame specific gender, race, and class subjects. Inherent in these architectural designs is the process of creating subject positions that are given the power to see and to be seen. See Colomina, "The Split Wall."

57. Reading bodies and cities as mutually defining and therefore proposing a new way of understanding the relationship between bodies and the built environment, Elizabeth Grosz writes, "The body, however, is not distinct from the city for they are mutually defining. Like the representational model, there may be an isomorphism between the body and the city. But it is not a mirroring of nature in artifice; rather, there is a two-way linkage that could be defined as an *interface*. What I am suggesting is a model of the relations between bodies and cities that sees them, not as megalithic total entities, but as assemblages or collections of parts, capable of crossing the thresholds between substances to form linkages, machines, provisional and often temporary sub- or micro-groupings" ("Bodies-Cities," 108).

58. The most intimate sites of the interior that extend from one's body to the space of domesticity become the most alienating experience of the familiar. See Freud, "The 'Uncanny.'"

59. Ong, *Neoliberalism as Exception.*

Chapter 1. Cartographies of Socialism and Post-Socialism

1. Dai, "Imagined Nostalgia." Dai traces the commodification of cultural nostalgia in the 1990s through a variety of literary productions.

2. Rancière, *Figures of History*, 32.

3. See the collection of footage on workers' strikes in Harun Farocki's film *Workers Leaving the Factory.*

4. Siegert, *Cultural Techniques*, 201.

5. Li, "Gongye ticai, gongye zhuyi yu 'shehui zhuyi xiandai xing.'" According to Li, industrial-themed literature produced in the first seventeen years of PRC history (1949–66) has comparatively less artistic achievement than works featuring rural or revolutionary topics. While attributing the reason to China's late industrialization, Li further cites the irresolvable conflicts between industrialism and socialism that required time and the accumulation of collective cultural experiences before they could develop meaningfully. Filmed shortly before the People's Republic of China was officially established, *Resplendent Light* was designed to launch the cinematic prototype of industrial factory film and to help create the class image of the Chinese proletariat. Compared to the proletariat literary and cinematic traditions in Euro-American, Soviet, and Japanese cultures, for example, proletarian literature and films in China are fewer in number.

6. For a detailed intellectual history of the end of Chinese socialism and mass depo-liticization, see Wang, *The End of the Revolution*.

7. Huang, *Beijing 798*, 16–20.

8. There are multiple publications about Beijing 798 that celebrate the struggle of a group of artists against the Beijing municipal government to preserve the factory as a site for independent art making. For example, see Lei and Qi, *Beijing 798*.

9. See Mars and de Waal, "Beijing and Beyond," 53.

10. Toscano and Kinkle, *Cartographies of the Absolute*.

11. See the chapter "Seeing Socialism," in Toscano and Kinkle, *Cartographies of the Absolute*, 78–100. For a thorough discussion of cognitive mapping, see Jameson, *Postmodernism*.

12. See this book's introduction for a discussion of Engels's industrial horror.

13. For a discussion and a list of scenes featuring workers leaving the factory, see Farocki, "Workers Leaving the Factory."

14. Banerjee, *We Modern People*, 90.

15. Coopersmith, *The Electrification of Russia*, 121.

16. For a nuanced discussion of electricity in Russian science fiction, see the chapter "Generating Power" in Banerjee, *We Modern People*, 90–118.

17. Schivelbusch, *Disenchanted Night*.

18. Huang, *Zhongguo jinxian dai dianli fazhan shi*, 30–31.

19. See Li, *Zhongguo dianli gongye fazhan shiliao*. Li's book includes a comprehensive history of the expansion of imperialism in China through the lens of electricity.

20. Li, *Zhongguo dianli gongye fazhan shiliao*, 118–39. In chapter 6, "Jiuyiba yihou de dongbei dianli gongye" (Northeast China's electricity industry after the Mukden Incident), Li explains that by 1937 Japan had successfully monopolized electricity in the Northeast and was continuing the expansion of electricity infrastructure during wartime with massive construction projects of hydroelectric dams and thermoelectric power plants.

21. Electricity equipment and power plants were important targets of attack during the Chinese Civil War and the Cold War in Asia. In the immediate aftermath of the Chinese Civil War in 1950, for example, a play titled *Guangming de shouwei zhe* (The guardian of light) was produced. The story is set in 1950 in Shanghai, where workers in a suburban hydroelectric power plant relentlessly protected equipment during the air strike launched by Chiang Kai-shek.

22. Li, *Zhongguo dianli gongye fazhan shiliao*, 165.

23. Between 1937 and 1941 as many as thirty thousand Chinese people were sent to Japanese labor camps to help construct hydropower dams, and thermoelectric power plants spread throughout the region. See Li, *Zhongguo dianli gongye fazhan shiliao*, 120.

24. The puppet state Manchukuo (1932–45), created by Japan, is mentioned in passing. In discussing the extent of the mechanical damage, the technician reports that several generators were already broken during the semicolonial period. Japanese engineers tried to fix them without success.

25. Heidegger, *The Question concerning Technology*, 20, 27.

26. Banerjee, *We Modern People*, 92.

27. Mihai Craciun wrote an interesting but short comparative study on Soviet and Chinese views on the socialist city, "Ideology Shenzhen."

28. Craciun, "Ideology Shenzhen," 47.

29. See Visser, *Cities Surround the Countryside*.

30. Craciun, "Ideology Shenzhen," 49.

31. Lefebvre, *The Urban Revolution*, 15.

32. Film production was extremely limited during the Cultural Revolution. During the early years, film activity almost came to a complete halt. But between 1971 and 1976, thirty-seven imported feature films were screened in Beijing. The production of narrative films gradually resumed after 1971, and between 1973 and 1976 seventy-six narrative films were produced. See Pang, "Colour and Utopia." Interestingly, even in this study of films that portray harvests or agrarian representations, notable tensions between the countryside and the city can be observed.

33. Rofel, "Rethinking Modernity," 97.

34. Toscano and Kinkle elucidate the purpose of Jameson's cognitive mapping as a method: "In this respect, the mapping or figuring of capital is not a question of accuracy or resemblance, in which aesthetic forms would be a mere instrument for knowledge, but constitutes a kind of force-field in which our conceptions of both modes of production and aesthetic regimes are put to the test" (*Cartographies of the Absolute*, 21–22).

35. From a historical analysis of policies, Kim Wing Chan concludes, "The overall urbanization policies in China have been motivated primarily by the considerations of rapid industrialization, similar to those in other Soviet-type economies, instead of China's special ideological commitment to rural development" (*Cities with Invisible Walls*, 5–6).

36. See the chapter "Economic and Philosophical Manuscripts" in Marx, *Early Writings*, 279–400.

37. Pang describes the dominant official ideology in late Cultural Revolution films as the "combination of revolutionary realism and revolutionary romanticism" that juxtaposes reality and fantasy, which sometimes support and sometimes distort each other ("Color and Utopia," 268).

38. Toscano and Kinkle, *Cartographies of the Absolute*, 92.

39. Lefebvre, *The Production of Space*, 54, 37–46, 54. Lefebvre is mostly commenting on early Soviet Russia's socialist architectural urbanism, which he compares to the urbanisms of China and Cuba.

40. Lefebvre, *The Production of Space*, 54.

41. See detailed discussions of zoning as a post-socialist experiment in chapter 4.

42. In Susan Buck-Morss's discussion of the relationship between humans and machines in Soviet Russia, she concludes that socialist technological advancement is conceptualized as humans making machines to enhance human existence within nature, rather than to exploit nature (*Dreamworld and Catastrophe*, 64).

43. Consider the incidents of workers' suicides at Foxconn's Shenzhen factories, a Taiwan-based company and one of the world's largest electronics manufacturers. The

subsequent media attention highlights the gap of information divided by the factory gate. See Chan, Pun, and Selden, *Pingguo beihou de sheng yu si*.

44. Chan, Pun, and Selden, *Pingguo beihou de sheng yu si*, 178. The local police force was regularly called upon to suppress protesting workers. On September 23, 2012, for example, five thousand policemen, government officials, and paramedics were called to the Foxconn factory in Taiyuan (in northern China), where eighty thousand workers worked in the factory city that produced Apple iPhones.

45. Harvey, *Rebel Cities*, xiv.

46. Butler and Athanasiou, *Dispossession*, 19.

47. Commenting on the door's social function, Bernhard Siegert writes, "Doors and door sills are not only formal attributes of Western architecture, they are also architectural media that function as cultural techniques because they operate the primordial difference of architecture—that between inside and outside. At the same time they reflect this difference and thereby establish a system comprised of opening and closing operations" (*Cultural Techniques,* 193).

48. See Dai, "Imagined Nostalgia."

49. See Chan, Pun, and Selden, *Pingguo beihou de sheng yu si*. The last section of the book details workers' protests throughout Foxconn factories during the late 2000s and early 2010s in China.

50. See Harvey, *Rebel Cities*, xvii.

51. Lefebvre, *The Urban Revolution*, 38, 40.

52. Foucault's "Des Espaces Autres" was published in the French journal *Architecture-Mouvement-Coutinuité* in October 1984. The article was based on a lecture Foucault gave in March 1967. See the first footnote in Foucault and Miskowiec, "Of Other Spaces." Lefebvre wrote *The Urban Revolution*, where he discusses heterotopy, around the time of the May 1968 uprising in Paris; the book was published in 1970.

53. See Lefebvre, *The Urban Revolution*, 81.

54. Harvey, *Rebel Cities*, xvii.

55. The video was commissioned as part of the project "What Are They Doing Here?" that was run by the Siemens Art Program from 2000 to 2006. The project invited Chinese artists to spend six months in residency at industrial facilities across the country. See Hodge, "Cao Fei."

56. Lefebvre, *The Urban Revolution*, 38. Lefebvre insists that utopia has nothing in common with the abstract imaginary but is at the very heart of the real. This idea corresponds to the search for sparks of the urban revolution in the textures, senses, and materialities of everyday life.

57. See Donald, "The Poetics of the Real in Jia Zhangke's *24 City*." For information about factory relocation during the Cold War, see Shapiro, "War Preparations and Forcible Relocations."

58. See Schultz, "Moving Portraits."

59. In an interview, Jia explains the reason he mixes fictional performances of workers' experiences, performed by some of the most well known actresses in Chinese cinema, with interviews given by real workers. In the process of filming what he

originally envisioned as a "documentary to record workers' oral history," Jia discovered the difficulty of telling the "truth as such." He says, "Every interviewee gave me the urge to imagine the rest of the story. There were words unspoken, sentences half finished. I thought I could only fully comprehend these real people's feelings through imagination." In other words, the insertion of the fictional performances in the form of the interview is partially to fulfill the filmmaker's urge to literalize, see, and hear the excessive gap between embodied histories of Chinese industrial modernity and the invisible process of modernization at large. See Deppman, "Reading Docufiction,"189.

60. Deleuze, *Cinema 1*, 99, 96–97.

Chapter 2. Intimate Dystopias

1. *Amélie* grossed roughly US$40 million at the box office in France alone, a sum rarely achieved by French films at home. See Lovejoy and Bonnaud, "The Amélie Effect," 36–38. There are numerous similarities between *Baober in Love* and *Amélie*, including the films' narrative, cinematographic composition, color scheme, and poster design.

2. Elizabeth Grosz writes, "If utopia is the good place that is no place, if utopias, by their very nature, involve the fragile negotiation between an ideal mode of social and political regulation and the cost that must be borne by the individuals thus regulated, then it is clear that they involve not only the political and social organization of space and power—which Plato and More have recognized and specifically addressed—but also two elements that remain marked, if unremarked upon, in their works: the notion of time as becoming (the utopic as a dimension of the virtual, an admixture of the latency of the past and the indeterminacy of the future, the mode of linkage between an inert past, conceived as potential, and a future not yet in existence)" ("Embodied Utopias," 137–38).

3. These questions are also raised in Grosz's reading of Plato, Thomas More, and Luce Irigaray, where she traces the figuration of the body in each philosophical tradition ("Embodied Utopias," 143–50).

4. Under intense pressure to quickly produce commodifiable femininity with market value, *Baober in Love* is based on the lighthearted French romantic comedy *Amélie* (dir. Jean-Pierre Jeunet, *Le fabuleux destin d'Amélie Poulain*, 2001), an international blockbuster featuring a whimsical female protagonist played by Audrey Tautou and picturesque portrayals of Parisian Montmartre. Transforming the Parisian city into an idyllic and "pretty" landscape, *Amélie* differs drastically from the gritty and alienating representations of postwar French society found in the New Wave cinemas of François Truffaut, Jean-Luc Godard, and Jacques Rivette. Accused of "whitewashing" ethnically diverse Paris and intentionally beautifying the urban landscape, the film transforms both bodies and cities in the pursuit of the commodified aesthetics of beauty. Dudley Andrew, for example, cites a comment from *Cahiers du cinema*'s response to Serge Bourguignon's *Sundays and Cybèle* (*Les dimanches de Ville d'Avray*, 1962) in the critique of *Amélie*: "Nothing in the look, everything in the smile. To please is its major obsession. It doesn't matter whether what it shows is false, unseemly, or stupid, so long as it's done prettily. There is no cliché this film recoils from, whether it be poetic,

literary or cinematographic" ("*Amélie*, or Le Fabuleux Destin du Cinéma Français," 37). For the comment on "whitewashing," see Steinberg, "The Thoroughly Conformist World of *Amélie*." Eager to try this formula for success, *Baober in Love* borrows *Amélie*'s unique red-and-green color scheme and transposes the French Amélie's vision of triviality—her distinctive ability to note details that no one else does—to the Chinese Baober, resulting in the two films' strikingly similar visual appearance and aesthetics. Amélie makes this observation, which functions like a motto for the film, from her favorite spot in a movie theater: "I like noticing details that no one else does." From the sensation of sinking her hand into a full bag of grain to the pleasure of cracking the sugar-coated crust of crème brûlée with a teaspoon, the world of Amélie and her friends is composed of all kinds of eccentric rituals and secret pleasures found in the most mundane activities of everyday life.

5. Gayatri Chakravorty Spivak defines "identities" not as names but as the cultural field where identities are produced: "Names like 'Asian' or 'Africa' or 'Madhuban' . . . are not anchored in identities. They are incessant fields of recoding that secure identities" (*Outside in the Teaching Machine*, 238).

6. Davis and Yeh, *East Asian Screen Industries*.

7. Davis and Yeh, *East Asian Screen Industries*. After China's accession to the WTO, foreign countries such as the United States have increasingly exerted influence on China's trade policies. China's accession to the WTO is arguably the most dramatic change that has happened in the Chinese film industry, since it puts China's national domestic cinema in direct competition with foreign films.

8. Curtin, *Playing to the World's Biggest Audience*.

9. For detailed analyses of Li's early films, produced in the 1990s, see Lu, "Culture and Violence."

10. Although the era of economic reform began in the late 1970s, Jason McGrath has deftly illustrated the persistence of socialist cultural production systems (e.g., the socialist film studio system and literary institution system) that played determinate roles in shaping the forms and content of cultural texts. As McGrath observes, "It was not until the early 1990s that the fundamental *cultural* logic of the People's Republic of China underwent a basic market-driven rupture" (*Postsocialist Modernity*, 2).

11. For a cultural analysis of how the transformative definitions of the city were recoded from spaces of consumption to spaces of production in cinematic productions of the first seventeen years of the socialist era, see Shi, *Zhuti de shengchan jizhi*.

12. Grosz explores the concept of "bodies-cities" as an interconnected network where the meanings and functions of the body and the city are mutually defining: "What I am suggesting is a model of the relations between bodies and cities that sees them, not as megalithic total entities, but as assemblages or collections of parts, capable of crossing the thresholds between substances to form linkages, machines, provisional and often temporary sub- or micro-groups" ("Bodies-Cities," 108).

13. For a detailed but concise history of the shifting definitions of femininity in twentieth-century China, see Barlow, "Femininity."

14. Barlow, "Femininity," 391.

15. See Merleau-Ponty, *Phenomenology of Perception*, 235–82.

16. Merleau-Ponty, *Phenomenology of Perception*, 235.

17. Barlow, *The Question of Women in Chinese Feminism*, 16.

18. Berlant and Warner, "Sex in Public."

19. Deborah Davis makes the point that since income disparity grew during the economic reform era, women are now more likely to approach marriage as the primary institution through which to acquire property. See Davis, "Who Gets the House?"

20. Benjamin, "Paris, Capital of the Nineteenth Century," 154.

21. As China moves into a market economy under a socialist regime, there is no longer any written rule for governance, but "an unwritten law that binds members of a community together and implicitly encourages them to transgress the written law as a mark of their common bond" (Žižek, *The Metastases of Enjoyment*, 37). See Lu, "Culture and Violence."

22. See Guo, "A Gender Study on Housing Rights of Women in Urban China." While housing is a serious urban social problem not unique to Chinese society, women in China are at a particular disadvantage due to the lack of legal recognition of the issue and the lack of legal housing rights for women.

23. Dong, "Historicizing Gender," 94.

24. Mao, "Note to 'Women Are Now on the Labor Front.'"

25. For a philosophical discussion of the "desiring machine" in capitalism, in which desires produce realities, see Deleuze and Guattari, *Anti-Oedipus*.

26. See "Foundations of Progressive Chinese Feminism" in Barlow, *The Question of Women in Chinese Feminism*, 64–126. In an intellectual history of "progressive feminism" in the 1920s and early 1930s, Barlow traces the presumption of species evolution and its influence on the social theory of women's emancipation.

27. For an intellectual history of market feminism, see "Socialist Modernization and the Market Feminism of Li Xiaojiang" in Barlow, *The Question of Women in Chinese Feminism*, 253–301.

28. Yuan, "Kan xia lai zhenxiang shi kongbupian."

29. See Karatani, *Origins of Modern Japanese Literature*, 27.

30. Poe, "The Philosophy of Furniture."

31. Colomina, "The Split Wall."

32. In addition to the creation of Chinese editions of international home decor magazines, such as *An di* (*Architectural Digest*) and *Jiagu lang* (*Elle Decoration*), there also have been at least fifty different domestic and imported fashion and interior decor magazines accessible to Chinese readers since the 1990s. A few examples are *Ruili jia gu* (*Rayli Home*), *Sheji shidai* (*Interni*), and *Lixiang Jia* (*Ideat*).

33. Davis, "When a House Becomes His Home."

34. Property titles or rental agreements are typically listed under the husbands (63 percent) rather than the wives (23 percent). See footnote 26 in Davis, "When a House Becomes His Home."

35. Most historical studies on Chinese industrialization focus on the introduction of Soviet managerial systems. For example, see Kaple, *Dream of a Red Factory*. For a general history on factories, see Huang, *Beijing 798*.

36. See Poe, *Complete Stories and Poems*.

37. "Chen Kun jingcai cheji huo biao'yang."

38. Because the *hukou* system was intended to restrict travel and movement under Mao's rule, most migrant workers spent years working in the city without residential benefits such as health care and access to the education system for their children. Although the film never directly engages the issue of domestic migration, we get a glimpse of migrants' lives when one of Yanni's neighbors gives her a job wrapping one hundred pirated DVDs in plastic bags for one RMB.

39. See Wang, "Gender and Sexual Differences in 1980s China."

40. Freud, "The 'Uncanny,'" 210, 212.

41. Spivak, *Outside in the Teaching Machine*, 166. Spivak explores the state of gestation that is left out of classical Marxist texts from a Marxist-feminist approach. In "The Mother," Beauvoir provides a detailed deconstruction of the mother as a social role and the presumption of women's "natural" enjoyment and desire for "maternity" as an illusion.

42. Spivak, *Outside in the Teaching Machine*, 169.

43. Beauvoir, "The Mother," 495.

Chapter 3. The Post- as Media Time

1. See Nornes, "Bulldozers, Bibles, and Very Sharp Knives," 50.

2. See Chow, "China as Documentary." Chow uses the term *hypermediality* in her discussion of Jia Zhangke's *24 City* (2008), a documentary film in which the filmmaker seamlessly integrates interviews of factory workers that are performed by professional actors as well as nonactors. She argues that *24 City* is a conceptual project that introduces a different understanding of "China as documentary." In the case of Jia, Chow is referring to the hypermedial nature of the so-called documentary with which Jia's film engages.

3. See Virilio, *Open Sky*, 134.

4. The notion "nothing happens" is taken from Ivone Margulies's monograph on Chantal Akerman, *Nothing Happens*.

5. Crary, *24/7*, 122.

6. In *Rhythmanalysis*, Lefebvre challenges traditional Marxism's emphasis on the teleological development of time. Lefebvre emphasizes "lived" time that is mediated through the body instead.

7. Jason McGrath points out that while "postcommunism" is commonly used in other post-socialist states, it is not an applicable term in China, where the Communist Party's single-party rule continues through the present day. He cites Kevin Latham, who has argued, "The 'post' of 'postsocialism' in the Chinese context does not signify a straightforward 'after' in either logical or chronological terms" (McGrath, *Postsocialist Modernity*, 13).

8. See a more detailed discussion of the sound-image economy in Akerman's film in Butler, "Bordering on Fiction," 4.

9. See Chow, "China as Documentary."

10. The idea to conduct an archaeology of documentary time is inspired by Malin Wahlberg's monograph, *Documentary Time*.

11. Derrida and Stiegler, *Echographies of Television*, 105.

12. Cheng, "Three Questions on China's 'Belt and Road Initiative.'" The initiative was first proposed by President Xi Jinping when he visited Central Asia and Southeast Asia in 2013. Cheng and the commentators he cites observe the similarity between the current initiative and the discontinued Develop the West Initiative. Citing William Overholt, Cheng notes earlier comparisons between China's global vision and the US economic expansion strategy toward Europe, Asia, and Africa in the postwar era. However, China's expansion plan covers a terrain that is currently war-torn and unstable, leading Cheng to conclude that the initiative is still highly volatile.

13. See "The Overexposed City" in Virilio, *Lost Dimension*, 25–48.

14. See "The Perspective of Real Time" in Virilio, *Open Sky*, 22–34. This notion of the intensified present is developed by Virilio in his continued critique of the military-industrial complex of speed, war, and telecommunication.

15. Chow, "China as Documentary."

16. Lefebvre, *Rhythmanalysis*.

17. Although Lefebvre lays out more consistent methods for the proposed rhythmanalytical project in *Rhythmanalysis*, the book complements various conceptual threads in *The Production of Space* and *Critique of Everyday Life*. Often criticizing the historical materialist approach as overemphasizing the immediately visible, Lefebvre has been consistently revising the spatial theory that he saw in Marx. The critique of space extends beyond factories and manufacturing towns and production and consumption, thus calling for new critical approaches to the production of space in capitalism. In the case of *Rhythmanalysis*, space is conceived as temporal repetitions of time that form habits, rituals, and cycles. See also Lefebvre, *Marxist Thought and the City*.

18. Lefebvre, *Rhythmanalysis*, 77.

19. Ricoeur, *Memory, History, Forgetting*.

20. See Pickowicz and Zhang, *From Underground to Independent*. The essays in this collection mainly address questions of aesthetics, individual filmmakers, and alternative channels of distribution. It is interesting to note that one of the earliest publications on the subject does not address the question of technology, the means of producing and distributing documentary records.

21. For an in-depth study on "small-screen realities," addressing a wide range of small-screen cultures of production and consumption in the digital age, see Voci, *China on Video*.

22. McLuhan, *Understanding Media*. From the perspective of a media theorist, the independent documentary movement in China may be read as the effects of new media technology creating and enabling new kinds of sociality and network connections. The focus on media technology as the fundamental driver of the movement shifts emphasis to the study of media platforms from the traditional focus on individual artists and filmmakers.

23. Nornes, "Marking the Body," 30.

24. Chow, *Entanglements*, 4 (italics in the original).

25. Chow, "China as Documentary," 27.

26. Lippit, *Ex-Cinema*, 1.

27. Spivak, "Translator's Preface," xii.

28. See "Exergue Ex-Cinema" in Lippit, *Ex-Cinema*, 1–14.

29. Rofel, *Desiring China*, 13.

30. For a discussion of the acceptance of electric lighting, see Dikotter, *Things Modern*, 133–44. Additionally, Leo Ou-fan Lee discusses the opening passage in Chinese writer Mao Dun's novel *Midnight* (*Ziye*), where Shanghai's urban modernity is captured in the phrase "LIGHT, HEAT, POWER," written in English in the Chinese text. See Lee, *Shanghai Modern*, 3–5.

31. See "Screen Events of Velocity and Duration" in Wahlberg, *Documentary Time*, 79–100. Wahlberg discusses a number of early Euro-American city films in detail.

32. "Ba xiaofei chengshi biancheng shengchan chengshi."

33. For a detailed study of the history of the industrialization of light and the social transformation of light created in Euro-American countries, see Schivelbusch, *Disenchanted Night*.

34. Hell and Schönle, *Ruins of Modernity*, 1, 9.

35. The idea of "strange loops" comes from Douglas Hofstadter's *Gödel, Escher, and Bach*. While observing the relationships between patterns of repetition in mathematics, art, and music, Hofstadter explains that his ultimate goal is to understand how animate beings come out of inanimate matter. This study contributes to the understanding and development of artificial intelligence.

36. See Harvey, *A Brief History of Neoliberalism*. Aside from Harvey's account of the origin of neoliberalism as an attempt to rejuvenate a capitalist system that is deemed no longer profitable, the chapter on China's post-socialist economy raises an interesting question that Harvey describes as an exception to the formula and the historical development of neoliberalism. Citing the prominent role of the state in China's economy, Harvey's description of China's state-led neoliberalism is also a record of intrigue and ambivalence. Rather than subsuming the China case under the grand historical narrative of neoliberalism, China's post-socialist economy calls for a closer examination of the post- as a new economic experiment.

37. See a detailed discussion of the observational mode in Nichols, *Introduction to Documentary*, 142–71.

38. Doane, "Real Time," 24.

39. Robinson, *Independent Chinese Documentary*, 30.

40. Zito, "The Act of Remembering," 23.

41. Sniadecki, "The Cruelty of the Social," 60.

42. For example, Ou Ning's *Meishi Street* (*Meishi jie*, 2006) adopts footage filmed by the documentary's protagonist in an experiment that gives the camera to the filmed subject.

43. Doane, "Real Time," 24.

44. The term *orogeny* is introduced in part A of *Stratum* in an intertitle superimposed in scenes of characters walking around the demolition site. Against the background of sand and debris, the intertitle reads in English, "The orogeny refers to the certain kind of geological events: Part of the earth crust is under stress, where rock

layers become drastically deformed, they are extensively folded and rise up to form new mountains. As the earth crust is unstable during this process, earthquake often happens simultaneously."

45. Parikka, *A Geology of Media.*

46. Virilio, *Open Sky*, 28.

47. Virilio, *The Vision Machine.*

48. Doane, *The Emergence of Cinematic Time*, 222.

49. Rodowick, *The Virtual Life of Film*, 141.

50. See Merleau-Ponty, *Sense and Non-Sense.*

51. The expression "waning indexicality," reminiscent of Jameson's concept of "waning affect" in the era of late capitalism, comes from Rodowick's description of the difference between the photograph and the digital image (*The Virtual Life of Film*, 145).

52. For example, see Zhang, *Chinese Modernism in the Era of Reforms.*

53. See the chapter "*Capital* in Its Time" in Jameson, *Representing Capital*, 93–108.

54. Heidegger, *The Question concerning Technology.*

55. Parikka, *A Geology of Media*, 37.

56. See Moore, introduction.

57. Liu, "Cong Feng."

58. Liu, "Cong Feng."

59. See Hell and Schönle, *Ruins of Modernity.*

60. Doane, *The Emergence of Cinematic Time*, 145.

61. Adorno, *Aesthetic Theory*, 23.

62. Elsaesser, introduction, 13.

63. See Kittler, *Literature, Media, Information Systems.*

64. Gould, *Glenn Gould Reader*, 28.

65. Service, "Glenn Gould."

66. Gould, *Glenn Gould Reader*, 331, 347, 338.

67. For a detailed discussion of the incorporation of a filmmaking analogy in Gould's recording techniques, see Broesche, "Glenn Gould, Spliced."

68. Hecker, "Glenn Gould, the Vanishing Performer."

69. Hecker, "Glenn Gould, the Vanishing Performer," 81.

70. The notion of transcended emotions is drawn from composer Philip Glass's discussion of Samuel Beckett. Having composed music for several of Beckett's plays, Glass discusses the transmedial affinity that his compositions have with Beckett's experimental approach to theater. See "Return to New York" in Glass, *Words without Music*, 201–17.

71. Gould describes the *Goldberg Variations* in the following way: "I do not think it fanciful to speculate upon supramusical considerations, even though we are dealing with possibly the most brilliant substantiation of a ground bass in history, for in my opinion the fundamental variative ambition of this work is not to be found in organic fabrication but in a community of sentiment. Therein the theme is not terminal but radial, the variations circumferential, not rectilinear, while the recurrent passacaille supplies the concentric focus for the orbit" (*Glenn Gould Reader*, 28).

72. See "Reel China 2014—Schedule." In the note prepared for *Stratum's* debut in the Seventh Reel China at New York University, the filmmaker explains the rationale for the music's incorporation in English: "Without any prior knowledge of the film, the music they performed strikingly echoed the film's style and content, generating an impressive effect. Having obtained the permissions of the musicians as well as Li Xianting Film Fund, 7th Reel China at NYU will project the film with the recorded music. Our sincere thanks for Ms. Liu Sola and Mr. Liu Yijun for their kind permission and generous support. Copyright of the music resides with the musicians. Recording on any devices during the exhibition is strictly prohibited."

73. Hofstadter, *Gödel, Escher, Bach*, 9.

74. Toscano and Kinkle, *Cartographies of the Absolute*, 201.

75. Hell and Schönle, *Ruins of Modernity*, 1.

76. Zhang, "Dream-Walking in Digital Wasteland."

77. Derrida, *Archive Fever*, 68.

78. Virilio, *The Vision Machine*.

Chapter 4. Post-Socialism in Hong Kong

1. "HK Filmmaker Fruit Chan's 'The Midnight After' Is a Hit."

2. There are several books that provide detailed analyses and histories of the protest movement. See Garrett, *Counter-hegemonic Resistance in China's Hong Kong*; Cai, *The Occupy Movement in Hong Kong*; and Lim and Ping, *Contextualizing Occupy Central in Contemporary Hong Kong*.

3. In addition to the driver's dancing scene, the film makes a reference to the monumentality of bodies occupying the space of transit through David Bowie's song "Space Oddity," about a fictional astronaut's launch into space. Released in the months preceding the Apollo 11 space mission that put men on the moon in 1969, the song simulates Major Tom's space journey through his calls with Ground Control. Transmitted as a cipher in Morse code, the lyrics of "Space Oddity" are broadcast through cell phone signals from an unknown caller in the film. The insertion of human bodies in the open spaces designed for nonstop mobility is accompanied by a sense of exhilaration and relief, leaving its consequences indistinct and intangible. Like each step on the moon, each step on Hong Kong's expressway is monumental, yet its concrete meaning escapes the categories of comprehension in the empirical world.

4. Butler, *Notes toward a Performative Theory of Assembly*, 8.

5. Fong, *Hong Kong's Governance under Chinese Sovereignty*. Fong observes the rising number of political protests after 1997. In 2012 the number of protests reached a record level of 7,529. This includes the annual July 1 protests that have taken place since 1997.

6. Shih, "Is the Post- in Postsocialism the Post- in Posthumanism?," 28.

7. Ong, *Neoliberalism as Exception*.

8. Easterling, *Extrastatecraft*, 39. This is a summary of a study by the sociologist and political scientist Xiangming Chen that is incorporated in Easterling's analysis. See Chen, "The Evolution of Free Economic Zones."

9. Lefebvre, *Urban Revolution*, 1, 41.

10. There are multiple studies that are useful for thinking about how global transportation is radically transforming urban landscapes. For the restructuring of urban centers around international airports, see Kasarda and Lindsay, *Aerotropolis*. For a detailed analysis of airports in Southeast Asian cities—Hong Kong, Bangkok, Kuala Lumpur, Singapore, and Shenzhen's Bao-an—see Hirsh, *Airport Urbanism*. For a detailed historical analysis of how containerization and the invention of container shipment changed the world, including their impact on the rise of China's special economic zones, see Levinson, *The Box*. Last but not least, two publications in Chinese detail the history of the controversial construction of the new Hong Kong International Airport in Chek Lap Kok and the Airport Core Program. See Zhou, *Meiguiyuan de gushi*, and the bilingual edition, Smith, *Kowloon*.

11. Solomon, "It Makes a Village."

12. Li, "Hong Kong Home Prices Scale New Peak."

13. The principle of "one country, two systems" was created by Deng Xiaoping in the early 1980s. While the original idea was to grant relative autonomy to former British colonies such as Hong Kong and Macau for at least fifty years, it is still unclear what will happen after the agreement expires in 2047 for Hong Kong and in 2049 for Macau. See Wong, "One Country, and Two Systems."

14. See Lefebvre, *The Production of Space*. How does one account for space and its significance in the understanding of capitalism? Responding to and challenging Marx's *Capital*, Lefebvre reframes Marx's original emphasis on production and redirects attention to reproduction, repetition, and reproducibility. Space is not only produced but reproduced as the reproducible. The critiques introduced in *The Production of Space* (as well as numerous other books written by the author) center on ways of unraveling space as a historical process that reproduces social behaviors, rhythms, patterns, perceptions, representations, and histories. For a quote on space as the reproducible, see Lefebvre, *The Production of Space*, 337.

15. Lefebvre, *The Production of Space*, 57.

16. Yu, *Gangdao hai'anxian*.

17. Hong Kong International Airport is built on the artificial island of Chek Lap Kok off the coast of Lantau. The planning of the new airport began in the early 1980s, but construction took place amid heated controversy and public debate from 1991 to the airport's opening in 1998. For a summary of the debate, see Zhou, *Meiguiyuan de gushi*.

18. Cartier, "Restructuring Urban Space," 65–71.

19. For an example of the city's aggressive vertical expansion, see Frampton, Solomon, and Wong, *Cities without Ground*. As part of the city's urban gentrification project, the land that once housed the Kai Tak Airport has been divided into different development zones and publicly auctioned to developers. Strong interest from mainland developers pushed prices above market value, creating a bidding war among investors. In addition to the excessive speculation, the higher prices have also meant higher asking prices for the housing units that will be constructed on these sites. There are numerous news articles on this topic. For a representative report, see Li, "K Wah International Prices K. City at Kai Tak above Taikoo Shing."

20. Butler and Athanasiou, *Dispossession*.

21. While not refuting the legitimacy of concerns over Hong Kong's democracy, the point I am making here is to clarify that "1997" is not a singular event that happened in a single year. The PRC and British governments reached an agreement in the Sino-British Joint Declaration signed in 1984 without Hong Kong's participation or consent. The way 1997 is treated as a singular event in scholarship on Hong Kong raises many concerns about tracing the continuities and discontinuities between two successive colonialities.

22. See Abbas, *Hong Kong*. Abbas's text is one of the most representative pieces of scholarship to discuss Hong Kong cinema as the desire to locate Hong Kong before its imminent disappearance in 1997. For studies that characterize post-1997 Hong Kong cinema as a resurgent or declining industry, see Davis and Yeh, *East Asian Screen Industries*, and Peng, *Huanghun weiwan*.

23. Adorno, *Aesthetic Theory*, 5.

24. Adorno does use the word *horror* to describe Germany after Hitler came to power, which he characterizes as "an age of incomprehensible horror" (*Aesthetic Theory*, 18).

25. The concept of becoming is present in almost all of Deleuze and Guattari's writings, in their discussions of "becoming minor," "becoming woman," "becoming animal," and "becoming machine." For a concise introduction to Deleuzian thought, see Smith and Protevi, "Gilles Deleuze." For a feminist reading of becoming, see Braidotti, *Metamorphoses*.

26. See Benjamin, *The Arcade Project*, and Jennings, *Dialectical Images*.

27. Sontag, "The Imagination of Disaster."

28. Virilio, *War and Cinema*, 4.

29. For a representative criticism of the commodification of ruins as ruin porn, see Toscano and Kinkle, *Cartographies of the Absolute*, 105–24.

30. See "Translators' Foreword" in Benjamin, *The Arcade Project*, ix–xiv. The foreword provides a context for understanding Benjamin's idea of the "dialectical image." The idea of the past coming alive in the actualization of a "now of recognizability" originates from this text.

31. Butler and Athanasiou, *Dispossession*. Although the book is devoted to the details of dispossession as a global condition, it also highlights the necessity of rethinking what possession means; possession is not simply the opposite of dispossession or repossession. See Butler and Athanasiou, *Dispossession*, 7–9, for a representative discussion in the first chapter.

32. For example, the case of Sir Gordon Wu and the development of Hopewell Holdings Limited provides a way to trace the infrastructural expansions taking place in South China as China entered the era of economic reform. According to Wu's biography, the Hong Kong native and trained engineer began thinking about the possibility of an infrastructural revolution in South China during his days at Princeton. As a student, Wu often traveled on the New Jersey Turnpike and the expressways on the East Coast, and he realized the profound transformative powers of an infrastructural network. Upon his return to Hong Kong, he created Hopewell Holdings Limited

in 1972. The company is responsible for the construction of expressways, bridges, and power stations connecting Hong Kong to China's special economic zones. The company's investment also extends to infrastructural projects in other developing countries, including Pakistan, India, Indonesia, the Philippines, and Thailand. See Sayer, *The Man Who Turned the Lights On*, and Campanella, *The Concrete Dragon*, 26–55.

33. Augé, *Non-places*, 78.

34. This is a term used by the architect Steven Smith in *Kowloon*.

35. Augé, *Non-places*, 79.

36. Hong Kong University Press has published several books dedicated to a close reading of Fruit Chan's films in the series New Hong Kong Cinema. See Cheung, *Fruit Chan's Made in Hong Kong*, and Gan, *Fruit Chan's Durian Durian*.

37. There is currently no nuclear power plant in Hong Kong. However, the city imports power from nuclear plants in close proximity across the border, such as Daya Bay Nuclear Power Plant in Guangdong, as well as from other power plants within China's borders. For an overview of China's post-socialist nuclear power expansion, see Kadak, "Nuclear Power."

38. Merleau-Ponty, *Phenomenology of Perception*. Merleau-Ponty's phenomenology contests the common assumption that behavior is triggered by external stimuli and the body is a passive object that receives and responds to stimulation from the external environment. Deconstructing the complex interaction between culture and nature, his phenomenology brings a radically new understanding of the human body and consciousness that has residual influences on later conceptualizations of strategies of resistance in political theory.

39. Lefebvre, *The Production of Space*, 407, 384, 363.

40. See "The 'Sensation' as a Unit of Experience" in Merleau-Ponty, *Phenomenology of Perception*, 3–14.

41. Zhou Xun's character has at least three names in the film, including Hong Kong, Dong Dong, and Fang Fang.

42. See chapter 3, "The Geopolitics of Desire," in Shih, *Visuality and Identity*, 86–116.

43. Plaza Hollywood, "Guan'yu women." The plaza has been in operation since 1997.

44. The discussion of the *fort/da* game appears in Freud, *Beyond the Pleasure Principle*.

45. Abbas, *Hong Kong*, 39.

46. For an example of Hong Kong's cultural imperialism, see Shih's analysis of *Her Fatal Ways* in *Visuality and Identity*, 86–116.

47. Lee, "Migrants in a Strange City."

48. Lippit, *Electric Animal*, 1.

49. Tsang, "Introduction to the Hong Kong Airport Core Programme," 3–4.

50. Merleau-Ponty, *The Primacy of Perception and Other Essays*, 3.

51. Mezzadra and Neilson, *Border as Method*, vii.

52. Bolchover and Hasdell, *Border Ecologies*.

53. Shadbolt, "Hong Kong's Border War over 'Green Buffer.'"

54. Banerjee, "What Lies Within."

55. The park was established by the Agriculture, Fisheries, and Conservation Department and the Hong Kong Tourism Board in 1998. See Hong Kong Wetland Park, "Background."

56. Virilio, *The Original Accident*.

Chapter 5. The Ethics of Representing Precarity

1. Chen, "Emotive Images and Their Reproductions in *Stray Dogs*," 173. Tsai Ming-liang and Lee Kang-sheng both attended publicity events organized by the Farglory Group.

2. Steyerl, *Duty Free Art*, 1.

3. Tsai, "Tsai Ming-liang's Notes," 99. I have slightly modified the original English translation for consistency.

4. Butler, *Precarious Life*, xiv–xv.

5. See Butler, *Frames of War*; Butler and Athanasiou, *Dispossession*; and Butler, Gambetti, and Sabsay, *Vulnerability in Resistance*.

6. For an example of reading Tsai's films for queer aesthetics, see Yeh and Davis, "Camping Out with Tsai Ming-liang."

7. See a detailed discussion on precaritization in Lorey, *State of Insecurity*.

8. Rangan, *Immediations*.

9. Tsai, *Jiaoyou*, 63–64.

10. Tsai, *Jiaoyou*, 223. The lake makes an appearance in Tsai's *I Don't Want to Sleep Alone* (2006) in Kuala Lumpur, for example, in an abandoned multilevel basement of a high-rise office building that stayed incomplete for ten years. Its dark and impenetrable depth becomes a reflective surface for the romantic hetero-homosexual triangle among a Bangladeshi male migrant worker, a homeless Taiwanese man, and a Taiwanese coffee shop waitress.

11. The question of the ethical encounter with the other is discussed in detail in the context of the post-9/11 world in Butler, *Precarious Life*.

12. Kristeva, *Powers of Horror*.

13. Kolakowski, *Metaphysical Horror*, 121.

14. For example, see Boon, Cazdyn, and Morton, *Nothing*.

15. Tsai and Qin, "Zhuanfang *Jin'gang jing* Tsai Ming-liang," translation by the author.

16. See Koay, "Cutting for Change," in which Tsai discusses his film set in Malaysia, *I Don't Want to Sleep Alone*.

17. Foucault, *The Birth of Biopolitics*, 45, 46.

18. Freud, "A Note upon the 'Mystic Writing Pad.'"

19. Williams, "Master Shots."

20. For example, Mary Ann Doane discusses the invention of the concept of the event in early cinema as a capitalist industrial strategy to create an economy of cinematic time. She writes, "The cinema participates in the rationalization of time characterizing the industrial age. 'Economy' is a fundamental value of the developed narrative film, and the efficiency of electricity is paralleled by the efficiency of narrative. Resolute linearity, efficiency, and economy are also crucial goals of scientific management in

its attempt to deploy the human body in labor with a maximum reduction of wasted time. 'Dead time' is, again, anathema" (*The Emergence of Cinematic Time*, 160).

21. Rancière, *The Politics of Aesthetics*, 13, 9.

22. Burgin, *The Remembered Film*.

23. Ruiz, *Poetics of Cinema*, 14.

24. Jean-Pierre Léaud started his acting career at the age of fourteen playing Antoine Doinel, Truffaut's semi-autobiographical character. Having worked with many of the representative directors of the French New Wave, including Jean-Luc Godard, Jean Eustache, Jacques Rivette, and Agnes Varda, Léaud may be considered the face of the French New Wave. Léaud appears in Tsai's *What Time Is It There?* when Lee Kang-sheng is watching Truffaut's *400 Blows* on TV and also in present time, when Léaud has a chance encounter with Chen Shiang-chyi in a Parisian cemetery. The Chinese actor Miao Tian has an even more significant relationship with Tsai's films. Meeting by chance many years ago on a TV drama set, Tsai quickly bonded with Miao, whom Tsai claims shares many similarities with his father. Miao eventually became the most significant actor and character in many of Tsai's films, including *Rebels of the Neon God* (1992), the groundbreaking portrayal of a father-son homosexual relationship in *The River* (1997), the return of the father spirit in *What Time Is It There?* (2001), and the tribute to the soon-to-be-demolished Fu He movie theater in Yonghe, Taipei, in *Goodbye, Dragon Inn* (2003), where there is a sequence that shows actors in King Hu's Dragon Inn watching themselves on screen in the movie theater. While many dismiss these setups as mere nostalgia for a bygone past, I am more partial to readings that explore the asynchronicity of temporalities in Tsai's works.

25. Artaud, *The Theater and Its Double*, 8, 101.

26. Deleuze, *Cinema 2*, 169 (italics in the original).

27. Kristeva, *Powers of Horror*, 1–2, 4.

28. See a detailed account of the introduction of plumbing technology in China's treaty port of Tianjin in Rogaski, *Hygienic Modernity*. Divided into foreign concessions, the city of Tianjin in the late nineteenth and early twentieth century provides the context for the notion of public health that transformed health into a state technology to manage ethnic boundaries, urban space, and consumer products.

29. Wojcik, *The Apartment Plot*. Wojcik distinguishes apartment living and the apartment plot as an emerging discourse in postwar America between 1945 and 1975, around the same time as the country's rapid suburbanization, that offered alternatives to the traditional understanding of the home as stable, family-based, and heterosexual.

30. Tanizaki, *In Praise of Shadows*, 5.

31. "2000 Seen By: An International Collection" is a series of films commissioned by La Sept Arte consisting of works from ten independent filmmakers. Each was asked to create a tale of what will happen when we enter the next millennium. This collective project shows that vision in ten different countries and from ten different perspectives.

32. Sontag, "The Imagination of Disaster," 212.

33. Bih and Chen, "Neo-Liberalism and the Invisibility of Women's Housing Problem in Taiwan."

34. In *The Hole* especially, dance performances are choreographed according to the songs of the Hong Kong singer and actress Grace Chang, one of the biggest stars of Hong Kong cinema during the Cold War. For a detailed discussion of Grace Chang's film and musical work and her cultural significance in the dance and musical genre (*gewu pian*), see Ma, *Sounding the Modern Woman*.

35. Abraham and Torok, *The Wolf Man's Magic Word*, xi–xlviii.

36. See Derrida, "*Fors*," xi.

37. The composer and singer Shu-run Huang's name is spelled here using the Wade-Giles system. The spelling in pinyin is Shu-jun Huang.

38. SARS (severe acute respiratory syndrome) is a respiratory disease caused by the SARS virus. Patients display flu-like symptoms at first and can later experience severe failure of the respiratory system. The pandemic broke out in Hong Kong in November 2002, seriously affecting Taiwan and South China, which adopted a quarantine system. It created widespread panic as it is spread by an airborne virus. In urban centers and public transportation systems, people wore professional surgical masks as a means of prevention. Many sociological studies have shown the long-term effects of SARS in terms of damaged relationships and human isolation.

39. See Cartier, "Diaspora and Social Restructuring in Postcolonial Malaysia."

40. For a detailed account of the repatriation of Chinese during the Malayan Emergency, see Chin, "The Repatriation of the Chinese as a Counter-Insurgency Policy."

41. Cartier, "Diaspora and Social Restructuring in Postcolonial Malaysia," 73–75.

42. Cartier, "Diaspora and Social Restructuring in Postcolonial Malaysia," 74.

43. Azizah, "Indonesian Immigrant Settlements in Peninsular Malaysia."

44. One of the most striking squatting scenes in the film occurs when Rawang's treasured mattress (which he shares nightly with the homeless Lee) is invaded by pests. After they throw out the bed, there is a shot of the two men with their bare backs to the camera, and Lee shows a rare moment of tenderness by gently scratching Rawang's back. Now that the mattress is gone, the couple has truly become homeless.

45. For example, the coffee shop boss, who is initially following the homeless Lee and Chen, gets lost in the building. As she descends the stairs, she accidently slips in a pool of water. The construction site is also a lover's nest. After the pest invasion, Rawang moves the mattress to the construction site, turning a haunting site into their temporary residence.

46. See Dolar, *A Voice and Nothing More*.

Epilogue

1. Rancière, *The Future of the Image*, 1.

2. Rancière, *The Future of the Image*, 6, 7.

3. For a discussion of Freudian psychoanalysis, the return of the repressed, and Hollywood cinema, see Wood, *Hollywood from Vietnam to Reagan*.

4. Agamben, "On Potentiality," 179, 81, 183.

Bibliography

Abbas, Ackbar. *Hong Kong: Cultures and the Politics of Disappearance*. Minneapolis: University of Minnesota Press, 1997.

Abraham, Nicolas, and Maria Torok. *The Wolf Man's Magic Word: A Cryptonomy*. Minneapolis: University of Minnesota Press, 1986.

Adorno, Theodor W. *Aesthetic Theory*. Translated by Robert Hullot-Kentor. Minneapolis: University of Minnesota Press, 1997.

Agamben, Giorgio. "On Potentiality." In *Potentialities: Collected Essays in Philosophy*, translated by Daniel Heller-Roazen, 177–84. Stanford, CA: Stanford University Press, 1999.

Andrew, Dudley. "*Amélie*, or Le Fabuleux Destin du Cinéma Français." *Film Quarterly* 57, no. 3 (2004): 34–46.

Artaud, Antonin. *The Theater and Its Double*. Translated by Mary Caroline Richards. New York: Grove Press, 1958.

Augé, Marc. *Non-places: Introduction to an Anthropology of Supermodernity*. Translated by John Howe. New York: Verso, 1995.

Azizah, Kassim. "Indonesian Immigrant Settlements in Peninsular Malaysia." *Sojourn: Journal of Social Issues in Southeast Asia* 15, no. 1 (2000): 100–122.

Balibar, Étienne. *Politics and the Other Scene*. Translated by Christine Jones, James Swenson, and Chris Turner. London: Verso, 2002.

Banerjee, Anindita. *We Modern People: Science Fiction and the Making of Russian Modernity*. Middletown, CT: Wesleyan University, 2012.

Banerjee, Bidisha. "What Lies Within: Misrecognition and the Uncanny in Hong Kong's Cityscape." *Inter-Asia Cultural Studies* 14, no. 4 (2013): 519–37.

Barlow, Tani. "Femininity." In *The Palgrave Dictionary of Transnational History*, edited by Akira Iriye and Pierre-Yves Saunier, 388–92. New York: Palgrave Macmillan, 2009.

Barlow, Tani. *The Question of Women in Chinese Feminism*. Durham, NC: Duke University Press, 2009.

Baudrillard, Jean. *Simulacra and Simulation*. Translated by Sheila Faria Glaser. Ann Arbor: University of Michigan Press, 1994.

"Ba xiaofei chengshi biancheng shengchan chengshi" [Transform consumption city to production city]. *People's Daily*, March 17, 1949.

Beauvoir, Simone de. "The Mother." In *The Second Sex*, translated by H. M. Parshley, 484–527. New York: Vintage Books, 1989.

Benjamin, Walter. *The Arcade Project*. Translated by Howard Eiland and Kevin McLaughlin. Cambridge, MA: Belknap Press of Harvard University Press, 1999.

Benjamin, Walter. "Paris, Capital of the Nineteenth Century." In *Reflections: Essays, Aphorisms, Autobiographical Writings*, translated by Edmund Jephcott, 146–58. New York: Harcourt Brace Jovanovich, 1978.

Benjamin, Walter. "The Work of Art in the Age of Mechanical Reproduction." In *Illuminations: Essays and Reflections*, translated by Harry Zohn, 217–51. New York: Schocken Books, 1968.

Berlant, Lauren, and Mark Warner. "Sex in Public." *Critical Inquiry* 24, no. 2 (1998): 547–66.

Bih, Herng-Dar, and Yi-Ling Chen. "Neo-Liberalism and the Invisibility of Women's Housing Problem in Taiwan." In *Women and Housing: An International Analysis*, edited by Patricia Kennett and Kam Wah Chan, 152–70. New York: Routledge, 2011.

Bockman, Johanna. *Markets in the Name of Socialism: The Left-Wing Origins of Neoliberalism*. Stanford, CA: Stanford University Press, 2011.

Bolchover, Joshua, and Peter Hasdell. *Border Ecologies: Hong Kong's Mainland Frontier*. Basel: Birkhauser, 2017.

Boon, Marcus, Eric Cazdyn, and Timothy Morton. *Nothing: Three Inquiries in Buddhism*. Chicago: University of Chicago Press, 2015.

Braester, Yomi. "Revolution and Revulsion: Ideology, Monstrosity, and Phantasmagoria in 1930s Chinese Cinema." In *Witness against History: Literature, Film, and Public Discourse in Twentieth-Century China*, 81–105. Stanford, CA: Stanford University Press, 2003.

Braidotti, Rosi. *Metamorphoses: Towards a Materialist Theory of Becoming*. Cambridge: Polity, 2002.

Broesche, Garreth P. "Glenn Gould, Spliced: Investigating the Filmmaking Analogy." *Music Theory Online* 22, no.4 (2016).

Brown, Wendy. *Undoing the Demos: Neoliberalism's Stealth Revolution*. New York: Zone Books, 2015.

Buck-Morss, Susan. *Dreamworld and Catastrophe: The Passing of Mass Utopia in East and West*. Cambridge, MA: MIT Press, 2002.

Burgin, Victor. *The Remembered Film*. London: Reaktion, 2004.

Butler, Judith. *Frames of War: When Is Life Grievable?* New York: Verso, 2009.

Butler, Judith. *Notes toward a Performative Theory of Assembly*. Cambridge, MA: Harvard University Press, 2015.

Butler, Judith. *Precarious Life: The Powers of Mourning and Violence*. New York: Verso, 2004.

Butler, Judith, and Athena Athanasiou. *Dispossession: The Performative in the Political.* Malden, MA: Polity, 2013.

Butler, Judith, Zeynep Gambetti, and Leticia Sabsay, eds. *Vulnerability in Resistance.* Durham, NC: Duke University Press, 2016.

Butler, Kristine. "Bordering on Fiction: Chantal Akerman's *D'Est.*" *Postmodern Culture* 6, no. 1 (1995). Accessed June 28, 2019. https://muse.jhu.edu/.

Cai, Yongshun. *The Occupy Movement in Hong Kong: Sustaining Decentralized Protest.* London: Routledge, 2017.

Campanella, Thomas J. *The Concrete Dragon: China's Urban Revolution and What It Means for the World.* New York: Princeton Architectural Press, 2008.

Cartier, Carolyn. "Diaspora and Social Restructuring in Postcolonial Malaysia." In *The Chinese Diaspora: Space, Place, Mobility, and Identity*, edited by Laurence J. C. Ma and Carolyn Cartier, 69–96. Lanham, MD: Rowman and Littlefield, 2003.

Cartier, Carolyn. "Restructuring Urban Space: The Mall in Mix-Use Developments." In *Mall City: Hong Kong's Dreamworlds of Consumption*, edited by Stefan Al, 65–71. Honolulu: University of Hawai'i Press, 2016.

Chakrabarty, Dipesh. *Provincializing Europe: Postcolonial Thought and Historical Difference.* Princeton, NJ: Princeton University Press, 2000.

Chan, Jenny, Ngai Pun, and Mark Selden. *Pingguo beihou de sheng yu si: Shengchanxian shang de Fushikang gongren* [Life and death behind Apple: Foxconn workers on the production line]. Hong Kong: Zhonghua shuju, 2015.

Chan, Kim Wing. *Cities with Invisible Walls: Reinterpreting Urbanization in Post-1949 China.* Hong Kong: Oxford University Press, 1994.

"Chen Kun jingcai cheji huo biao'yang, Luo Lixian zan qi ju dongzuo juxing qianzhi" [Chen Kun's stunt car driving skill receives praise; Luo Lixian sees a new action hero]. *Sina*, February 2, 2007. http://ent.sina.com.cn/m/c/2007-02-02/14541436762.html.

Chen, Tai-song. "Emotive Images and Their Reproductions in *Stray Dogs*." In *Stray Dogs at the Museum: Tsai Ming Liang Solo Exhibition*, edited by Mun-lee Lin and Ming-liang Tsai, 170–75. Taipei: Museum of National Taipei University of Education, 2016.

Chen, Xiangming. "The Evolution of Free Economic Zones and the Recent Development of Cross-National Growth Zones." *International Journal of Urban and Regional Research* 19, no. 4 (1995): 593–621.

Cheng, Lei, and Qi Zhu. *Beijing 798.* Hong Kong: Timezone 8, 2008.

Cheng, Leonard K. "Three Questions on China's 'Belt and Road Initiative.'" *China Economic Review* 40 (2016): 309–13.

Cheung, Esther M. K. *Fruit Chan's Made in Hong Kong.* Hong Kong: Hong Kong University Press, 2009.

Chin, Low Choo. "The Repatriation of the Chinese as a Counter-Insurgency Policy during the Malayan Emergency." *Journal of Southeast Asian Studies* 45, no. 3 (2014): 363–92.

Chow, Rey. "China as Documentary: Some Basic Questions (Inspired by Michelangelo Antonioni and Jia Zhangke)." *European Journal of Cultural Studies* 17, no. 1 (2014): 16–30.

Chow, Rey. *Entanglements, or Transmedial Thinking about Capture*. Durham, NC: Duke University Press, 2012.

Chung, Chuihua Judy, and Bernard Chang. *Great Leap Forward*. Cologne: Taschen, 2001.

Colomina, Beatriz. "The Split Wall: Domestic Voyeurism." In *Sexuality and Space*, edited by Beatriz Colomina, 73–128. New York: Princeton Architectural Press, 1992.

Coopersmith, Jonathan. *The Electrification of Russia, 1880–1926*. Ithaca, NY: Cornell University Press, 1992.

Craciun, Mihai. "Ideology Shenzhen." In *Great Leap Forward*, edited by Alice Chung, Chuihua Judy Chung, Jeffrey Inaba, Rem Koolhaas, Sze Tsung Leong, and Qingyun Ma, 44–155. Cambridge, MA: Harvard Graduate School of Design, 2001.

Crary, Jonathan. *24/7: Late Capitalism and the Ends of Sleep*. New York: Verso, 2013.

Curtin, Michael. *Playing to the World's Biggest Audience: The Globalization of Chinese Film and TV*. Berkeley: University of California Press, 2007.

Dai, Jinhua. "Imagined Nostalgia." In *Postmodernism and China (A Boundary 2 Book)*, edited by Xudong Zhang and Arif Dirlik, 205–21. Durham, NC: Duke University Press, 2000.

Davis, Darrell William, and Emilie Yueh-yu Yeh. *East Asian Screen Industries*. London: BFI, 2008.

Davis, Deborah S. "When a House Becomes His Home." In *Popular China: Unofficial Culture in a Globalizing Society*, edited by Perry Link, Richard Madsen, and Paul Pickowicz, 231–50. Lanham, MD: Rowman and Littlefield, 2002.

Davis, Deborah S. "Who Gets the House? Renegotiating Property Rights in Post-Socialist Urban China." *Modern China* 36, no. 5 (2010): 463–92.

Deleuze, Gilles. *Cinema 1: The Movement-Image*. Translated by Hugh Tomlinson and Barbara Habberjam. Minneapolis: University of Minnesota Press, 1986.

Deleuze, Gilles. *Cinema 2: Time-image*. Translated by Hugh Tomlinson and Robert Galeta. Minneapolis: University of Minnesota Press, 1989.

Deleuze, Gilles, and Félix Guattari. *Anti-Oedipus: Capitalism and Schizophrenia*. Translated by Robert Hurley, Mark Seem, and Helen R. Lane. Minneapolis: University of Minnesota Press, 1983.

Deppman, Hsiu-Chuang. "Reading Docufiction: Jia Zhangke's *24 City*." *Journal of Chinese Cinema* 8, no. 3 (2014): 188–208.

Derrida, Jacques. *Archive Fever: A Freudian Impression*. Translated by Eric Prenowitz. Chicago: University of Chicago Press, 1996.

Derrida, Jacques. "*Fors*: The Anglish Words of Nicolas Abraham and Maria Torok." In *The Wolf Man's Magic Word: A Cryptonomy*, edited by Nicolas Abraham and Maria Torok, xi–xlviii. Minneapolis: University of Minnesota Press, 1986.

Derrida, Jacques, and Bernard Stiegler. *Echographies of Television: Filmed Interviews*. Translated by Jennifer Bajorek. Malden, MA: Polity, 2002.

Dikotter, Frank. *Things Modern: Material Culture and Everyday Life in China*. London: C. Hurst, 2007.

Dirlik, Arif. *Complicities: The People's Republic of China in Global Capitalism*. Chicago: Prickly Paradigm Press, 2017.

Dirlik, Arif. "Postsocialism? Reflections on 'Socialism with Chinese Characteristics.'" *Critical Asian Studies* 21, no. 1 (1989): 33–44.

Doane, Mary Ann. *The Emergence of Cinematic Time: Modernity, Contingency, the Archive*. Cambridge, MA: Harvard University Press, 2002.

Doane, Mary Ann. "Real Time: Instantaneity and the Photographic Imaginary." In *Stillness and Time: Photography and the Moving Image*, edited by Peter Green and Joanna Lowry, 22–38. Brighton, UK: Photoworks/Photoforum, 2005.

Dolar, Mladen. *A Voice and Nothing More*. Cambridge, MA: MIT Press, 2006.

Donald, Stephanie Hemelryk. "The Poetics of the Real in Jia Zhangke's *24 City*." *Screen* 55, no. 2 (2014): 267–75.

Dong, Limin. "Historicizing Gender: A Study of Chinese Women's Liberation from 1949–1966." Translated by Casey M. Lee and S. Louisa Wei. *differences* 24, no. 2 (2013): 93–108.

Drucker, Peter. *Post-Capitalist Society*. New York: Harper Business, 1993.

Easterling, Keller. *Extrastatecraft: The Power of Infrastructure Space*. New York: Verso, 2014.

Elsaesser, Thomas. Introduction to *Early Cinema: Space, Frame, Narrative*, edited by Thomas Elsaesser and Adam Barker, 11–30. London: BFI, 1990.

Engels, Friedrich. *The Condition of the Working Class in England*. Edited by David McLellan. New York: Oxford University Press, 2009.

Farocki, Harun. "Workers Leaving the Factory." Translated by Laurent Faasch-Ibrahim. *Senses of Cinema* 21, July 2002. http://sensesofcinema.com/2002/harun -farocki/farocki_workers/.

Fong, Brian C. H. *Hong Kong's Governance under Chinese Sovereignty: The Failure of the State-Business Alliance after 1997*. London: Routledge, 2015.

Foucault, Michel. *The Birth of Biopolitics: Lectures at the Collège de France, 1978–1979*. Translated by Graham Burchell. New York: Palgrave, 2008.

Foucault, Michel, and Jay Miskowiec. "Of Other Spaces." *Diacritics* 16, no. 1 (1986): 22–27.

Frampton, Adam, Jonathan D. Solomon, and Clara Wong. *Cities without Ground: A Hong Kong Guidebook*. Rafael, CA: ORO Editions, 2012.

Freud, Sigmund. *Beyond the Pleasure Principle*. Translated by James Strachey. New York: W. W. Norton, 1989.

Freud, Sigmund. "A Note upon the 'Mystic Writing Pad.'" In *General Psychological Theory: Papers on Metapsychology*, edited by Philip Rieff, 211–16. New York: Collier, 1963.

Freud, Sigmund. "The 'Uncanny.'" In *Writings on Art and Literature*, edited by James Strachey, 193–233. Stanford, CA: Stanford University Press, 1997.

Gan, Wendy. *Fruit Chan's Durian Durian*. Hong Kong: Hong Kong University Press, 2005.

Garrett, Daniel. *Counter-hegemonic Resistance in China's Hong Kong: Visualizing Protest in the City*. New York: Springer, 2015.

Glass, Philip. *Words without Music: A Memoir*. New York: Liveright, 2015.

Gould, Glenn. *Glenn Gould Reader*. Edited by Tim Page. New York: Knopf, 1984.

Grosz, Elizabeth. "Bodies-Cities." In *Space, Time, and Perversion: Essays on the Politics of Bodies*, 103–10. New York: Routledge, 1995.

Grosz, Elizabeth. "Embodied Utopias." In *Architecture from the Outside: Essays on Virtual and Real Space*, 131–50. Cambridge, MA: MIT Press, 2001.

Guo, Hui-min. "A Gender Study on Housing Rights of Women in Urban China: Case Study of Single-Parent Female Domestic Workers' Group." In *Women and Housing: An International Analysis*, edited by Patricia Kennett and Kam Wah Chan, 171–86. Abingdon, UK: Routledge, 2011.

Halberstam, Jack. *Skin Shows: Gothic Horror and the Technology of Monsters*. Durham, NC: Duke University Press, 1995.

Harvey, David. *A Brief History of Neoliberalism*. Oxford: Oxford University Press, 2005.

Harvey, David. *Rebel Cities: From the Right to the City to the Urban Revolution*. New York: Verso, 2012.

Hecker, Tim. "Glenn Gould, the Vanishing Performer and the Ambivalence of the Studio." *Leonardo Music Journal* 18 (2008): 77–83.

Heidegger, Martin. *The Question concerning Technology, and Other Essays*. Translated by William Lovitt. New York: HarperCollins, 2013.

Hell, Julia, and Andreas Schönle, eds. *Ruins of Modernity*. Durham, NC: Duke University Press, 2010.

Hirsh, Max. *Airport Urbanism: Infrastructure and Mobility in Asia*. Minneapolis: University of Minnesota Press, 2016.

"HK Filmmaker Fruit Chan's 'The Midnight After' Is a Hit." *Star Online*, May 19, 2014. https://www.thestar.com.my/lifestyle/entertainment/movies/news/2014/05/19/a-hit-after-midnight/.

Hodge, David. "Cao Fei: Whose Utopia?" Tate. Accessed September 15, 2017. http://www.tate.org.uk/art/artworks/cao-whose-utopia-t12754.

Hofstadter, Douglas. *Gödel, Escher, Bach: An Eternal Golden Braid*. New York: Basic Books, 1979.

Hong Kong Wetland Park. "Background." Accessed May 12, 2017. https://www.wetlandpark.gov.hk/en/aboutus/index#Background.

Huang, Rui, ed. *Beijing 798: Zai chuangzao de "gongchang"* [Beijing 798: Reflections on the "factory" of art]. Chengdu: Sichuan meishu chubanshe, 2008.

Huang, Xi. *Zhongguo jinxian dai dianli fazhan shi* [A history of electric power technology in modern China]. Shandong: Shandong jiaoyu chubanshe, 2006.

Jameson, Fredric. *Postmodernism, or, The Cultural Logic of Late Capitalism*. Durham, NC: Duke University Press, 1991.

Jameson, Fredric. *Representing Capital: A Reading of Volume One*. New York: Verso, 2011.

Jennings, Michael. *Dialectical Images: Walter Benjamin's Theory of Literary Criticism*. Ithaca, NY: Cornell University Press, 1987.

Kadak, Andrew C. "Nuclear Power: 'Made in China.'" *Brown Journal of World Affairs* 13, no. 1 (2006): 77–90.

Kafka, Franz. *The Metamorphosis: Translation, Backgrounds and Contexts*. Translated and edited by Stanley Corngold. New York: W. W. Norton, 1996.

Kaple, Doborah A. *Dream of a Red Factory: The Legacy of High Stalinism in China*. New York: Oxford University Press, 1994.

Karatani, Kojin. *Origins of Modern Japanese Literature*. Translated by Brett de Bary. Durham, NC: Duke University Press, 1993.

Kasarda, John D., and Greg Lindsay. *Aerotropolis: The Way We'll Live Next*. New York: Farrar, Straus and Giroux, 2011.

Kittler, Friedrich A. *Literature, Media, Information Systems*. Edited by John Johnston. London: Routledge, 1997.

Koay, Allan. "Cutting for Change." *Star Online*, May 14, 2007. https://www.thestar.com .my/lifestyle/entertainment/movies/news/2007/05/14/cutting-for-change/.

Kolakowski, Leszek. *Metaphysical Horror*. Chicago: University of Chicago Press, 2001.

Kristeva, Julia. *Powers of Horror: An Essay on Abjection*. Translated by Leon S. Roudiez. New York: Columbia University Press, 1982.

Lee, Leo Ou-fan. *Shanghai Modern: The Flowering of a New Urban Culture in China, 1930–1945*. Cambridge, MA: Harvard University Press, 1999.

Lee, Vivian. "Migrants in a Strange City: (Dis-)locating the China Imaginary in Post-1997 Hong Kong Films." *Journal of Modern Literature in Chinese* 10, no. 1 (2010): 67–85.

Lefebvre, Henri. *Critique of Everyday Life*. Translated by John Moore. New York: Verso, 1991.

Lefebvre, Henri. *Marxist Thought and the City*. Translated by Robert Bononno. Minneapolis: University of Minnesota Press, 2016.

Lefebvre, Henri. *The Production of Space*. Translated by Donald Nicholson-Smith. Cambridge, MA: Blackwell, 1991.

Lefebvre, Henri. *Rhythmanalysis: Space, Time and Everyday Life*. Translated by Stuart Elden and Gerald Moore. New York: Continuum, 2004.

Lefebvre, Henri. *The Urban Revolution*. Translated by Robert Bononno. Minneapolis: University of Minnesota Press, 2003.

Lei, Cheng, and Zhu Qi, eds. *Beijing 798*. Chengdu: Sichuan meishu chubanshe, 2008.

Levinson, Marx. *The Box: How the Shipping Container Made the World Smaller and the World Economy Bigger*. Princeton, NJ: Princeton University Press, 2008.

Li, Daigeng. *Zhongguo dianli gongye fazhan shiliao: Jiefang qian de qishinian (1879–1949)* [The history of the industrialization of electricity in China: The seventy years before liberation (1879–1949)]. Beijing: Shuili dianli chubanshe, 1983.

Li, Sandy. "Hong Kong Home Prices Scale New Peak, 20 Years after 1997 Record." *South China Morning Post*, July 13, 2017. http://www.scmp.com/property/hong-kong-china /article/2094340/hong-kong-home-prices-scale-new-peak-20-years-after-1997.

Li, Sandy. "K Wah International Prices K. City at Kai Tak above Taikoo Shing." *South China Morning Post*, February 9, 2017. http://www.scmp.com/property/hong-kong -china/article/2069542/k-wah-international-prices-k-city-kai-tak-above-taikoo.

Li, Yang. "Gongye ticai, gongye zhuyi yu 'shehui zhuyi xiandai xing': 'Chengfeng-polang' zai jiedu" [Industrial topic, industrialism, and the 'modernity of socialism': Rereading *Riding the Wind and Waves*]. *Wenxue pinglun* [Literary criticism], no. 6 (2010): 46–53.

Lim, Tai Wei, and Xiaojuan Ping. *Contextualizing Occupy Central in Contemporary Hong Kong*. London: Imperial College Press, 2015.

Lippit, Akira. *Electric Animal: Toward a Rhetoric of Wildlife*. Minneapolis: University of Minnesota Press, 2000.

Lippit, Akira. *Ex-Cinema: From a Theory of Experimental Film and Video*. Berkeley: University of California Press, 2012.

Liu, Yajing. "Cong Feng: Cong guxiang chuzou, zai xiangcun jilu" [Cong Feng: Exiled from hometown to document the countryside]. *Xin jing bao* [Beijing news], February 8, 2013.

Lorey, Isabell. *State of Insecurity: Government of the Precarious*. New York: Verso, 2015.

Lovejoy, Alice, and Frédéric Bonnaud. "The Amélie Effect." *Film Comment* 37, no. 6 (2001): 36–38.

Lu, Tonglin. "Culture and Violence, Li Shaohong: *Bloody Dawn*." In *Confronting Modernity in the Cinemas of Taiwan and Mainland China*, 173–90. Cambridge: Cambridge University Press, 2002.

Ma, Jean. *Sounding the Modern Woman: The Songstress in Chinese Cinema*. Durham, NC: Duke University Press, 2015.

Mao, Zedong. "Note to 'Women Are Now on the Labor Front.'" In *Socialist Upsurge in China's Countryside*. Translated by Marxist Internet Archive, 1955. Accessed July 3, 2015, www.marxists.org/reference/archive/mao/selected-works/volume-5/mswv5_48.htm.

Margulies, Ivone. *Nothing Happens: Chantal Akerman's Hyperrealist Everyday*. Durham, NC: Duke University Press, 1996.

Mars, Neville, and Martijn de Waal. "Beijing and Beyond." In *Beijing 798: Reflections on Art, Architecture and Society in China*, edited by Huang Rui, 38–53. Hong Kong: Timezone 8, 2004.

Marx, Karl. *Early Writings*. Translated by Rodney Livingstone and Gregor Benton. London: Penguin, 1992.

Marx, Karl, and Friedrich Engels. *Karl Marx and Frederick Engels: Selected Works in Two Volumes*. Moscow: Foreign Languages Publishing House, 1962.

McGrath, Jason. *Postsocialist Modernity: Chinese Cinema, Literature, and Criticism in the Market Age*. Stanford, CA: Stanford University Press, 2008.

McLuhan, Marshall. *Understanding Media: The Extensions of Man*. New York: New American Library, 1964.

Merleau-Ponty, Maurice. *Adventures of the Dialectic*. Translated by Joseph Bien. Evanston, IL: Northwestern University Press, 1973.

Merleau-Ponty, Maurice. *Humanism and Terror: An Essay on the Communist Problem*. Translated by John O'Neill. Boston: Beacon Press, 1969.

Merleau-Ponty, Maurice. "Marxism and Philosophy," In *Sense and Non-Sense*, translated by Hubert L. Dreyfus and Patricia Allen Dreyfus, 125–36. Evanston, IL: Northwestern University Press, 1964.

Merleau-Ponty, Maurice. *Phenomenology of Perception*. Translated by Colin Smith. London: Routledge, 1962.

Merleau-Ponty, Maurice. *The Primacy of Perception and Other Essays on Phenomeno-logical Psychology, the Philosophy of Art, History and Politics.* Translated by James M. Edie. Evanston, IL: Northwestern University Press, 1964.

Merleau-Ponty, Maurice. *Sense and Non-Sense.* Translated by Hubert Dreyfus and Patricia Allen Dreyfus. Evanston, IL: Northwestern University Press, 1964.

Mezzadra, Sandro, and Brett Neilson. *Border as Method, or, the Duplication of Labor.* Durham, NC: Duke University Press, 2013.

Miller, James. *History and Human Existence: From Marx to Merleau-Ponty.* Berkeley: University of California Press, 1982.

Miller, Tom. *China's Asian Dream: Empire Building along the New Silk Road.* London: ZED Books, 2017.

Moore, Jason W. Introduction to *Anthropocene or Capitaloscene? Nature, History, and the Crisis of Capitalism,* edited by Jason W. Moore, 1–11. Oakland, CA: PM Press, 2016.

Moretti, Franco. "Dialectic of Fear." In *Signs Taken for Wonders: Essays in the Sociology of Literary Forms,* 83–108. New York: Verso, 1988.

Nichols, Bill. *Introduction to Documentary.* Bloomington: Indiana University Press, 2010.

Nornes, Abé Mark. "Bulldozers, Bibles, and Very Sharp Knives: The Chinese Independent Documentary Scene." *Film Quarterly* 63, no. 1 (2009): 50–55.

Nornes, Abé Mark. "Marking the Body: The Axiographics of the Visible Hidden Camera." In *DV-Made China: Digital Subjects and Social Transformations after Independent Film,* edited by Zhang Zhen and Angela Zito, 29–56. Honolulu: University of Hawai'i Press, 2015.

Ong, Aihwa. *Neoliberalism as Exception: Mutations in Citizenship and Sovereignty.* Durham, NC: Duke University Press, 2006.

Pang, Laikwan. "Colour and Utopia: The Filmic Portrayal of Harvest in Late Cultural Revolution Narrative Films." *Journal of Chinese Cinemas* 6, no. 3 (2012): 263–82.

Parikka, Jussi. *A Geology of Media.* Minneapolis: University of Minnesota Press, 2015.

Peng, Lijun. *Huanghun weiwan: Hou jiuqi Xianggang dianying* [Dusk is yet to arrive: Hong Kong cinema after 1997]. Hong Kong: Zhongwen daxue chubanshe, 2010.

Pickowicz, Paul G., and Yingjin Zhang, eds. *From Underground to Independent: Alternative Film Culture in Contemporary China.* Lanham, MD: Rowman and Littlefield, 2006.

Plaza Hollywood. "Guan'yu women" [About Us]. Accessed April 19, 2017. https://www.plazahollywood.com.hk/aboutus.

Poe, Edgar Allan. *Complete Stories and Poems of Edgar Allan Poe.* Garden City, NY: Doubleday, 1966.

Poe, Edgar Allan. "The Philosophy of Furniture." In *Selected Writings of Edgar Allan Poe: Poems, Tales, Essays and Reviews,* edited by David Galloway, 414–20. Harmondsworth, UK: Penguin, 1967. Originally published in *Burton's Gentleman's Magazine* (1840).

Rancière, Jacques. *Dissensus: On Politics and Aesthetics.* Translated by Steven Corcoran. New York: Continuum, 2010.

Rancière, Jacques. *Figures of History.* Translated by Julie Rose. Malden, MA: Polity, 2014.

Rancière, Jacques. *The Future of the Image*. Translated by Gregory Elliott. New York: Verso, 2007.

Rancière, Jacques. *The Politics of Aesthetics: The Distribution of the Sensible*. Translated by Gabriel Rockhill. New York: Continuum, 2004.

Rangan, Pooja. *Immediations: The Humanitarian Impulse in Documentary*. Durham, NC: Duke University Press, 2017.

"Reel China 2014—Schedule." NYU Center for Religion and Media. Accessed August 2, 2017. https://wp.nyu.edu/crm/reel-china-2014-schedule/.

Ricoeur, Paul. *Memory, History, Forgetting*. Translated by Kathleen Blamey and David Pellauer. Chicago: University of Chicago Press, 2004.

Robinson, Luke. *Independent Chinese Documentary: From the Studio to the Street*. Basingstoke, UK: Palgrave Macmillan, 2013.

Rockmore, Tom. "Merleau-Ponty, Marx, and Marxism: The Problem of History." *Studies in East European Thought* 48, no. 1 (1996): 63–81.

Rodowick, D. N. *The Virtual Life of Film*. Cambridge, MA: Harvard University Press, 2007.

Rofel, Lisa. *Desiring China: Experiments in Neoliberalism, Sexuality, and Public Culture*. Durham, NC: Duke University Press, 2007.

Rofel, Lisa. "Rethinking Modernity: Space and Factory Discipline in China." *Cultural Anthropology* 7, no. 1 (1992): 93–114.

Rogaski, Ruth. *Hygienic Modernity: Meanings of Health and Disease in Treaty-Port China*. Berkeley: University of California Press, 2004.

Ruiz, Raoul. *Poetics of Cinema*. Paris: Dis vois, 2005.

Sayer, Rosemary. *The Man Who Turned the Lights On: Gordon Wu*. Hong Kong: Chameleon Press, 2006.

Schivelbusch, Wolfgang. *Disenchanted Night: The Industrialization of Light in the Nineteenth Century*. Berkeley: University of California Press, 1995.

Schultz, Corey Kai Nelson. "Moving Portraits: Portraits in Performance in *24 City*." *Screen* 55, no. 2 (2014): 276–87.

Service, Tom. "Glenn Gould: A Wilfully Idiotic Genius?" *The Guardian*, September 20, 2012. https://www.theguardian.com/music/2012/sep/20/glenn-gould-wilfully-idiotic-genius.

Shadbolt, Peter. "Hong Kong's Border War over 'Green Buffer.'" CNN, April 4, 2012. http://edition.cnn.com/2012/04/04/world/asia/hongkong-border/.

Shapiro, Judith. "War Preparations and Forcible Relocations: How Factories Polluted the Mountains and Youths 'Opened' the Frontiers." In *Mao's War against Nature: Politics and the Environment in Revolutionary China*, 139–94. Cambridge: Cambridge University Press, 2001.

Shi, Jin. *Zhuti de shengchan jizhi: Shiqi nian dian'ying neiwai de shenti huayu* [The production of subjectivity: Discourses of the cinematic body in the seventeen year period]. Beijing: Beijing daxue chubanshe, 2014.

Shih, Shu-mei. "Is the Post- in Postsocialism the Post- in Posthumanism?" *Social Text* 30, no. 1 (2012): 27–50.

Shih, Shu-mei. *The Lure of the Modern: Writing Modernism in Semicolonial China, 1917–1937*. Berkeley: University of California Press, 2001.

Shih, Shu-mei. *Visuality and Identity: Sinophone Articulations across the Pacific*. Berkeley: University of California Press, 2007.

Siegert, Bernhard. *Cultural Techniques: Grids, Filters, Doors, and Other Articulations of the Real*. Translated by Geoffrey Winthrop Young. New York: Fordham University Press, 2015.

Smith, Daniel, and John Protevi. "Gilles Deleuze." In *Stanford Encyclopedia of Philosophy*, edited by Edward N. Zalta, winter 2015. https://plato.stanford.edu/archives /win2015/entries/deleuze/.

Smith, Steven. *Kowloon: Transport Super City*. Hong Kong: Terry Farrell and Partners, 1998.

Sniadecki, J. P. "The Cruelty of the Social: Xianchang, Intersubjectivity, and Interobjectivity." In *DV-Made China: Digital Subjects and Social Transformations after Independent Film*, edited by Zhang Zhen and Angela Zito, 57–75. Honolulu: University of Hawai'i Press, 2015.

Solomon, Jonathan D. "It Makes a Village." In *Mall City: Hong Kong's Dreamworlds of Consumption*, edited by Stefan Al, 93–105. Honolulu: University of Hawai'i Press, 2016.

Sontag, Susan. "The Imagination of Disaster." In *Against Interpretation, and Other Essays*, 209–25. New York: Farrar, Straus and Giroux, 1967.

Spivak, Gayatri Chakravorty. *Outside in the Teaching Machine*. New York: Routledge, 1993.

Spivak, Gayatri Chakravorty. "Translator's Preface." In *Of Grammatology*, by Jacques Derrida, ix–lxxxvii. Baltimore: Johns Hopkins University Press, 1997.

Stark, David, and László Bruszt, eds. *Postsocialist Pathways: Transforming Politics and Property in East Central Europe*. New York: Cambridge University Press, 1998.

Steinberg, Stefan. "The Thoroughly Conformist World of *Amélie*." *World Socialist Web Site*, August 28, 2001. http://www.wsws.org/en/articles/2001/08/amel-a28.html.

Steyerl, Hito. *Duty Free Art: Art in the Age of Planetary Civil War*. New York: Verso, 2017.

Tanizaki, Junichiro. *In Praise of Shadows*. Translated by Thomas J. Harper and Edward G. Seidensticker. London: Jonathan Cape, 1991.

Terada, Rei. *Feeling in Theory: Emotion after the "Death of the Subject."* Cambridge, MA: Harvard University Press, 2001.

Toscano, Alberto, and Jeff Kinkle. *Cartographies of the Absolute*. Alresford, UK: Zero Books, 2015.

Tsai, Ming-liang. *Jiaoyou* [Stray dogs]. New Taipei City: INK Yingxiang wenxue, 2014.

Tsai, Ming-liang. "Tsai Ming-liang's Notes." In *Stray Dogs at the Museum*, edited by Mun-lee Lin and Ming-liang Tsai, 95–163. Taipei: Museum of National Taipei University of Education, 2016.

Tsai Ming-liang and Qin Zhuanxi. "Zhuanfang *Jin'gang jing* Tsai Ming-liang" [Interview with *Diamond Sutra* Tsai Ming-liang]. *Douban*, September 8, 2012. https://site .douban.com/106383/widget/movie_info/9660423/info/20945442/.

Tsang, Donale. "Introduction to the Hong Kong Airport Core Programme." *Proceedings of the Institution of Civil Engineers, Civil Engineering* 126 (1998): 3–4.

Virilio, Paul. *Lost Dimension*. Translated by Daniel Moshenberg. Los Angeles: Semiotext(e), 2012.

Virilio, Paul. *Open Sky*. Translated by Julie Rose. New York: Verso, 1997.

Virilio, Paul. *The Original Accident*. Translated by Julie Rose. Cambridge: Polity, 2007.

Virilio, Paul. *The Vision Machine*. Translated by Julie Rose. London: BFI, 1994.

Virilio, Paul. *War and Cinema: The Logistics of Perception*. Translated by Patric Camiller. London: Verso, 1984.

Visser, Robin. *Cities Surround the Countryside: Urban Aesthetics in Postsocialist China*. Durham, NC: Duke University Press, 2010.

Voci, Paola. *China on Video: Smaller-Screen Realities*. New York: Routledge, 2010.

Wahlberg, Malin. *Documentary Time: Film and Phenomenology*. Minneapolis: University of Minnesota Press, 2008.

Wang, Hui. *The End of the Revolution: China and the Limits of Modernity*. New York: Verso, 2011.

Wang, Lingzhen. "Gender and Sexual Differences in 1980s China: Introducing Li Xiaojiang." *differences* 24, no. 2 (2013): 8–20.

Williams, Blake. "Master Shots: Tsai Ming-liang's Late Digital Period." *Cinema Scope*. Accessed October 31, 2017. http://cinema-scope.com/features/tiff-2013-cinema -scope-56-preview-stray-dogs-tsai-ming-liang-taiwanfrance/.

Wojcik, Pamela Robertson. *The Apartment Plot: Urban Living in American Film and Popular Culture, 1945–1975*. Durham, NC: Duke University Press, 2010.

Wong, Yiu-Chung. "One Country, and Two Systems: Where Is the Line?" In *Crisis: Hong Kong's Transformation since the Handover*, edited by Yiu-Chung Wong, 15–36. Oxford: Lexington Books, 2004.

Wood, Robin. *Hollywood from Vietnam to Reagan . . . and Beyond*. New York: Columbia University Press, 1986.

Yeh, Emilie Yueh-yu, and Darrell William Davis. "Camping out with Tsai Ming-liang." In *Taiwan Film Directors: A Treasure Island*, edited by Emilie Yueh-yu Yeh and Darrell William Davis, 217–48. New York: Columbia University Press, 2005.

Yu, Zhenyu. *Gangdao hai'anxian* [Coastline of Hong Kong]. Hong Kong: Zhonghua shuju, 2014.

Yuan Sun. "Kan xia lai zhenxiang shi kongbupian 'Lian'ai zhong de Baobei' qingrenjie shichong" [Like a horror film, *Baober in Love* losing favor]. *Renmin wang* [*People's Daily Online*], February 18, 2004. www.people.com.cn/GB/yule/1080/2345470.html.

Zhang, Xudong. *Chinese Modernism in the Era of Reforms: Cultural Fever, Avant-Garde Fiction, and the New Chinese Cinema*. Durham, NC: Duke University Press, 1997.

Zhang, Xudong. *Postsocialism and Cultural Politics: China in the Last Decade of the Twentieth Century*. Durham, NC: Duke University Press, 2008.

Zhang, Zhen. "Dream-Walking in Digital Wasteland: Observations on the Uses of Black and White in Chinese Independent Documentary." *Journal of Chinese Cinemas* 6, no. 3 (2012): 299–319.

Zhang, Zhen. "Song at Midnight: Acoustic Horror and the Grotesque Face of History." In *An Amorous History of the Silver Screen, 1896–1937*, 298–344. Chicago: University of Chicago Press, 2005.

Zhou, Bojun. *Meiguiyuan de gushi: Xianggang xin jichang wenti tantao* [The story of rose garden: The politics of Hong Kong Airport]. Hong Kong: Qingwen shuwu faxing, 1993.

Zito, Angela. "The Act of Remembering, the *Xiangchang* of Recording: The Folk/Minjian Memory Project in China." *Film Quarterly* 69, no. 1 (2015): 20–35.

Žižek, Slavoj. *The Metastases of Enjoyment: Six Essays on Women and Causality.* London: Verso, 1994.

Index

Note: Page numbers in *italics* refer to illustrations.

106, 108, 155; electrification in Soviet Russia and, 46; habiting-habitat distinction and, 64–65; imagination of disaster and, 161; utopia and, 66, 229n56

exception, zones of, 3, 13, 30, 147, 164, 191; border-crossing and, 178; crisis of embodiment in, 183; Hong Kong as, 150, 152, 158, 165, 172, 191; imaginary of socialist empires and, 151; as new sites of capital accumulation, 154

Ex-Cinema (Lippit), 112

Execution of Czolgosz with Panorama of Auburn Prison (Edison Studios silent film), 132

factory films, 28, 42, 62, 63, 226n5

factory ruins, 28, 40, *41*, 42

factory space, 23, 28, 39, 65; heterotopic, 42, 43; representation of, 43–44; socialist representation of bodies in, 57

Farglory Group, 185

Farocki, Harun, 35, 44–45, 59

fascism, 60

female body, 92, 95, 96, 97, 98

femininity, 29, 226n56; commodified, 80, 93; historically shifting concepts of, 99; male theatrical performance of, 73; in Republican era, 73; socialist, 75, 78, 169

femininity, post-socialist, 70, 71, 81–82, 98; birth of, 80; capitalist dream of the interior and, 86; coding process of, 88; commodified, 73–74, 85; post- trope and, 69–76

feminism, Chinese, 29, 71, 75, 79; architectural feminism, 99–100; discourses of evolution and, 79, 232n26; Mao-era state feminism, 72; US-based feminism contrasted with, 96

feminist blockbusters, 24, *75*

feudalism, agricultural economy and, 58

Fiery Youth [*Qingchun sihuo*] (Dong Kena film), 37, 49–58, *55*, *56*, 61

Fifth Generation filmmakers, 72

Foucault, Michel, 17–18, 63, 198–99, 224n30

Foxconn company: police suppression of workers and, 59, 229n44; protests in factories, 229n49; workers' suicides at factories, 59, 228n43

France, May 1968 protests in, 64, 153, 229n52

Frankenstein (Shelley), 5

Frankenstein, Dr., monster of, 4

Freud, Sigmund, 96–97, 170, 199, 208

future anteriority, 40, 75, 106

Future of the Image, The (Rancière), 218

gender, 170, 172, 177; gender equality, 78, 79, 88; gender hierarchy, 23; gender violence, 72, 81, 87, 91; home ownership and, 85, 232n34; identities, 71, 74; state language of gender emancipation, 78; subordinated under class interests, 29; Taiwan housing crisis and, 206

gentrification, 76, 82, 115, 128, 139; conversion of socialist-era factories, 86; real estate speculation and, 238n19

geopolitics, 4, 25, 52, 59, 157; Cold War and, 74; conception of Chinese cinema and, 71; desires and anxieties shaped by, 105; factory interior envisioned and, 63; geographical dichotomies and, 151; Hong Kong and, 178; post- trope and, 68; precarity and, 187–88; Taiwan and, 197; of the visible, 109

Germany, East, 40, 86, 104

Glass, Philip, 236n70

Godard, Jean-Luc, 136, 230n4, 242n24

Goldberg Variations (Bach): Gould's performances of, 131, 135–37, 236n71; played in reverse, 118, 119, 131, 135–39, 236n71

Goodbye, Dragon Inn (Tsai Ming-liang film), 209, 242n24

gothic literature, Euro-American, 4

Gould, Glenn, 131, 135–37, 236n71

Gramsci, Antonio, 10

Grosz, Elizabeth, 70, 226n57, 230n2, 231n12

Guangming de shouwei zhe [*The guardian of light*] (play), 227n21

Guomindang Party, 6, 46, 48

Halberstam, Jack, 4–5

Harvey, David, 19, 235n36

Hegel, G. W. F., 10, 18

Heidegger, Martin, 48–49, 129

Hell, Julia, 113, 151

heteronormativity, 71, 76, 97, 98, 197, 204

heterosexuality, 72, 79, 88, 242n29; capitalist social hierarchy and, 92; patriarchy and, 216

heterotopia, industrial, 42, 58–63

Hitchcock, Alfred, 89, 91

Hofstadter, Douglas, 139, 235n35

Hole, The [*Dong*] (Tsai Ming-liang film), 198–99, 205–8, 243n34

Hollywood film industry, 71
Hollywood Hong Kong (Fruit Chan film), 166,
167, 169–75, 171, 178
homelessness, 29, 77, 78, 81, 87
homophobia, 60
Hong Kong, 4, 8, 21, 189; Airport Core
Program, 176; as city without bodies, 147,
148, 156; as colonial-era treaty port, 154, 211;
as corporeal landscape, 169–78; Frontier
Closed Area during Cold War, 179; hybrid
culture of, 158; infrastructural boom
(1980s–90s), 154, 166; International Airport
at Chek Lap Lok, 156, 238n17; nature
reserve on border with China, 179, 180, 181,
241n55; neoliberal post-socialism and, 149;
"one country, two systems" and, 1, 2, 172,
173; post-socialism in, 2–3, 150–59; protests
after handover to PRC, 150, 161, 237n5; as
quintessential Chinese city, 23; real estate
market, 154, 238n19; SARS pandemic in,
210, 243n38; Sino-British Joint Declaration
(1984) and, 239n21; as space/zone of exception, 24, 30, 150, 152, 158, 165, 172, 191.
See also Umbrella Movement
Hong Kong cinema, 30, 150, 156, 182; blockbusters marketed to mainland audience,
183; historical continuities and, 157; Marxist
phenomenology and, 159–62
horror, 23, 91, 132, 183; aesthetic style of, 25;
affect of, 23; body-centered, 6, 23–24; in
Chinese cinema, 6; defined, 5–6; gendered
embodiments and, 72; genealogy of, 5;
horror-comedies, 24; industrial, 44, 219;
metaphysical, 194; precarity and, 187
housing, 76, 85; crisis landscape and, 199;
dissolution of socialism and, 85–86; lack of
affordable housing, 78, 154, 163, 206; legal
housing rights for women, 232n22; shortage
of housing in Malaysia, 212. See also apartments, urban
Hu, King, 202, 242n24
Huang Weikai, 30, 103, 140
Hui, Ann, 178, 179
hukou system, 233n38
humanism, post-socialist, 62
Humanism and Terror (Merleau-Ponty), 10
human rights, 25, 171
hypermediality, 4, 25–26, 101, 102, 218,
223n1

I Don't Want to Sleep Alone [Hei yanquan]
(Tsai Ming-liang film), 210–15, 213, 215,
241n10, 243nn44–45
image: as condition of reality, 27; future of the
image, 3, 31, 158–59, 187–88, 218–19; radical
transformations in meaning of, 25; reality
in relation to, 26; technologies of image
capture and distribution, 27
imaginaries, 13, 28, 76, 107, 189; Cold War, 109;
consolidated, 34; of the future in the present, 107; geopolitical, 19, 150–51; of global
empires, 216; of global neoliberalism, 73;
post-socialist femininity and, 72; of post-
socialist time, 106, 140; of socialist industrial
modernity, 37; urban, 72, 73, 76, 90, 206
imperialism, 18, 20, 46, 191
indexicality, 116, 127–28, 236n51
India, 107, 195
industrialism, 37, 44, 54, 59, 61
industrialization, 35, 46, 67, 145; capitalist,
167; China's late entry into, 37, 226n5; mass
dreams of, 57; post-socialist, 58; rapid,
228n35; representation of time and, 134; socialist, 49, 51, 52; Soviet managerial systems
and, 232n35; as transnational process, 59;
urbanization tied to, 50, 55
Industrial Revolution, 4, 61
In Praise of Shadows (Tanizaki), 204–5
interior design/decoration, 76, 79, 87; magazines, 85, 232n32; male interior decorator,
90, 92
interior space: commodified dream of, 90;
"dreams of the interior," 76–79; of factory,
37, 44; socialist-era factories converted to
housing, 86–88, 88; space-time of production, 36. See also phantasmagorias of the
interior
intersubjectivity, 11

Jameson, Fredric, 44, 129, 228n34, 236n51
Japan: documentary practices in, 111;
Malaysian-Chinese migrant workers in,
212; wartime occupation of Northeast
China, 47–48, 227n20, 227nn23–24
Jeunet, Jean-Pierre, 70
Jia Zhangke, 39, 59, 63, 66, 115, 233n2
Jia Zhangke, films of: A Touch of Sin (2013),
59–61; 24 City (2008), 39, 63, 66–68, 115,
229–30n59, 233n2

migrants/migrant workers, 171, 175, 179, 205, 210, 212, 214

mimesis, 26

mise-en-abîme, 28, 172

misogyny, cultures of, 72

modernity, industrial, 9, 29, 34; factory space and, 29; mass dreams of, 43; nostalgia for, 39; social imaginaries and, 37; socialist imaginary of, 53

monsters/monstrous bodies/monstrosity, 4, 24, 93, 219; benevolent, 7; sound technology and, 6

More, Thomas, 70, 230n2

Moreau, Jeanne, 201

Moretti, Franco, 4

"Mother, The" (Beauvoir), 97, 233n41

music, diegetic, 215

Nanjing, Treaty of (1842), 211

nature-culture interaction, 168, 197, 216, 240n38

Neilson, Brett, 178–79

neoliberalism, 16, 67, 113, 118; art production and, 186, 188; as attempt to rejuvenate capitalist system, 235n36; "with Chinese characteristics," 18, 19–20; crisis landscape and, 199; Eurocentric developmentalist model of, 18; as exception, 152; heteronormativity and, 76; housing crisis and, 206; imaginaries of, 73; possible socialist origin of, 22; post-socialism and, 2; redefinition of the state and, 18; violence in production of space, 3; worldwide expansion of, 17, 19

New Sensationalism, 7

Night and Fog [Tinshuiwai di ye yu mo/Tianshuiwei de ye yu wu] (Ann Hui film), 179, 181–82

No. 89 Shimen Road (Shu Haolun film), 115

noise, 126, 194, 196–97, 201; landscape and politics of, 210; narrative sounds contrasted with, 209; phenomenological experience of, 188

nonplaces, 156, 165, 166, 221

Nornes, Abé Mark, 102, 111

nostalgia, 5, 39, 60, 109, 122, 242n24; abandonment of, 63; Hong Kong as subject of, 175; for labor, 54; nostalgia films, 24; origin of post-socialist nostalgia, 57; post-socialist, 28, 134; for socialism, 61; socialist industrial landscape and, 33–34, 59; utopic pursuit of transcendent feelings, 139; without origin, 62

Notes Toward a Performative Theory of Assembly (Butler), 149–50

Occupy movements, 1, 26

Of Grammatology (Derrida), 112

"Of Other Spaces" ["Des Espaces Autres"] (Foucault), 42

Open Sky (Virilio), 125

oral histories, 116, 125, 130, 131, 133, 138, 230n59

Orientalism-Occidentalism dichotomy, 151

origins, reinvention of, 129

OSRAM Lighting Factory (Foshan), 65–66

Ou Ning, 115, 127

Pankejeff, Sergei (Freud's "wolf man"), 208

paranoia, 77, 89, 91, 92, 93, 96

patriarchy, 70, 78, 79, 94, 214, 216; Confucian, 76; property and, 87; Taiwan's housing crisis and, 206

Pearl River Delta, 65, 152, 155, 163

perception, 11, 115, 167, 185; blind spots in field of, 140; body as theory of, 75; expanded boundaries of, 200; phenomenological study of, 168; social function of art and, 202; speed of, 142

performance art, 31

performativity, bodily, 75, 100, 205

phantasmagorias of the interior, 29, 83, 84, 85–86, 94

phantom of the opera, 4, 6

Phantom of the Opera, The (Rupert Julian film), 6, 7

phenomenology, 8, 31, 64, 72, 127

phenomenology, Marxist, 9, 10, 11, 149, 166–67; Hong Kong cinema and, 183; theorization of the body, 12

Phenomenology of Perception (Merleau-Ponty), 10, 11, 240n38

philosophy, Western, 194, 195

"Philosophy of Furniture, The" (Poe), 83

Piano in a Factory, The [Gang de qin] (Zhang Meng film), 33, 39, 61–63

piracy, video, 25

Plato, 70, 230n2

plumbing technology, 204

Poe, Edgar Allan, 83, 89, 91

post-capitalism, 14, 18

post-colonialism, 15

post-communism, 104–5, 233n7

post-industrialism, 39, 59

post-socialism, neoliberal, 2, 4, 12, 99–100, 113; cultural logic of abstraction, 164; developmentalist temporality of, 130; in Eastern Europe, 106; emergence in China, 13–20; forces of resistance in era of, 24; as global phenomenon, 153, 219; in Hong Kong, 150–59; regime of visibility, 29; temporal logic of, 14; visual culture of, 58; zones of exception and, 13. *See also* neoliberalism

post- trope, 13–14, 19, 58, 220; as geopolitical imaginary, 68, 69; as imaginary of the future, 107; as media event with documentary impulses, 110–13; as temporalized and spatialized imaginary, 15

post-X neoliberalism, logic of, 15, 16, 18, 22, 43; factory visibility and, 34; new economic rationality and, 14; technologies of space and, 22; violence in production of post-X spaces, 23; ways of seeing, 43

PRC film industry, 71, 231n7; Fifth Generation filmmakers, 72; socialist film studio system, 231n10

precarity (precarious life), 31, 185, 199, 209, 213, 217, 221; Asian urban space and, 216; buried histories of violence and, 214; cruelty of existence and, 202; neoliberal management of, 20; nonbeing and, 60, 187–88; "precariat," 59–60

pregnancy, psychological (imagined), 69, 70, 71, 94–100

Primacy of Perception, The (Merleau-Ponty), 177

Production of Space, The [*La production de l'espace*] (Lefebvre), 11–12, 22, 223n17, 234n17; on deconstruction of spatial categories, 168; on reproducibility of space, 155, 238n14

productivity, 37, 49, 54, 66, 115

proletariat, 4, 45, 54, 59, 226n5

property ownership, 76, 79, 85, 86, 232n19

"Prospects of Recording, The" (Gould), 136

Public Toilet (Fruit Chan film), 166

"Question Concerning Technology, The" (Heidegger), 48–49

racism, 60

Rancière, Jacques, 8, 27, 44, 201; on cinematic images of workers at factory gate, 34–35;

definition of the image, 219; on images and apocalyptic discourses, 218

real, Lacanian, 214

Reality Is the Future of the Past [*Xianshi shi guoqu de weilai*]. See *Disorder*

Rear Window (Alfred Hitchcock film), 89

Rebels of the Neon God [*Qingshaonian Nezha*] (Tsai Ming-liang film), 207, 209–10, 242n24

relationalities, 24

Religion [*Xinyang*] (Cong Feng film), 130

repetition, 12, 22, 113, 122, 139; city-body linkage and, 149; of desires, 203; documentary and, 133, 144; in everyday life, 105, 106, 108, 155; musical ruin-in-reverse and, 135, 136; rhythmanalysis and, 108; temporality of capitalism and, 129; urban planning and, 50

representation, 185, 189; archaeology of media history and, 129; limits of, 43; speed of, 142; technologies of, 5; of time, 103, 144; transmedial, 54; of the unrepresentable, 66, 72

resistance, 10, 13, 45, 221; aesthetics and, 4, 27, 217; body as site of, 11, 149, 167–69, 183, 202; cinema and, 161; differential body and, 12; in era of hypermediality, 24–28; factory interior as site of, 63, 65; femininity and, 74, 75; future devoid of, 220; image-making as practice of, 185; "lived experience" as, 11; nothingness and, 216; reimagined, 3; ruin gazing and, 116; space of, 11, 15, 157, 183; in state-sanctioned space, 42

Resplendent Light [*Guangmang wanzhang*] (Xu Ke film), 37, *38*, 42, 44–51, 55, 226n5; mass dreams of socialist industrialism and, 61; socialist light of work and production, 114–15

reterritorialization, 30, 68, 77; Belt and Road Initiative and, 107; border-crossing and, 151; end of Cold War and, 205; of post-socialist global geography, 154; violent, 182

revolution, 3, 9, 10; affective rehearsals of, 221; communist uprisings in early twentieth century, 37; definition of, 26; end of, 220; "gender equality" and, 78; industrial, 53, 54; infrastructural, 30, 154; media, 4, 25, 102; proletarian/workers', 49–51, 62; of the sensible world, 8, 26, 27; sensory, 218; technological, 37; urban, 22, 25, 63, 65, 147, 229n56

Rhythmanalysis (Lefebvre), 233n6, 234n17

rhythmanalytical project, 108, 145, 234n17

Ricoeur, Paul, 108

special economic zones, 13, 19, 22, 68, 163; economic development reoriented to, 58; Hong Kong and, 165, 178, 179, 181; invisibility of factory interiors, 58–59; invisible spaces of labor in, 34; new factory cities in, 29; nuclear energy and, 167, 240n37; post-socialism and, 152; workers' protests in, 62–63

species-being, 53, 97

species-life, 53, 55, 97–98

Spivak, Gayatri Chakravorty, 97, 112–13, 231n5, 233n41

Steyerl, Hito, 186

Stolen Life [*Shengsi jie*] (Li Shaohong film), 72, 94–95, 95, 233n38

"strange loops," 116, 118, 139, 235n35

Stratum 1: The Visitors [*Diceng 1: Laike*] (Cong Feng film), 102–3, 144, 237n72; cinematic and musical ruin-in-reverse, 128–33; digital memory and, 116–28; hypnotic rhythm of repetitive movement, 122, *122*; musical ruin-in-reverse and transmediality, 133–40; orogeny (geological term) as metaphor, 123, *124*, 131, 235n44; ruin-in-reverse images, 116, *117*, 118, *119*; "strange loops" in, 116, 118; surveillance-style footage, 116, 121, 125–26, *126*. See also *Goldberg Variations* (Bach), played in reverse

Stray Dogs [*Jiaoyou/Excursions*] (Tsai Mingliang film), 184–87, *186*, 192, *193*, 199–200, *200*

Street Angel [*Malu tianshi*] (Yuan Muzhi film), 114

Sundays and Cybèle [*Les dimanches de Ville d'Avray*] (Serge Bourguignon film), 230n4

surveillance, 18, 89, 103, 111, 146; in factories, 59; surveillance-style footage, 116, 121, 125–26, *126*, 142, 144; technologies of, 220; ubiquity in Chinese urban spaces, 142

Taipei, city of, 23, 184, 210

Taiwan, 4, 17, 24, 170; as apocalyptic landscape, 191–92, 198; Foxconn company based in, 59, 228n43; lifting of tariffs on foreign films, 71; neoliberal approach to housing, 206; as precarious island, 188; SARS pandemic in, 210; in state of nonbeing, 189–91

Tang Dynasty Band (Tangchao yuedui), 138

Tanizaki Junichiro, 204–5

technology: dystopian, 59; as mode of revealing, 48; "standing reserve" and, 129; of state surveillance, 220

Terada, Rei, 8

terror, war on, 187

Thatcher, Margaret, 176

Theater and Its Double, The (Artaud), 202

Tiananmen Square massacre (1989), 3, 15, 17, 220

Tianjin, city of, 242n28

Tie Xi Qu: West of the Tracks (Wang Bing film), 39, 115

time/temporalities, 6, 61, 201; accelerated speed of commerce routes, 107; affect of horror and, 23; archaeological layers of, 106, 108, 109; beyond socialism, 34; electric light and representation of, 114; of filmmaking, 25; geological, 120, 123, 125; industrialized, 115; legibility of, 127, 128; "lived" time mediated through the body, 104, 106, 233n6; Marx's theory of Capital and, 11; naturalized progression of, 138; performativities of, 30; post-socialist, 105, 120, 121, 128, 139, 140; post- trope and, 15; real time, 120, 121; repetition of waiting, 104–10; ruin-in-reverse as turning back of time, 131, 134; social production of, 108; synchronization of global time, 155; technology and the everlasting present, 125; teleological development of, 107, 233n6; temporal experience in era of the post-, 101–4; time lag between production and distribution, 112; urban as time-making machine, 113–16

Tin Shui Wai, border town of, 179, *180*, 181–82

Toscano, Alberto, 56

Touch of Sin, A [*Tian zhuding*] (Jia Zhangke film), 59–61

town-country distinction, 49, 228n32

Truffaut, François, 190, 230n4, 242n24

Tsai Ming-liang, 31, 184–85, 187, 189; influenced by French New Wave cinema, 190; metacinema of, 190, 191, 194, 205; philosophy of sound in film, 210, 215

Tsai Ming-liang, films of: *Diamond Sutra* (2012), 195; *Goodbye, Dragon Inn* (2003), 209, 242n24; *The Hole* (1998), 198–99, 205–8, 243n34; *I Don't Want to Sleep Alone* (2006), 210–15, *213*, *215*, 241n10, 243nn44–45; *Journey to the West* (2014), 196, *196*; *Rebels of the Neon God* (1992), 207, 209–10, 242n24; *The*

www.ingramcontent.com/pod-product-compliance
Lightning Source LLC
Chambersburg PA
CBHW030343270326
41926CB00009B/941